WORK AT HOME with a REAL JOB ONLINE

- Work anytime from anywhere
- Cut the cost of commute
- Jobs leading to career or just extra income

Written and compiled by AnnaMaria Bliven
"The Prosperity Princess"
©Copyright 2016 AnnaMaria Bliven

Work at Home with a Real Job Online
AnnaMaria Bliven

Copyright © 2016 AnnaMaria Bliven

Bliven Publishing
Blanchardville, Wisconsin
Library of Congress Control Number: 2016902583

ISBN: 978-1-940243-94-8
All rights reserved.

Book design by AnnaMaria Bliven.

This book has been compiled from several websites using the verbiage thereof. The graphics are Google images labeled for legal reuse.

AnnaMaria Bliven
Visit my website at: http://work-at-home-jobs-online.com
Printed in the United States of America

TABLE OF CONTENTS

INTRODUCTION

Most people who hear the words: "work at home" think "oh, that's just another scam," and dismiss the idea altogether. But I am living proof that there really is a legitimate work at home online jobs work force, and I am one of them.

I have been earning income and extra income working jobs at home and online since 2002. From 2002 to the present time, I have figured out exactly what it takes to get hired and stay hired to work at home at an online job. I wrote: Get A Real Job Online in 2013 with listing companies and the online job opportunities, and now I am following that up with this book.

This book will be more instructional than the first book as well as informational. You will learn the three steps it takes to get to the interview stage, along with techniques to keep and advance in your job after you are hired. You will also be shown the different types of job boards for online jobs which will expedite the time it takes to search for an online job opening.

I also want to show you how it is possible to be putting money in your pocket while you are waiting to be contacted for a job interview (this information is even applicable to people seeking on site jobs and perfect for college students). The jobs I am referring to are called "Mini or Micro Tasks*," and do not have qualifications you need to meet; all you do is register to work the tasks. However, the more skills you have that match the tasks, the more money you can make.

Please note: All workers are required to submit tax information. U.S.-based workers need to submit a tax ID or Social Security number. Non-U.S. citizens living outside the United States also need to submit an IRS tax form. U.S. citizens living outside the United States may not work for some of the companies.

*The companies listed in this book have been checked for legitimacy. There is no guarantee that you will get a job, but if you are determined and diligent, you most likely will land a job online.

*Keep in mind that the Micro Task jobs are always available for fast ways to earn money.

If you are disabled there are certain amounts of money you can make that will not affect your Benefits. Consult your SSI and SSDI office for details.

There is a great many benefits to working at home and it is a super privilege. I refer to this as a "super privilege" because you can actually have a special work-life balance that is only possible when you work at home.

Chapter 1

GENERIC VERSUS GENRE JOB BOARDS

It is important to know that there are two different types of job boards for work at home online jobs.

Generic online job boards such as Monster.com and Indeed.com, for example, list work at home online open job positions in all genres, so if you are looking for an IT position, you have to weed through all the types of positions and look for the IT listings mixed in with all the others. On the other hand, Genre specific internet job boards list job openings only in the one genre. For example, only IT related online jobs are listed which makes it easier and faster to see the ones you are qualified and interested.

See a listing of **Generic Work At Home Job Boards***:

Monster.com

Indeed.com

Careerbuilder.com

Ratracerebellion.com

Myemploymentoptions.com

Flexjobs.com (they require a fee to use their job leads)

Workersonboard.com

Moneymakingmommy.com

WAHM.com

Makemoneyfromonlinejobs.com

Realwaystoearnmoneyonline.com

Homewiththekids.com

Snagajob.com/job-search/q-work+at+home

Dreamhomebasedwork.com

There may be more of these types of sites; this is not an exhaustive list

Genre Job Boards are as follows (these are examples, and there are many more):

Computer technology jobs (varied): Dice.com / powertofly.com

Customer Service: liveops.com / workathomesolutions.com

Freelancer: freelance.com

Gaming tester: gamingjobzone.com

Higher Education: highered.com / connectionsacademy.com / scholarlyhires.com

Insurance: greatinsurancejobs.com

Nursing: sironahealth.com / Work from home Nursing Jobs

Transcription: athreon.com

Virtual Assistant: womenforhire.com

Chapter 2

ARE YOU PREPARED TO WORK AT HOME?

I hear a lot of people talk about "wouldn't it be nice to work at home and not have to commute to work?" I also hear people say "I want to work at home, can you help me get a job so I can stay at home?" I agree, working at home is a great experience, if you are prepared with the following:

A. Schedule your work time and work your scheduled time. Your employer hired you to produce work and be dependable.

B. Eliminate distractions. Make sure you can work in a place where there are no noise, sound or sight distractions (especially when working with a headset talking to customers)

C. Perform your work task with excellence. As a worker working at home, you are on the honors system and expected to produce excellent work.

In addition, there is certain equipment and accounts you will need to perform your work task, communicate with your employer and get paid. Here are the items you will need to be successful:

1. Computer with internet connection
2. Internet DSL works best
3. Phone with a land line (especially for some call center online jobs)
4. Access to a fax machine, scanner (to send application and application materials (i.e. social security card, driver's license, certification, etc.)
5. The working location needs to be in an area of no distractions. (Some companies require you be where there is no background noise)
6. Email address

7. Checking account

8. PayPal account

9. Commitment to perform your work tasks with excellence.

10. Determination ---diligence and most of all------CONFIDENCE with a positive attitude.

If you have this equipment, place at home set apart and a workable at home schedule and determination, you have what it takes to succeed working at home.

In the next Chapter, I teach the three steps to getting to the interview stage.

Chapter 3

THREE BASIC STEPS TO SEEKING, FINDING, AND APPLYING FOR WAH ONLINE JOB

There is a 3-step process to getting a work at home real online job: (**Seek / Find / Apply**)

1. **Seek:** This step is when you do an internet search to find a work at home online type of job you are experienced and interested to work. For example: if you are interesting in a Customer Service Online Chat position, you would type the following in the search box: "Work at home chat jobs"

Screen shot of what the list might look like:

So, now you would read the list and decide which of these online chat job positions interest you the most.

You might want to continue the "seeking" using one of the listing, such as the one from "www.workathomewoman.com

By clicking on this link, this is what you might see:

So, now we have a list of companies that hire people to work at home as Chat Agents:

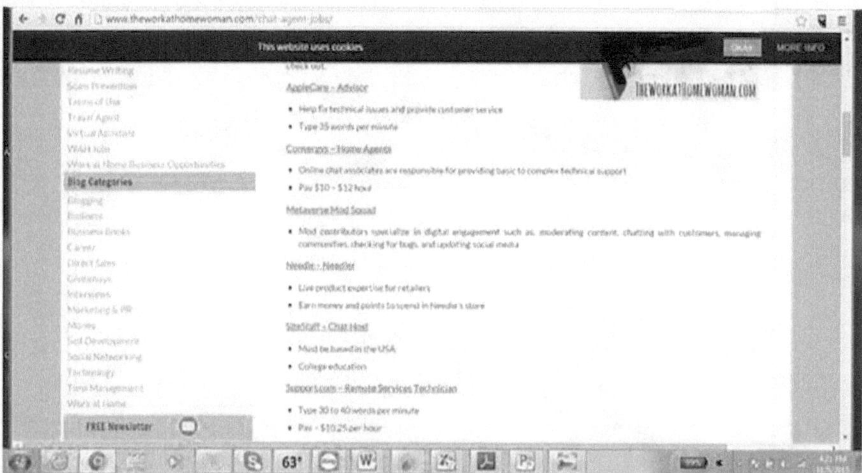

2. **Find**: this is the step when you look at the list and decide which one(s) are closer to the kind of job you wish to apply for.

If you see a job opening you are qualified to do, then click on the link to the company's website:

For example, let's say you are interested in the "AppleCare-Advisor" position. You click on the link and this is what you see:

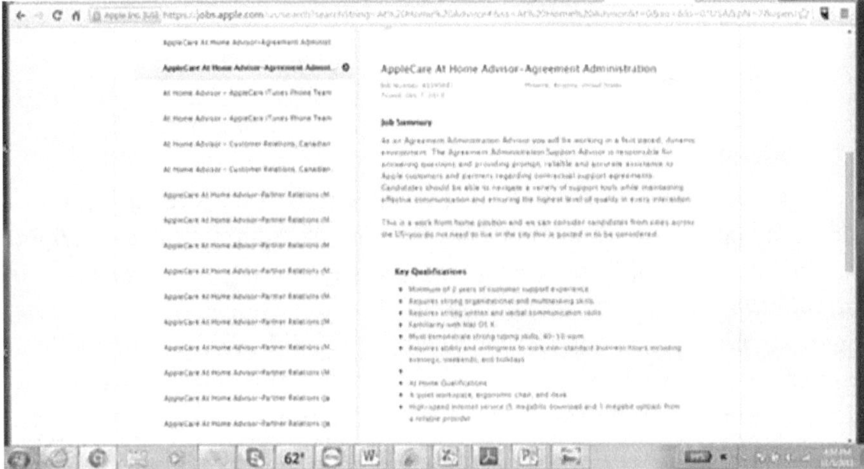

Let's say that you like what you read about this position and you meet the Key Qualifications. You think to yourself, "This is definitely a job I can do and want to do," and you are ready to proceed to applying for the job. Now you are ready for step 3.

3. **Applying** for the job position. This step may sound self-explanatory, but this is the one step most people do incorrectly and then wonder why the company never called them for an interview.

Follow these directions very carefully and you are more likely to get called for a job interview.

First of all, not all job positions are applied for the same way. Some require only an email inquiry and then you are emailed further instructions. Some require only a resume be sent with an optional cover letter. Then, there are other online job openings when you apply for them with an online application, an essay question and an assessment. Believe me when I tell you that I have used all of these methods when applying for a work at home online job, and did so very successfully!

Secondly, the company will tell you how they want you to apply for their job. Pay very close attention to what they want and make sure to give them everything they require.

Lastly, applying for a work at home online job, most of the time, is not easy to do. It requires careful reading, making sure to pay attention to details. Let me show you what I mean.

Let's say for example, you are applying for this job:

Job Summary

As an Agreement Administration Advisor you will be working in a fast paced, dynamic environment. The Agreement Administration Support Advisor is responsible *for answering questions and providing prompt, reliable and accurate assistance* to Apple customers and partners regarding contractual support agreements. Candidates should be able to navigate a variety of support tools while maintaining **effective communication and ensuring the highest level of quality** in every interaction. This is a work from home position and we can consider candidates from cities across the US-you do not need to live in the city this is posted in to be considered.

Key Qualifications

- Minimum of 2 years of customer support experience.
- **Requires strong organizational and multitasking skills.**
- **Requires strong written and verbal communication skills**
- **Familiarity with Mac OS X.**
- Must demonstrate strong typing skills, *40-50 wpm*
- Requires ability and willingness to work non-standard business hours including **evenings, weekends, and holidays**
- At Home Qualifications
- A quiet workspace, ergonomic chair, and desk
- High-speed Internet service (5 megabits download and 1 megabit upload) from a reliable provider

Description

•Serve as a point of contact for Apple, Apple's customers and our partners by ***answering questions and providing assistance in resolving contract issues*** for customers. •Process contract maintenance requests received via internet chat using a variety of internal tools from regions worldwide.   •Handles requests to speak to management regarding exception requests or customer satisfaction issues. •Provide support for Apple contracts including Enterprise level agreements. •Process and manage day to day chat business efficiently and ***ensure service levels are met and key performance indicators are met.*** Ability to make sound decisions by identifying issues which require escalation, report issues and problems by following the appropriate escalation channels.

There are some key details that must be noted and addressed. I highlighted them in **bold and *italicized***. The **bold** highlighted details are to be addressed in the resume, and the ***italicized*** highlighted details are addressed in the cover letter.

Some of these highlighted details will be addressed in the resume and some will be addressed in a cover letter (or in an essay question).

At the bottom of the webpage where this job description was posted, the applicant was given three options:

Email the job to a friend, Add to Favorites or Submit Resume.

The next screen looks like this:

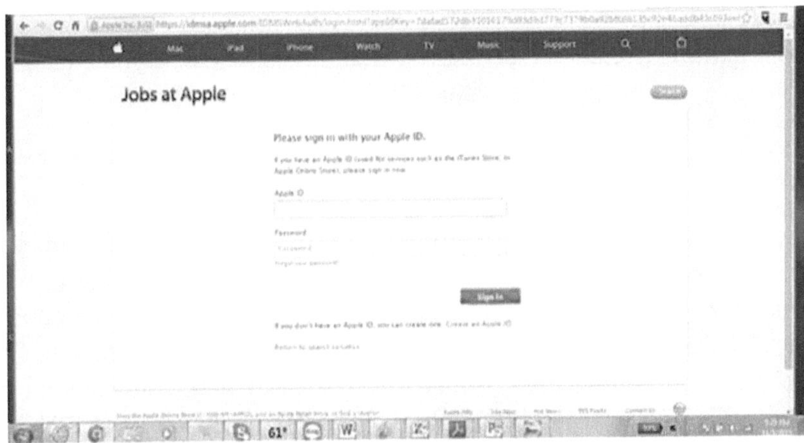

So, in this case, you do not even begin applying for this job without first logging into the site.

After you log into the site, you are then given a place to upload a pre-written resume. Now, what most people do at this point is go into their computer file, grab their resume in the file and upload it. If that pre-written resume in the file already includes all the details that are highlighted, then great, wonderful, it is possible HR will notice your resume and you will be contacted for an interview.

But, more than likely, that pre-written resume in the computer file has generic information regarding your work experience and does not address any of the highlighted details.

So, if your resume needs to address the highlighted details, you do so with measurable results. For example, let's say you worked three years as a Customer Service Representative for a catalog company like "Lands' End." You worked in their Call Center and achieved high level performance goals. You can post in bullet points the following:

Lands' End Call Center, Customer Service Representative Call Center 2003-2006

- Answered phone calls and replied to customer emails answering questions and provided assistance in resolving ordering issues with a 90 percent customer satisfaction rating.
- Received awards every month for achieving top performance levels for upsells and customer satisfaction.

In your Skills and Abilities section you would be sure to post you type 40-50 wpm.

Do you see how making mention of these achievements in your resume makes you appear to HR as a viable and sought after job candidate?

Now, if you were given an opportunity to submit a cover letter with your resume, then you would make sure to add that you are available to work evenings, weekends and holidays. You would also mention you are familiar with Mac OS X and you have more than two years experienced as a Customer Service Representative, with strong organizational, multi-tasking and verbal skills. But be aware there are other mentions that need to be made, and those have to do with addressing the culture of the company.

Are you compatible with the Company's Culture?

This is a very serious question that must be answered to the satisfaction of HR, or you will not hear from them for an interview. Some of the companies will state their cultural beliefs with their job description, but in most cases, you have to do your homework!

In this case, if this was the company with the job opening, the cultural information can be found in the "About" section of the website and all you would need to do is click on: About Support.com.

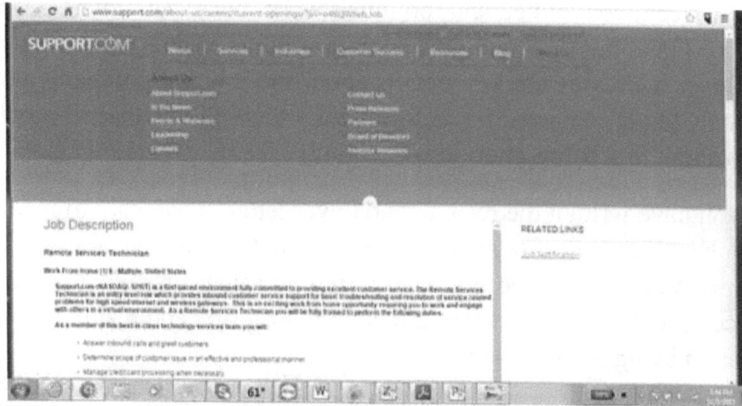

You want to be aware of the company's mission statement, goals and objectives, beliefs and what type of person works for them. This is a big clue as to the kind of applicant they are searching for to work for them.

Here are the cultural beliefs of this company:

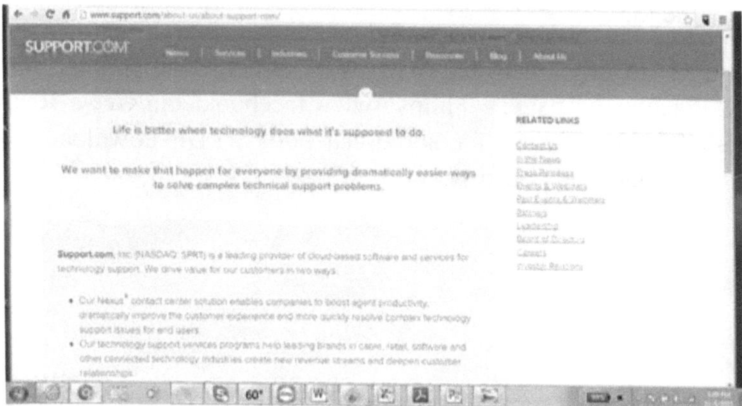

So, if Support.Com was the company with the job opening you are applying for, you would be sure to mention how you subscribe to working as a team to ensure customers receive service to solve complex technical support problems. Then read the rest of the webpage and you will see more statements regarding diversity and innovation as two characteristics most valued in their workforce. If you want to stand out from among the hundreds or thousands of other applicants, you will be sure to mention how you believe as they believe and can demonstrate that in one or two sentences. This, my friend is the way to get noticed as a potential applicant HR wants to interview!

This may seem convoluted and too much work, but I can almost guarantee that if you take the time and go the extra mile to ensure your resume and cover letter addresses the key details about the job and company, you are very likely to get contacted for an interview. After all, there is no way to get hired without first being interviewed, right?

After you have written the resume and cover letter, make sure to read them over, or have someone else read them over to make sure there are no spelling or grammatical errors. I do not need to tell you that misspelled words and sentences that do not make sense are definite turn-offs and result in your job application being filed in file #13.

In these short 9 pages, I have shared with you the first three steps in getting a work at home online job. This is the method I have used over and over again since 2002 to get work at home online jobs for income and extra income.

Needless, to say, these first three steps were repeated many times until I got a job. When I was contacted for a job interview, there was a certain technique I used to prepare for the interview that 90% of the time worked successfully and I got the job.

Stay tuned to my website: www.work-at-home-online-jobs.com and to my Facebook page: https://www.facebook.com/**Get-a-Real-Job-Online**-590709354357568 for additional books, PDF downloads, digital courses, webinars and podcasts.

Chapter 4

KNOW THE DIFFERENCE BETWEEN A SCAM AND A LEGITIMATE ONLINE JOB

There are many work-at-home online job seekers who are afraid of being "scammed" while they are seeking online employment. According to the "scam meter" found at (http://www.ratracerebellion.com/index.html), there are 53 scams to 1 legitimate online job. However, in the past 14 years, I have been scammed 5 times and employed 11 times. I know exactly what to do to keep from getting scammed and how to ensure you get contacted for an interview that could lead to being hired.

Scams:

- Scams always require payment of some amount to get started.
- There is usually a lengthy video or sales page prior to requesting you pay some amount of money to get started (which is usually a low amount) and then more sales pages/videos tempting you to spend more money (usually a higher amount)....and this is repeated until you get to the end of all the offerings or you click "no, not interested" at some point.
- Reviews are generally negative.

Legitimate online jobs:

- Legitimate online jobs require an application and most of them will also require you pass a profile and/or skills assessment for FREE.
- There is usually a job description noting education, experience and skills requirements, and company description, mission and objectives.
- There is an application process prior to hiring.
- Reviews are generally positive.

Chapter 5

WORK AT HOME ONLINE JOBS LISTING

Please note: These jobs were cut and pasted from the actual websites and were available at the time of publishing

ADMINISTRATION/EXECUTIVE

AdminClericalOnlineJobs
(http://www.adminclericalonlinejobs.com/)

We are a fast growing highly rated Media and Marketing Company looking for new associates. Almost everything we do is 100% web-based and most of our Services are conducted online. This web site is designed to give you information about our web-based telecommute position and will help you with your decision to begin working today.

Are you looking for extra income to get out of debt and pay off bills? Have you been laid off? Tired of going to job interviews with 200 other people applying for the same job? If this sounds like what you have experienced then why not consider making your own destiny?

This is an entry level opportunity and no experience is required to begin working immediately.

The Right Place. The Right Team

Flexible Full & Part Time Openings

Easy Data Entry Form Filling Jobs

Home Based Admin Clerical Online Jobs

ADP
(http://jobs.adp.com/job/rpo-recruiting-client-relationship-manager-52989263?SID=1011&rb=INDEED&rx_campaign=Indeed16&rx_group=100169&rx_job=52989263&rx_source=Indeed)

RPO Recruiting Client Relationship Manager

JOB DESCRIPTION:

ADP RPO is hiring a Recruiting CRM. Strong relationships are the foundation of our success. The Client Relationship Manager (CRM) is responsible for developing a partnership with our client accounts by working directly with the client staffing team, hiring managers (Manager or Director level), or account team to develop and enhance strategies to ensure successful delivery of staffing services. Individuals must be highly consultative, have the ability to perform a variety of functional tasks, work within a team environment, and exhibit a commitment to our peers and clients. The Recruiting CRM is responsible for managing the recruitment efforts and hiring process for complex accounts and positions requiring he/she to lead the intake process with hiring managers develop sourcing strategies and develop relationships with client contacts on a regular basis. The primary focus of the roles is to identify and select top level candidates for key openings within the assigned client(s). The role is responsible for building and managing relationships within assigned operating unit in order to fully understand the needs of the client. Other responsibilities may include, but are not limited to the following: phone interviewing, offer negotiation, education, training, and managing of administrative resources to support the account.

We strive for every interaction to be driven by our CORE values: Insightful Expertise, Integrity is Everything, Service Excellence, Inspiring Innovation, Each Person Counts, Results-Driven, - Social Responsibility.

RESPONSIBILITIES:

- Requisition Management/Pipeline Management which includes candidate screening, as well as database management (consistently reviewing and assessing pipeline for each requisition and dispositioning candidates accordingly).

- Manage profitability of Account via development of comprehensive, effective and innovative sourcing and selection strategies in order to efficiently attain top level candidates.
- Consistently consult and collaborate with hiring managers regarding expectations, challenges and strategies.
- Develop process improvements, implement solutions and share best practices with account team members and client partners.
- Lead weekly meetings with hiring managers and account teams to discuss and assess candidate and requisition status and health; Internet research and job posting responsibility and pipeline status movement.
- Perform and/or manage passive recruiting through RMS resources as necessary to attract top level candidates.
- Consult regarding phone interviewing strategies and analysis of completed interviews, including behavioral interviews, of potential candidates to select top level candidates for clients.
- Accurately forecast and request transitional hours in a timely manner; leverage resources to maximize productivity and pipeline management.
- Review candidate profile, experience and telephone interview responses and decide final disposition of candidate (i.e.. eligible for hire, not eligible for hire, second round interview eligible, or transfer to another requisition because of skill set match)
- Furthermore, sell identified and selected candidates to client hiring managers, as well as advise top level candidates on a client's opportunity including culture fit, knowledge gaps and value proposition.
- If applicable, negotiate and present compensation packages to candidate for acceptance.
- Metric analysis, interview guide development, SLA adherence and report generation.
- Interpret and analyze data and present back to client and account manager so that enhancements can be made to the hiring process such as revisions of behavioral based interview guides, job descriptions, compensation packages, and success indicators.
- Development and delivery of presentations to client human resource partners and hiring managers.

- Provides back up to Account Manager in areas of reporting, coaching, mentoring and sharing of best practices.
- Performs other related duties as assigned.

QUALIFICATIONS REQUIRED:

- Bachelor's Degree required.
- 3-5 years' Experience with a thorough understanding of recruitment practices.
- PREFERRED QUALIFICATIONS: Preference will be given to candidates who have the following:
- Demonstrated professional growth within HR, Staffing and/or Talent Acquisition Skills and Abilities.
- Proven ability to design, develop and implement strategic solutions.
- Ability to interact effectively with all levels of the organization both internally and externally
- Technical - Business Knowledge
- Demonstrated ability to manage priorities within tight deadlines and high client expectations
- Client Focus/Service Orientation
- Communication Skills - written and verbal, coupled with interpersonal skills.
- People Management- embraces the concept of managing up and down.
- Manages expectations across all levels of the organization and communicates appropriately both internally and externally.
- ATS System - ability to report and leverage the ATS and manipulate data to share a story internally and externally.

Software in the Cloud; Experts on the Ground:

ADP powers the working world with comprehensive solutions that drive business success. Consistently named one of the "Most Admired Companies" by FORTUNE® Magazine, and recognized by Forbes® as one of "The World's Most Innovative Companies," ADP has over a half-million clients around the globe and 65 years of experience as one of the largest providers of human capital management solutions world-wide.

Assistant Match

(http://www.assistantmatch.com/become-a-virtual-assistant/)

- Virtual Assistants

Assistant Match accepts applications from experienced, talented virtual assistants. The majority of the work is part-time and all work is completed from your home office. See the website for further information and online application.

Availity

(http://www.availity.com/about-us/careers-availity/search-jobs/?gnk=job&gni=8a7886f85132d80c0151370469802f4e&gns=Indeed)

Hospital Solution Specialist

GENERAL DESCRIPTION

The Hospital Solution Specialist will collaborate with the Hospital Solutions team with onsite and remote support for clients for pre- and post-implementation. The level of support will include assessing internal patient access revenue cycle workflow, business rules, and policies. The Hospital Solution Specialist will work under the supervision of the Sr. Hospital Solutions Specialist to identify, demonstrate, and recommend modifications or changes to the client's current workflow that will improve performance and upfront collections using Availity Patient Access solution(s). The Specialist will participate in prospective and new client business and strategy discussions, and support strategic Patient Access redesign meetings at prospective clients to support ongoing sales efforts.

KEY RESPONSIBILITIES

- Manages the implementation timeline, system workflow, business process and results delivery based on customer requirements using Availity processes and tools

- Participate with Hospital sales team as needed onsite for client strategy and discovery meetings. Provide industry expertise during active key sales processes and pre and post implementation

- Reports status and progress of new business partners as well as adoption and utilization

- Provides subject matter expertise on how hospital revenue cycle processes and functions can be impacted by Patient Access workflow and process redesign – Provide extensive experience to drive repeatable process design, workflow automation, and significant cash improvement through Availity solutions
- Assist sales team to drive overall sales achievement results
- Assist as needed with the Hospital Patient Access Sales organization to assist with deal strategy, and client strategy meetings
- Identify opportunity to "pull-through" RCM/Clearinghouse opportunities in Hospital Patient Access deals
- Assist Sr. Hospital Solutions Specialist with building and design standard and recommended flowcharts and presentations, and policies when required
- Various other tasks as required by Sr. Hospital Solutions Specialist and RVP of Hospital Solutions to support evolving corporate objectives

The above cited duties and responsibilities describe the general nature and level of work performed by people assigned to the job. They are not intended to be an exhaustive list of all the duties and responsibilities that an incumbent may be expected or asked to perform.

EDUCATION AND EXPERIENCE

- Bachelor's degree or the equivalent work experience
- Minimum of five (5) years' experience in the healthcare industry (finance and/or administrative sectors), preferably managing patient access and/or revenue cycle operations
- Prefer experience in supporting health systems from vendor/consulting perspective
- Ability to work with Senior executive level within health system

SKILLS AND KNOWLEDGE

- Excellent verbal and written communication skills as well as excellent presentation skills.
- Prior experience writing, developing and presenting written proposals and presentations.

- Demonstrated ability to work in a fast-paced, deadline driven environment
- Proven ability to manage multiple tasks
- Experience with multi-tasking and project coordination
- Able to think on your feet, react quickly, and maintain composure in stressful situations.
- The ability to function collaboratively with a diverse team, both directing and taking direction.
- Apply creativity and judgment in developing new approaches and solutions
- A team player who can also work independently and is a self-starter

Blue Zebra Appointment Setting

(http://www.bluezebraappointmentsetting.com/Careers.aspx)

-Administrative Assistant

Ideal candidates will have 7+ years serving the business-to-business marketplace, 5+ years of experience within a sales or appointment setting environment, 3+ years of experience with ACT contact management or CRM software, Microsoft Word, Excel, and MS Outlook software. See website for more details.

Capital Typing (http://www.capitaltyping.com/employment-application)

Virtual secretary providing administrative office support for individuals, professionals, SME's and large corporations

Foundation Medicine

(https://careers-foundationmedicine.icims.com/jobs/1371/account-executive-kansas/job)

Account Executive (may require the applicant to live in a certain state)

Overview:

Foundation Medicine is seeking an Account Executive (AE) to develop and grow a territory and to exceed sales goals for Foundation Medicine's fully informative genomic profiling test, FoundationOne™. This encompasses the creation and implementation of a territory business plan as well as the specific sales strategy within a defined geographic region. The AE will be responsible for managing business results, sales activities, and cross functional initiatives in their respective territory. He/She will be responsible for making the day to day decisions required to manage a productive territory, retain existing customer base of business while growing sales through new account acquisition. Securing and analyzing relevant information, knowledge of territory, market intelligence, environmental factors and political landscape, to identify key issues and committing to action after developing alternative solutions that take into consideration strategic objectives, resource constraints and organizational values. The successful AE will also be responsible for a positive ROI within their specified territory. This may be a position covering several states requiring frequent travel.

RESPONSIBILITIES:

- Achievement of territory sales objectives; revenue and expenses
- Development and execution of a territory business plan that aligns with the regional and national strategy
- Direct execution of sales strategies and tactics, and implementation of sales and marketing plans.
- Maintain profitable sales to expense ratio.
- Manage individual territory activities, ensuring return on investment spends.
- Maximize sales pull-through opportunities that are aligned with FMI's managed care strategy to achieve or exceed revenue targets.
- Develop and maintain key customer relationships with target audiences; assists in developing business solutions that are mutually beneficial; applies broader business scenarios and customer-focused models to achieve breakthrough results.
- Maintain high level of product and market knowledge.
- Assist in programs designed to promote or facilitate product sales and the FMI culture/image.
- Participate in cross functional teams that support all customer facing roles within the assigned geographic region.
- Identify client-bill contracting opportunities with academic medical centers, large cancer centers, health systems, and other strategically important key accounts.

- Full compliance with FMI's CRM solution for the defined geographic region.

QUALIFICATIONS:

Leadership – The successful candidate must be a high energy, charismatic leader who is first a talented, strategically oriented, highly ethical business executive with strong executive presence and presentation skills. He/she will have the skills and ability to quickly gain credibility and respect with both the internal and external constituents. He/she will participate by example to ensure a good and compliant working environment, while at the same time maintaining accountability for delivering upon commitments.

Driving Results – The successful candidate will have an accomplished track record in growing complex organizations. History of success maintaining key relationships, demonstrated ability to drive strategic sales/marketing solutions, demonstrated ability to execute sales strategy focusing on net sales growth while leveraging existing customer relationships into increasing market share and developing and executing plans to deliver new channels of distribution.

Building and Managing Relationships – The successful candidate will have comfort and experience interacting with key strategic accounts, thought leaders and Key Opinion Leaders (KOLs) instrumental and other influential healthcare executives in the oncology commercial and research/development continuum that defines the operating complexity of the biotechnology / Personalized Medicine / MDx industry.

- A minimum of 5 years of experience in a relevant industry/commercial environment (pharmaceutical, diagnostics, research products) as a sales professional.
- Bachelor's degree required.
- Deep domain knowledge of the Diagnostic Services industry. Molecular Diagnostic experience strongly preferred.
- Experience selling Oncology based tests and services into the Pathology and/or Oncology clinical communities preferred
- Experience within complex selling environments required.
- Direct experience in either the diagnostics (preferred) or pharmaceutical market.

- Ability to travel required
- Abilities: (Abilities as evidenced through activities or behaviors that are similar to those required on the job, including dealing with ambiguity, action oriented, self-development, and decision quality)
  - Able to prioritize and align organizational goals and objectives; enables innovation through quick decision making and encourages a sense of urgency; ensures rigor in operational excellence and focuses on outcomes with clear measures and metrics.
  - Interpersonal flexibility to effectively interact with a broad range of personnel.
  - Ability to develop and utilize cross-functional relationships to facilitate the accomplishment of work goals and objectives.
  - Advanced presentation skills and business acumen a necessity.
  - Ability to work effectively with minimal direction from the Regional Sales Manager.
  - Problem solving, decision making and technical learning.
  - Advanced written and oral communication skills.
  - Strong administrative skills. Sophistication to manage business in complex environments.
- Demonstrates FMI's Values by acting with integrity, respect and trust.
- Knowledge: (Proficiency in a body of information that can be applied directly to accomplish a task, e.g. knowledge of molecular diagnostics, genomics, personalized medicine, knowledge of particular oncology drugs)
  - Comprehensive understanding and experience with various industry trends and market segments and industry trends. Clear knowledge of regional market trends.
  - Knowledge and application of strategic planning, and development sales strategy and tactical implementation within your specified territory.
  - Expertise in health care with emphasis on molecular diagnostics, genomics, biotechnology, pharmaceuticals, and oncology.

Medical Science Liaison

More information about this job:

Overview:

Foundation Medicine is aiming to build a high-performing, experienced Medical Science Liaison Team to round out our highly respected Medical Affairs Team specifically related to developing and enhancing a strong network of Key Opinion Leaders (KOLs) to support the commercial and scientific efforts and objectives of the company. We are seeking multiple field-based, highly trained Medical Science Liaisons (MSLs) with strong clinical and/or scientific backgrounds and excellent communication skills to initiate and sustain an exchange of scientific information with key external customers and internal teams. Activities include conducting scientific presentations to health care providers, emphasizing the medical and scientific strengths of the company's existing products, well as with any future company development initiatives. The MSL will address scientific questions, as well as promote and develop access to key thought leaders in their assigned region and utilize these relationships to collaborate where appropriate on educational and research opportunities. This position will report to the VP, Medical Affairs and will require approximately 70% travel. At this time we are considering candidates that are based in any location in the Continental United States.

RESPONSIBILITIES:

- Function as a regional MSL specializing in Medical Affairs interactions and initiation and exchange of scientific information with key opinion leaders and other physicians in the oncology and pathology settings
- Facilitate education regarding FMI products in the hematology/oncology and pathology communities as a scientific expert through presentations and scientific exchange
- Help identify and establish relationships with key opinion leaders, clinical and research leaders including academicians, clinicians, medical directors and other HCPs, and provide regular support and education regarding disease state awareness and FMI clinical data
- Respond to scientific/genomic inquiries from HCP customers promptly

- Assist with identification of investigator initiated studies, guiding through the approval process, and monitoring study progress
- Facilitate involvement in national, regional and local scientific forums including symposia, tumor boards and training meetings
- Contribute to scientific messaging for promotional materials, provide competitive insight and work with managers to provide leadership and strategies to develop advocates for the company
- Develop and create materials such as slide decks, training materials, white papers, monographs, case report summaries, clinical synopses
- Integrate efforts with Medical Affairs for organization of scientific advisory boards, key opinion leader management, coordination of clinical trials, and execution of publication strategy
- Gather market intelligence on competitor products and new products in development.

REQUIRED SKILLS

- General understanding of the field of oncology; knowledge of oncogenomics and targeted therapy
- Fundamental understanding of principal cancer patient management algorithms and clinical utility of laboratory-developed molecular tests
- Familiarity with CLIA, LDT, Sunshine Act (2013), AdvaMed Guidelines
- Business acumen (market analysis, market access strategy, territory planning) combined with exceptional interpersonal communication ability
- Existing key opinion leader relationships a plus
- Ability to train/teach others
- Strong matrix management skills
- Ability to travel (domestic) extensively (70%), often at short notice
- Self-motivated

EDUCATION AND EXPERIENCE

- Advanced scientific or medical degree (PhD, PharmD, MD)

- 3 or more years of MSL experience in a diagnostics, biotech or pharmaceutical company. Oncology experience is required.

New Market Corporation

(https://newmarket-corporation.workable.com/jobs/88024)

Accounting Administrative Assistant

DESCRIPTION:

We are looking for a detail-oriented, meticulous, and experienced Administrative/Accounting Assistant to help support in the accounting department. This position is being created due to growth in our company and we are looking for the right person to build upon. Our hope is for this person to build a long-term career with a successful and growing company that aligns with both our goals and their goals alike. We pride ourselves on building employee capital and rewarding those who work hard.

REQUIREMENTS:

- At least 2-5 years of experience as an Administrative Assistant with general accounting/bookkeeping experience and possibly banking experience.
- Proficiency in Microsoft Office, Excel and Quick-books.
- Strong problem solving skills.
- Strong attention to detail.
- Ability to work independently with minimal supervision.
- Assist in verifying daily time logs.

ReachOut Healthcare America

(https://reachout-healthcare-america.workable.com/jobs/96062)

Administrative Assistant

DESCRIPTION:

The Healthcare Administrative Assistant provides administrative support to the Director and select additional team members. This includes a full range of administrative and programmatic duties, and requires the ability to handle a broad range of items on a proactive, professional and discreet basis.

REQUIREMENTS:

1. High School Diploma or equivalent required.

2. Ideal candidates will have experience in the healthcare industry, with data analysis and administrative assistant experience. Candidates should have excellent communication skills both written and verbal, high attention to detail, in depth understanding of excel, be highly organized and positive, team player attitude.

3. Minimum one year's experience in an administrative position required; experience in the healthcare industry strongly preferred.

4. Responsible for managing deadlines and communications to the team and assign appropriate roles in project scenarios.

5. Maintain necessary files in support of department's activities.

6. Implements and enforces policies and procedures set by management and in line with Company policies.

The Healthcare Administrative Assistant provides administrative support to the Director and select additional team members.

Responsive Translation

(http://www.responsivetranslation.com/company/jobs/)

Business Development Administrator/Inside Sales

The business development administrator will assist the sales department in identifying and qualifying sales prospects using a program of email, social media linking and phone research to develop a list of qualified prospects for the sales team. This is a remote position. The successful candidate should reside in a North American or South American time zone. This is a great opportunity for someone interested in mastering the consultative sales process earning big commissions while working at home.

Freelance Project Managers

Seeking freelance project managers to work on a temporary and/or part-time basis for contract work. Project managers will be responsible for handling all aspects of a translation engagement, which may include desktop publishing, audiovisual or software localization tasks to ensure a great customer experience and a high-quality deliverable prepared in an ISO 9001

QA environment. We are looking for people with the skillsets and collo-quial fluency in English best suited to the needs of our Fortune 500 clientele. Successful candidates will be able to demonstrate a history of marshaling diverse teams for great outcomes. This is a remote assignment, but candidates should reside in a North or South American time zone. The successful candidate will be able to offer a robust IT presence that will ensure reliable and uninterrupted communication with clients and other team members. Knowledge of Trados is a must. Experience in pre- and post-edited machine translation workflows is a valuable plus.

Sage

(https://careers-sage.icims.com/jobs/11843/san-accountant-advocate-i/job?mode=job&iis=Internet%2FJob+Board+%28Specify+Job+Board+below%29&iisn=Indeed.com&mobile=false&width=970&height=500&bga=true&needsRedirect=false&jan1offset=-420&jun1offset=-360)

SAN Accountant Advocate I

OVERVIEW:

Sage has an immediate opening for a Sr. Accountant Advocate. This position will focus efforts on providing an Extraordinary Customer Experience to the Accounting professionals in the Sage Accountants Network/Accountant Partner Program (SAN/APP) program. Responsibilities include new member on-boarding, new member recruitment, member engagement, training and development, as well as being a liaison between SAN/APP members and Sage. Going above and beyond every day to deliver an Extraordinary Customer Experience to SAN/APP members is the most critical piece of this role. In addition, this role will work with the top Global Associations driving Sage awareness within these firms.

RESPONSIBILITIES:

- Deliver an Extraordinary Customer Experience (ECE) to the Sage Accountants Network members through exemplary customer service and by meeting customer expectations of knowledge, empathy and professionalism

- Deliver value added presentations, workshops, webinars and other educational content to associations, partners, and other industry groups on behalf of Sage.

- Respond to member inquiries directing to the appropriate people within Sage that can solve customer problems.
- Meet individual goals and contribute towards departmental goals for quality, productivity, sales and sales adherence
- Update and maintains customer database as necessary
- Communicate effectively and efficiently in a fast paced team environment
- Ensure SAN/APP member satisfaction by forming US-based advisory group (not in existence today)
- Ensure new SAN/APP members are up and running on the software and are aware of training resources and availability, which may involve welcome calls
- Represent accountant customer needs and goals within the organization to ensure quality
- Proactively contact SAN/APP members to educate, inform and gather information about how to best service them and their clients
- Build relationships and value with accountant customers to encourage new and repeat business opportunities
- Research and pursue opportunities for account growth and new business in specific geographical areas
- Communicate accountant customer goals and represent the SAN/APP member interests to the Partner Programs team
- Use social media to establish trust in the SAN/APP program and convey program messages
- Regularly post content from the SAN/APP program on Facebook, Twitter, Linked In and other social media websites
- Join and participate in other Social Media groups and organizations that tie into the Sage Partner Programs strategy
- Protect company proprietary and confidential information
- Other duties as assigned

QUALIFICATIONS:

- Bachelor's degree in Finance/Accounting, Business or Marketing or equivalent work experience

- Previous customer experience is required
- Working knowledge of Sage 50 would be an asset
- Working knowledge as an accounting professional would be an asset
- Ability to work well with peers, managers, and administrative personnel in order to accomplish objectives and build relationships across the business
- Ability to identify and analyze problems, propose solutions, and anticipate problem areas before initiating action and implementing solutions
- Must have excellent organizational and time management skills
- Ability to multi-task and prioritize is critical
- Excellent interpersonal and communication skills
- Excellent attitude and spirit of cooperation
- Professional telephone manner
- Ability to work with minimal supervision
- Working knowledge of MS Office applications, especially Word and Outlook
- Ability to learn quickly and apply knowledge to practical use

Virtual Office Temps (http://www.virtualassistantjobs.com/)

- Virtual Assistants

VOT (Virtual Office Temps) recruits professional virtual assistants to work from home providing clerical and administrative support. Register on their site to be considered for work.

Xerox
(http://xerox-virtual.jobs/virtual-usa/director-of-business-operations-xerox-human-resource-services/42EC00C4A9C44BC4A1583B6A6525120B/job/)

Director of Business Operations, Xerox Human Resource Services in United States

Within Xerox, Human Resource Services brings the full spectrum of human resource, benefits, and healthcare consulting and outsourcing to our advisory, technology, and administration solutions. Here you'll discover an innovative, high-energy environment that inspires top achievement. As a prestigious highly successful leader in providing employee benefit, actuarial, outsourcing and HR management consulting services, we have the strong resources, solid reputation and global reach to enrich your work life and enhance your career.

Position: Director of Business Operations, Xerox Human Resource Services•Responsible for directing the activities of the Business Operations function. •Ensures that business group standards around client profitability, pricing, contracts, and equipment investments and real-estate are maintained. •Oversees the development and implementation of client and contract performance metrics and tools. •Provides leadership and direction for diverse and complex functions, including risk/quality, operational/organizational excellence, automation, management reporting, and information technology in support of the business group. •Contributes to the development of the organization's business strategy. •Interprets business strategy and develops organizational objectives to align with this strategy. •Leads process improvement initiatives through use of measurements, accountability, analysis and consideration of process alternatives in order to arrive at best practices. •Manages multiple teams of professionals.

Behaviors We Value: Agility • Nurturing • Creativity • Integrity • Accountability • Vision • Client value driven • Positivity • Emotional intelligence • Thought leader • Trusted advisor • Collaborative

KEY RESPONSIBILITIES:

- Evaluate actual results against expected performance and communicate areas for improvement • Establish, evaluate, and implement performance metrics to track business performance; measures and analyze actual performance and make recommendations for improving profitability where needed

- Review and analyze forecasts and recommend changes where appropriate; in partnership with Finance, update forecasts for both current performance and new development to provide management with a current perspective of the business

- Collaborate with cross-functional groups to propose and manage creative solutions for improving coordination, collaboration, and communication; in certain situations, coordinate and drive to resolution cross functional initiatives impacting financial performance

- In partnership with Finance, develop and manage budget and expenses

- Lead overall reporting and analysis for organization focused on operational reporting, proactive monitoring and identifying opportunities for improvements

- Develop and implement holistic operational review and scorecard process to provide single view of operations across primary business verticals and horizontals, and in total

- Drive the leadership team to clear, efficient and accountable decision-making

- Establish a consistent, best-in-class, strategic approach for change management and organizational effectiveness in order to increase employee adoption and usage while minimizing resistance

- Network effectively across the broader Xerox organization to internal services and solutions as well as to increase operational efficiency and mitigate corporate risk

- Lead and grow a high performing team of professionals; direct training and education to staff on metrics and tools to improve financial performance. Foster people development through leadership and example

- Demonstrate the highest level of integrity and honesty

EXPERIENCE:

- Generally requires 12 years related experience in Finance, Information Systems, Business Process Improvement or Operations

- Deep financial management (P&L/Budget/Cost Containment)

- Demonstrated business process improvement success

- Excellent data visualization and creative PowerPoint skills

- Excellent Word, Excel skills

Education Bachelor's Degree or Equivalent - Field of study-Finance, Accounting, Economics, Statistics or Information Systems preferred

CERTFICATIONS - PMP, Lean, BPI or Six Sigma preferred

Xerox is an Equal Opportunity Employer and considers applicants for all positions without regard to race, color, religion or belief, sex, age, national origin, citizenship status, marital status, military/veteran status, genetic information, sexual orientation, gender identity, physical or mental disability or any other characteristic protected by applicable laws. People with disabilities who need a reasonable accommodation to apply or compete for employment with Xerox should contact (in the US) accommodations@xerox.com.

BI-LINGUAL WORK AT HOME JOBS

Bi-lingual call center

1-800-FLOWERS
(http://ww30.1800flowers.com/template.do?id=template8&page=9000&conversionTag=true)

New York-based floral company regularly hires for at-home call center jobs on a temporary basis for seasonal employment. It does occasionally hire permanent (particularly bilingual), at-home call center agents as well.
Must live in the following states: Florida, New Mexico, New York, Ohio, Oklahoma, Texas or Virginia.

Advanis (http://www.advanis.ca/available-positions)

Canadian market research company hiring for virtual call center jobs and mystery shopping jobs.
Bilingual jobs in French or Spanish available for the home call center jobs.
Must live in Canada for call center jobs

Home Based Telephone Research Interviewer Locations: Your home Salary: Hourly wage as advertised, please call or email for more detail Start Date: Immediately Hours of Operation: Monday through Friday 3-10 pm MST (5-12 pm EST) and Saturdays 10-5pm MST (12-7 pm EST) Advanis is a Market and Policy Research company that has been doing surveys since 1997 and we are looking for telephone interviewers. We offer fully paid training and a set wage. You need: • a good command of the English language • excellent customer service skills • a typing speed of 30 wpm • a quiet, private place in your home • a computer with high speed Internet service • a phone line in the office space – if you wish to leave your phone line available for people to call in on ,you would need to have a second (separate) phone line • a landline phone. No cellphones. • a corded headset with a noise cancelling microphone. No cordless phones or speaker phones. • a personal computer (PC or Mac) Bilingualism (French, Spanish, or other) is an asset, but not essential. As a remote agent, you would receive additional benefits such as: • the ability to claim a portion of household expenses such as Internet, power, rent, or mortgage • no transportation cost to come to work and no parking costs • great web community to provide you with the support you need to do a great job • flexible scheduling that works with your home life Application Procedure Applications will only be accepted through our online application form available on our website. We thank all applicants for their interest; however, only candidates under consideration will be contacted.

Affiliated Computer Services, Inc. (http://www.acs-inc.com/)

FORTUNE 500 companies, owned by Xerox, provides business process outsourcing (BPO) and Information technology solutions. Company offers part-time employment (paying $10/hr) for home call center agents, bilingual (Spanish) preferred.
Use "work at home" a keyword in company's careers database.

Alorica (http://www.apply.westathome.com/applynow.html)

Alorica's customer service agents are employees who handle billing, sales or technical troubleshooting calls for the company's clients. They are paid on a per-minute rate, per-call or minimum wage. Training is paid. Some bilingual jobs are available

Alpine Access (https://jobs.alpineaccess.com/)

Home-based agents take in-bound customer service and sales call for various clients.
Reps at this Business process outsourcer (BPO) are paid at an hourly rate of around $9, and training is paid.

Requires a minimum commitment of 20 hours per week with up to full-time hours available.

Bilingual jobs in Languages such as Spanish, Mandarin and Cantonese available.

Apple At-Home Advisors (http://www.apple.com/jobs/us/aha.html)

Apple at Home is a work at home call center program from Apple that is part of the company's Apple Care department. Use the keyword "home" in the company's job database. It recruits French and English bilingual agents who live within 100 miles of Markham, Ontario.

American Express (http://jobs.americanexpress.com/key/work-from-home-jobs.html)

The travel division of American Express hires bilingual virtual travel agents and call center agents with experience in reservation systems in the U.S., U.K., Canada and Australia. Use "virtual" "telecommute" or "work at home" as keywords to find a job online in its database.

Assurian (https://www.asurion.com/asurion/en/home/?referral=newcorp)

Extended warranty company pays home-based customer care reps $9-10 per hour to take in-bound calls. It hires both work-at-home and office-based call center agents to troubleshoot and provide customer service for its clients. New hires who live within 50 miles of a brick-and-mortar training site must train there; others can train virtually. The company's clients include Best Buy, Lowe's DirecTV, Wal-Mart, GameStop, AT&T and Gateway.
Hires agents bilingual in Spanish/English also.

BSG - Third Party Verification (http://www.bsgclearing.com/contact_us/careers/)

Agents take inbound calls to do third party verification for utility, cable and financial services clients. Agents can choose shifts as short as two hours. Pay is $8.50/hour for English-only agents and $9/hour for bilingual agents.

Languages needed include Korean, Vietnamese, Spanish, Cantonese, Mandarin, Tagalog, Arabic, Armenian, Bosnian, Cantonese, Farsi, German, Indonesian, Korean, Mandarin, Persian, Polish, Somalia, Russian, Turkish, Ukrainian and Yugoslavian.

Century Link
(http://www.centurylink.com/Pages/AboutUs/CompanyInformation/ Careers/)

Formerly CenturyTel and EMBARQ, CenturyLink is a provider of voice, broadband and video services for consumers and businesses in 33 states.
Work at home call center jobs pay around $10-11/per hour.
Bilingual encouraged to apply. Search job database using "work at home."
Work at home jobs are based in FL, IN, KS, MN, MO, NC, NE, NJ, NV, OH, PA, SC, TN, TX, VA, and WY.

Hilton Hotels (http://jobs.hiltonworldwide.com/en/?cntry=united- states)

Hotel chain's Hilton@Home program hires motivated, work-from-home sales agents for customer care and reservations. New hires receive in-depth training and support.
Bilingual jobs in Spanish or Portuguese earn $1 per hour more.
$47/hr in Part-time job openings. Requirements: Must have a computer.

JetBlue (http://www.jetblue.com/work-here/job-descriptions.aspx)

Airline hires some home-based customer service representatives as employees.
Bilingual ability may be required for some call center jobs. Travel to Salt Lake City, UT, office may be required.

LiveOps (http://join.liveops.com/)

Company hires independent-contractor, call-center agents, including licensed Insurance agents, for a variety of positions including outbound sales, bilingual customer service (Spanish and French) and financial services.

TeleTech@Home

(http://www.teletechjobs.com/athome-en-US)

Global business process outsourcing (BPO) company hires associates in some U.S. states and the U.K. To work from home as call agents and other fields. TeleTech@Home's call center agents are employees, not independent contractors.

These call center agents perform sales, customer service, and technical support. Agents bilingual in Spanish, German, French, Catalan, Dutch and many other languages are hired. Pay is $9-10/hour.

U-Haul

(http://jobs.uhaul.com/contact_center.aspx?jobtype=workfrom home)

Work at home call center agents take incoming calls from customers dialing specific U-Haul moving centers across the US and Canada. English/French bilingual agents needed in Canada. Representatives answer general questions, take reservation and/or provide roadside assistance. Paid training.

Ubiqus

(http://www.ubiqus.com/GB/recruitment.htm)

Ubiqus is an Equal Opportunity Employer. It considers all positions without regard to race, religion, color, sex, national origin, age, disability or other categories as proscribed by federal, state or local law.

Fill out our online application. If we are interested in your credentials, we will contact you by email or telephone:

Note: Transcriptionist Applicants, please read our disclaimer before beginning your application

> Verbatim Transcriptionist
> Medical Transcriptionist
> Summary Writer
> Medical Summary Writer

Translator

Interpreter

Foreign Language Transcriptionist

Audio Technician

Audience Response Technician

VIP Desk
(https://www.vipdesk.com/employment/login.aspx?ReturnUrl=%2femploy
ment%2fapplicant%2fmyhomepage.aspx&cc=635220487313204132)

Home shoring company specializes in delivering concierge and virtual call
center services for the "high-value customers" of its corporate clients. Its
home-based agents handle customer requests via phone, e-mail, and chat
and research and fulfill requests from customers in the United States and
abroad. Offers full- and part-time hours but agents must commit to certain
availabilities.
Fluency in English is required. Fluency in French, German, Spanish or Italian is a plus.

Working Solutions
(http://www.workingsolutions.com/work-at-home-agents/)

Company contracts with agents to do call center and data entry jobs for
clients.
Pay ranges from $7.20 to $30 an hour. Call center projects include order processing, reservations, Customer service, sales, market research and technical
support.
Applicants who successfully complete a two-part online test are placed on
a list and notified when a project becomes available. Hires agents Bilingual
in 32 different languages including Mandarin, Portuguese, Bengali, Spanish,
Italian, French, German, Greek, Vietnamese, Tagalog, Punjabi, Japanese,
Hindi, Romanian, Polish, Russia and Arabic.
Accepts agents from outside the U.S. for some projects.

Bi-lingual Translation/Transcription/ Interpretation

Aberdeen

(http://workathomemoms.about.com/od/dataentrytranscription/fl/Work-at-HOme-Company-Profile-Aberdeen-Captioning.htm)

Bilingual Jobs: Translation, Transcription

Company provides captioning, transcription and translation services and hires transcribers, real time captioners, editors and translators to work at home and in its office in Orange County, CA.

Transcription jobs pay $1-$1.50 per audio minutes; real time captioners are paid $75/hour.

Acclaro (http://www.acclaro.com/localization-jobs)

Bilingual Jobs: Localization, translation
Agency hires experienced freelance translators and other localization professionals to work from home.

Appen Butler Hill (https://erec.appen.com/sap/bc/webdynpro/sap/hrrcf_a_unreg_job_search?sap-client=300#)

Bilingual Jobs: Translation Review
Hires language consultants and data annotators who evaluate online search results as well as translators and transcriptionists. Looks for candidates with experience in linguistics, especially computational; software testing and library science plus a native-level fluency in more than one language other than English.

Capital Typing
(http://www.capitaltyping.com/employment-application)

Language Translation Service is provided in Spanish, French and German.

CSC (http://www.csc.com/careersus/flxwd/16005-careers)

Bilingual Jobs: Translation, Media Monitoring
Company offers IT-enabled business solutions and services to businesses. Jobs in its database indicate whether it is remote. Hires for telecommute jobs in IT, management and translation.

DialogOne
(http://dialog-one.com/career/)

Dialog One is committed to delivering the very best cross cultural communication solutions to meet our client's needs. We are always looking for highly skilled professionals and reliable agents such as freelance translators, interpreters, cultural mediators, marketing professionals, desktop publishers, webmaster with foreign language skills and other professionals to help us meet our clients' globalization strategies.

Minimal Qualifications:
Minimum 2 years of College Education
Excellent verbal and written communication
Fluent in both native and acquired languages
Experience working with inter-cultural environments
The ability to pass "Proficiency Exam"
Criminal background check
Drug test
Provide Two (2) letters of recommendations

Dialog One offer numerous advantages:
Opportunities to support in a variety of services and time frames.
An agent relations department dedicated to assist while you are collaborating with Dialog One access to work opportunities in a variety of specialties and fields of interest accumulate and balance your work experience with a company that accredits your experience.

GlobaLink Translations Ltd.
(http://www.globalinktranslations.com/work_with_us.asp?section= workwithus)

Bilingual Jobs: Translation, Translation Review, Localization Canadian company assists clients with translation and cultural adaptation needs.
Its translation jobs are for both translators and translation reviewers.

Google
(http://workathomemoms.about.com/od/webdesignmarketing/p/Google-Ads-Quality-Rater.htm)

Bilingual Jobs: Translation Review/Quality Rater
Hires ads quality raters who evaluate the accuracy of Google web advertising and communicating the effectiveness of web layouts and information using an online tool.

The requirements include a BA/BS Degree (or equivalent experience); fluency in a specific language as well as English; an understanding of the culture of the speakers of the specific language; web research and analytic capabilities, high-speed Internet connection and U.S. work authorization. Languages include Chinese, Japanese, Korean, Russian, Italian, German, Spanish, Turkish and more.

Language Line Solutions

(https://www.languageline.com/company/careers/)

Bilingual Jobs: Interpreter
Interpreters are tasked with quickly understanding and instantly communicating an idea across two languages, while retaining the meaning of the original message. This requires a high level of proficiency in both languages because some concepts do not always translate literally from one language to another. A qualified interpreter will be capable of performing this action without delay and in a manner that effectively facilitates the conversation until its completion.

LanguagesUnlimited (http://www.languagesunlimited.com/)

Bilingual Jobs: Translation, Interpretation
Company hires linguists on a freelance basis for translation jobs as well as on-site and telephone interpretation and transcription services. To apply, register in company's database.
Languages include Japanese, Chinese, Spanish, English, French, German, Russian, Bengali, Hindi, Portuguese and more.

Linguistic Systems

(http://www.linguist.com/for-translators-overview.htm)

Bilingual Jobs: Translation, Interpretation
Requirements include two years' experience, college degree, access to email and knowledge of use basic translation software tools. Company seeks "language professionals with in depth knowledge in a professional field (such as medicine, software, finance, and engineering, interpreters or narrators (voice-over professionals) living in the New England area." Online

application includes translating a short text for each language pair you wish to qualify in. Permit to work in U.S. required.

LiveOPs (http://cloud.liveops.com/glp-liveops-multichannel-demo. html?gclid=CITD-8bxl7sCFbQWMgodTRkA1g)

Industry:
Call Center: at home insurance jobs: licensed insurance agents
Based in Santa Clara, CA, this privately held company provides call center outsourcing to clients using only U.S.-based home call center agents. Its more than 20,000 virtual call center agents are all independent contractors.

Types of Work at Home Opportunities:
Most calls are inbound sales calls; however there are several types of center agent positions:
Advanced sales agent - According to LiveOPs web page, the average advanced sales agent can invoice $9.62 per 30 minute block.

Outbound agents - According to LiveOPs web page, the average Outbound Agent makes $5.25 per 30 minute block but incentives are available.

Bilingual agents - French and Spanish
Roadside assistance agent -inbound/outbound sales, customer service and dispatch.

Network Omni (http://www.networkomni.com/about-careers.asp)

Hires experienced freelance language specialists as independent contractors. Minimum requirements are 3 years professional experience in translation or interpretation, college degree and knowledge in specific subject areas, such as legal and financial matters, marketing writing, medical and general business. Also have freelance opportunities for desktop publishers and localization engineers.

Pacific Interpreters (http://www.pacificinterpreters.com/careers/)

Bilingual Jobs: Translation, Interpretation
Company hires telephonic interpreters and translators for the medical industry.
U.S. citizenship/work permit and experience in medical industry required.

Quicktate/iDictate

(http://workathomemoms.about.com/od/workathomejobprofiles/p/Quick-tate-Idictate.htm)

Bilingual Jobs: Transcription
Company provides transcription of short audio files, such as voicemails and dictated notes, by hiring work-at-home transcribers. Quicktate pays $.0025 per word and iDictate and Quicktates medical transcription work pay $.0050 per word. Successful QuickTate transcriptionists may receive work from iDictate, which transcribes a wider range of documents. Bilingual, particularly Spanish and English, transcribers needed but other languages such as French, Italian, German, Chinese, Farsi, Portuguese and Japanese desired as well.

Responsive Translation (http://www.responsivetranslation.com/company/jobs/)

Bilingual Jobs: Translation, Interpretation
Hires freelance translators and on-site interpreters. College degree required. Email resume for consideration. Languages include English, Dutch, Haitian, Creole, Korean, Hebrew, Farsi, Russian, Spanish, Polish, Japanese, Arabic, Mandarin, French, Amharic, Portuguese and more.

SDL (http://www.sdl.com/aboutus/careers/careers.html)

Bilingual Jobs: Translation
Global information Management Company hires freelance translators for translation jobs. The company is a supplier of localization services to the IT, engineering, e-business & multimedia sectors, and experience in those and other business sectors are helpful.
Requirements are a minimum 2 years freelance (or 1 year in-house) translation experience, but the company says it accepts "translators with relevant experience.

Telelanguage (http://www.telelanguage.com/careers)
Bilingual Jobs: Interpretation, Translation
Company offers opportunities for both on-site and telephone interpreters.

Translators.com

(http://www.translatorscafe.com/cafe/default.asp)
Bilingual Jobs: Interpretation, Translation
Bid site for translation and interpretation services offers thousands of opportunities in a huge variety of Languages.

Ubiqus

(http://www.ubiqus.com/GB/recruitment.htm)

Ubiqus is an Equal Opportunity Employer. It considers all positions without regard to race, religion, color, sex, national origin, age, disability or other categories as proscribed by federal, state or local law.

Fill out our online application. If we are interested in your credentials, we will contact you by email or telephone:

Note: Transcriptionist Applicants, please read our disclaimer before beginning your application

Translator

Interpreter

Foreign Language Transcriptionist

WordExpress (http://www.wordexpress.net/freelance-position.html)

Bilingual Jobs: Translation, Interpretation, Desktop Publishing, Sales, Voice Talent Santa Monica, CA-based company hires for freelance translation jobs in more than 100 different languages from anywhere in the world. Other positions include sales managers and reps, interpreters, desktop publishers and voice talent.

Worldlingo (http://www.worldlingo.com/en/company/jobs.html)

Bilingual Jobs: Translation, Interpretation
Requirements for generalist translators or proofreader are 5 years continuous translation experience in a commercial environment, membership of the

professional translation association, university degree from a recognized institution and Trados 5 Freelance.

Bi-lingual Writing and Teaching

About en Español
(http://weblogs.about.com/b/2011/09/20/writing-jobs-for-spanish-bloggers-open-At-about-com.htm)

Bilingual Jobs: Writing
About.com contracts guides, which are experts in many fields, to write online content for its Spanish-language site About en Español. Must be fluent in English and Spanish. Pay for this work at home jobs starts at $675/month.

Appen
(https://erec.appen.com/sap/bc/webdynpro/sap/hrrcf_a_unreg_job_search?sap-client=300#)

Linguist: Croatian, Danish, Dutch, Estonian, Finnish, Japanese, Malay, Romanian, Montenegrin, Armenian, Assamese, Hong Kong, Kazakh, Japanese, Indonesian, Hebrew, Arabic, Korean, Lithuanian, Macedonian, Thai, Lithuanian, Korean, Arabic, and others.

Annotator: Romanish

Data Annotator: French, German, Italian, Japanese, English (India), English (UK),

AuraLog
(http://www.homejobsformom.com/job/auralog.)

Compensation increases with page view growth.
Bilingual Jobs: Teaching
Hires online language tutors to work in conjunction with "Tell me more" Language software.

Connections Academy
(https://www.connectionsacademy.com/careers/home.aspx)

Bilingual Jobs: Teaching
Connections Academy "a school without walls", is a virtual educational program serving K-12 Students throughout various states in a non-Classroom-based environment. It hires certified Teachers for online teaching jobs.
This includes foreign language teacher for K-12 German, French and Spanish.

EduFire (http://edufire.com/why_teach)

Bilingual Jobs: Teaching
Types of Online Teaching Jobs: Adult Education, Languages, Exam Prep (This company does not hire Online tutors but provides a service of putting together students and tutors and providing online tools for tutoring. It charges 15 percent commission on all fees collected by tutors.)

Gofluent (http://www.gofluent.com/web/us/careers)

Bilingual Jobs: Teaching
Teaching English by phone, gofluent seeks home-based trainer who are native English speaker and are Bilingual in French, Italian, German, Russian and Korean.
They hire only from Kansas, Missouri, New York, Oregon, and Pennsylvania and Canada.

SMARTTHINKING.com
(https://careers-smarthinking.icims.com/jobs/intro)

Bilingual Jobs: Teaching
The Washington, D.C.-based education organization hires part-time (usually 9-20 hours per week), work-at-home tutors for many subjects (including foreign languages) for students of varying abilities and ages. Tutors may work from anywhere in the world as long as they have computer and Internet access (and a U. S. bank account).
Peak season for hiring is May-August and November-December every year. Most tutors are paid on an hourly basis. Paid training.
Hires graduate and undergraduate as well as high school students.

Worldlingo (http://www.worldlingo.com/en/company/jobs.html)

Bilingual Jobs: Proofreading, Editing, Writing, Desktop Publishing, Sales, Voice Talent
Requirements for generalist translators or proofreader are 5 years continuous translation experience in a commercial environment, membership of the professional translation association, university degree from a recognized institution and Trados 5 Freelance.

CHAT ROOM CUSTOMER SERVICE REPRESENTATIVE

(The companies listed are the ones with job openings at
the time of publishing)

Apple At Home Advisor (https://jobs.apple.com/us/search?)

Apple has a work at home call center program that hires college and non-students full-time or part-time. You must be within 100 miles of specific locations. Check their site for more details.

Arise
(http://www.ariseworkfromhome.com/getting-started/join-an-ib)

Arise is a well-known and highly trusted company offering work at home chat jobs. However, Arise is very different from most any other work at home company. In order to contract work through Arise's clients you would have to incorporate yourself as a business and pay for training. Only some of Arise's clients offer work at home chat jobs. However, the handfuls that do are well known brands.

While it may take a lot of time and some investment to contract to Arise-it can be very well worth every bit of your efforts. The positions usually pay well (reportedly $9-19/hour depending on the client) and they have a highly flexible scheduling system. Remember though that working with Arise means you are starting your own home based business.

Join an Independent Business as a Client Support Professional
Not Ready to Start Your Own Business?

If you're not ready to start your own business, but still want see if the call center industry is right for you, a great way to give it a try is to join an existing business in the Arise Vendor Network as a Client Support Professional. It's a first step to learn about the industry, and the details of providing services to clients using Arise infrastructure, before choosing to start your own company.

- As a Client Support Professional with an existing business in the Arise Network, you will work for that independent business.
- Every business in the Arise network is different, and the work arrangements (from home, contractor, employee, local call center) vary.
- Arise does not endorse any one independent business and we encourage you to visit our Facebook page and talk with the tens of thousands of members of our Independent Business community.

The admissions process is the same no matter which path you choose.

1. Fill out a profile
2. Take a voice assessment
3. Pass a background check ($7.95 paid directly to the background check company)
4. Enroll in and pass the basic course "CSP 101" which provides details about the Arise infrastructure and systems ($5 - $99 class fee – some independent businesses offer reimbursement, follow Arise on Facebook for updates on special pricing)
5. *It is at this point that you have the opportunity to register your small business – or let us know that you have joined an existing company as a CSP. Engage with Independent Businesses on our Facebook Page or reach out to the "Arise Premiere Partners" – the top performing businesses in our network.*
6. After you've completed the Admissions Process, you have the opportunity to select a client program and enroll in a certification course – upon completion you get to service a particular brand based on your arrangement with the Independent Business you join.

Capital Typing
(http://www.capitaltyping.com/employment-a pplication)

Capital typing hires Chat support specialists to assist customers' online providing answers and customer support. See their website for more details.

My Live Pro (http://mylivepro.com/jobs-mylivepro)

Growth, diversity, work-life balance and recognition…
..You'll find all that and more as a member of our LivePRO Managed Live Chat Team. We conduct our business at the highest ethical standards so that our Clients trust us to "Do the right thing". We are committed to earning that same trust from our employees, which is why we aim to ensure that our team members receive respect, support an opportunities for development.
With our recent growth, we have significantly expanded our geography, further enhancing job opportunities for energetic, ambitious and talented people like you.

Our Live Chat Agent Job Description- Part Time IC
We provide Managed Live Chat Solutions for leading business organizations across the country. Our clients trust us to save them time and money while helping them provide legendary service to their website Visitors.
We're looking for part-time Live Chat Agents to respond to Live Text Chats on behalf of our clients. As a LivePRO Chat Agent, you'll receive full training from a dedicated mentor and will be supported by our proprietary internal tools.

KEY BENEFITS:
- Professional Involvement in cutting edge industry
- Work from Home with a flexible schedule
- Dynamic work environment
- Fun company culture

PRIMARY RESPONSIBILITIES:
- Answer text chats and respond to live visitor requests.
- Promptly identify, research, and resolve visitor requests using the Internet and internal tools.

- Project a professional company image on behalf of our clients through text chat interaction
- Provide visitors with client's basic products and/or services information.
- Promote clients' products and/or services.
- Categorize and assign chat sessions appropriately.
- Recommend process improvements.

KEY REQUIREMENTS:

- Must be over 18 years old, flexible, responsible and dependable
- Legally permitted to work in the United States
- Reside in continental United States (not Alaska or Hawaii)
- Must pass a background check
- Maintain your own records and pay your own taxes
- Must have
  - Attention to detail with a superior customer service attitude
  - A home office workspace, snappy computer and reliable Internet connection
  - Computer Savvy / Ninja-like Internet Research abilities
  - Good self-management and motivation
  - Ability to employ common sense with on-the-spot decision making
  - An intermediate understanding general business operations and related resources
  - Professional verbal and written communication skills and the ability to type 30 wpm
  - DSL or Cable Modem connection to the internet
  - A monitor capable of displaying at least 1024 X 768 pixels
  - A sound card installed with speakers or headphones
  - Personal System requirements should be a PC based workstation with 2 GB memory recommended, the ability to run Microsoft.NET Framework 2.0 or higher, and the latest edition of Firefox browser.

So, if being a part-time Professional Live Chat Agent sounds like the rewarding challenge you've been looking for, watch for details for upcoming openings!

Needle.com
(https://pincushion.needle.com/needlers/welcome/)

Chat online for clients such as Coach, Overstock,etc …
Needle has partnered with several internet retailers to provide shoppers with live product expertise from fans like you who know and use their products.

If selected, you will:
Chat online with customers and help them find the right products
Set your own schedule, work as a 1099 contractor
Compensated with cash, plus earn points to redeem for cool products.

Post Loop (http://www.postloop.com/)

Get paid to comment on various forums online. Forums owners and bloggers need user participation. Attracting visitors to a forum or blog is not easy. People struggling with this come to Post: Loop for help. Post Loop provides a list of the forums and blog posts needing your participation. You participate and you get paid.

Pays via Paypal everyday as long as you have reached your payment minimum.

Presto Expert (http://www.prestoexperts.com/)
Get paid chatting online as an expert, answering people's questions.
Must be an expert in the fields of:

Education
Technology
Counseling
Health
Design
Business
Social Media
Shopping
Coaching
Legal
Home Lifestyle

Site Staff (http://sitestaff.com/careers/)

Chat Host: Accepting applications for true service-minded professionals that feel the way they communicate with people makes a difference in their lives.

Talk 2 Rep (http://chk.tbe.taleo.net/chk05/ats/careers/jobSearch.jsp?org=TALK2REP&cws=1&org=TALK2REP)

Talk 2 Rep provides online customer chat support that pays based on your performance. While Needle.com keeps its focus primarily on Customer Support, Talk2Rep is focused on Sales. This is a bit more cut-throat and not as relaxed. I understand the scheduling is semi-flexible but steady and consistent.

Beware: Your pay is dependent on making sales!

Televate (www.televate.com/our-company/careers)

Live Chat Customer Service Assistant: Answer customer questions and resolve issues via live chat.

COMPUTER TECHNOLOGY

BCD   Travel   (http://www.bcdtravel.com/get-to-know-us/careers/search-global-jobs/)

QIK Developer

JOB SUMMARY:

Placement on the Point of Sale (POS) Development team with a focus GDS programming technologies in an effort to increase agent productivity and decrease errors. Responsible for POS version control and upgrades as required. Respond to industry changes that affect the POS standard packages. Establish a proactive approach to addressing and solving customer challenges at the POS. Specific skill to include QIK Developer plus general programming experience.

ESSENTIAL DUTIES:

- Program and customize POS code for automation initiatives
- Provide a proactive and consultative approach to POS development; design solutions that increase agent productivity while decreasing errors
- Gain master proficiency with Sabre QIK Developer, including email and database integration.
- Participate in "scope of work" and ROI for new project requests and technology solutions
- Work with other technology teams and industry suppliers to evaluate best practices and implementation of technology solutions
- Ability to prioritize work and work independently
- Analyze GDS host functionality updates to determine impact
- Special projects as needed
- Assume and perform other duties and responsibilities, not specifically outlined herein, as is proper and inherent to the position

TRANSFERABLE SKILLS (Competencies):

- Proficient in Sabre QIK Developer
- Sabre GDS experience
- Ability to learn mid-office systems, back office systems, fulfillment, and online procedures
- Strong customer service, analytical, organizational, and prioritization skills
- Ability to work independently with minimal supervision
- Proficient in word processing, spreadsheet, and presentation software.
- Professional manner and appearance

QUALIFICATIONS:

- Excellent verbal & written English communication skills
- Minimum 3 years programming experience or equivalent education
- Strong problem solving and process reengineering skills
- Ability to travel as needed (less than 10%)

Cisco

(https://jobs.cisco.com/job/Offsite-Consulting-Systems-Engineer-Commercial-NY/308134100/)

Consulting Systems Engineer

DESCRIPTION:

Want to be at the forefront of the Computer Networking industry? With the acquisition of Meraki, Cisco formed the Cloud Networking Group and created the fastest growing group within the company. Quickly becoming known as the most successful acquisition in Cisco's history, the Cloud Networking Group is crushing its sales targets and continuing to win new logos in the commercial and enterprise markets.

We are looking for a rising star that is highly motivated, technically savvy and passionate to join Cisco's Cloud Networking Group (CNG) as our next Consulting Systems Engineer. In this role, your primary responsibility will be to team up with a rockstar Product Sales Specialist and perform technical pre-sales activities for new and existing opportunities. This position is based in your home office with frequent travel to regional Cisco offices and customer sites. Utilizing your in-depth knowledge of CNG's networking solutions and our competitors' offerings, you will clearly demonstrate the advantages to both prospects and partners. We highly leverage our pre-sales engineers which mean you have the opportunity to make great money while contributing to the success of the entire organization. This territory will cover commercial accounts in New York, New Jersey, and Connecticut.

RESPONSIBILITIES:

Act as the technical subject matter expert, thoroughly understanding products, features, functions, and benefits while being able to communicate to customers of every enterprise level

Understand customer requirements for wireless networks and explain how Cisco Meraki will integrate with current infrastructure, as well as service future needs.

Create product documentation for customers and perform competitive analysis regarding competing products.

Perform site surveys and provide onsite deployment assistance on large deployments

Provide technical guidance to channel partners and assist them in effectively selling the Cisco Meraki solution

DESIRED SKILLS & EXPERIENCE:

Field pre-sales experience required; ASE / CSAP grads preferred

Expert knowledge of 802.11a/b/g/n wireless networks, site surveys, requirements gathering, deployment challenges.

Solid understanding of wired networks, including firewalls, content filters, routing/switching, VLANs, etc.

Understand wireless security methodologies, including 802.1x w/ RADIUS integration

Proven track record of 5-10 years in a pre-sales technical role, such as solutions architect, systems engineer, sales engineer, etc.

Knowledge of sales cycle, strong verbal and written communication skills, and proven negotiation techniques.

Great relationship building skills, tenacity, resilience and presentation skills

CCIE, CWNP, CWDP, CCNA preferred.

Strong organizational skills with the ability to multi-task and set priorities

Ability to travel 50+%

BS or MS degree in computer science, computer engineering or related discipline required.

Deis (https://deis.com/careers)

DevOps Support Engineer - US and EU (Remote)
Technical Support | Remote

The Engine Yard Services & Support team is responsible for assisting the ever growing number of Engine Yard customers with expert advice on deploying, managing and scaling Ruby on Rails or PHP applications. Our customers, who include some of the largest Rails and PHP sites on the web, expect timely, knowledgeable, thorough, double-checked, well-researched and accurate responses and service.

REQUIREMENTS:

- You have experience building and deploying Ruby on Rails or Docker Based Applications.
- You are familiar and have experience with a majority of technologies in our stack https://support.cloud.engineyard.com/hc/en-us/articles/205408398-Engine-Yard-Gentoo-12-11-Technology-Stack
- You are detail-oriented and have excellent verbal and written communication skills.
- You are a troubleshooter at heart and enjoy diving in the deep end, figuring things out, and solving problems.
- Linux skills. You will spend a large part of your day over ssh to our slices and servers. You must be at home on the command line.
- Ability to work remotely 8:00 AM to 5:00 PM (EST or PST) and some weekends.

SKILLS/EXPERIENCE:

- You have deployed and managed high-volume Web Based applications.
- You have existing expert knowledge of at least a handful of our stack technologies: https://support.cloud.engineyard.com/hc/en-us/articles/205408398-Engine-Yard-Gentoo-12-11-Technology-Stack
- Basic knowledge of DNS, CDN, load balancing, firewalls, VPNs, SMTP, SSL, etc. — all the things that make the web work.
- Interested in Deis and containers
- You are able to multitask and prioritize multiple incoming requests without freaking out and/or dropping one of the balls.
- You consider yourself well rounded, enjoy learning new things, and can pursue answers/ solutions on your own.
- You are ready to step up your skill set and work with some of the brightest minds in Ruby and Rails and Containerization.
- Experience matters as you will be expected to aid expert developers. That being said, the ability to learn, adapt and to communicate well are the top requirements of the job.

Freelancer

(https://www.freelancer.com/?t=o&utm_expid=294858-349.DOy8iXfo
SOueIj4bX0Qyjw.2#rac)

Work computer tech projects as a freelancer. You browse jobs, apply for
work and get hired and earn money. Sign up for free.

Guru   (http://www.guru.com/d/jobs/)

Work computer tech projects as a freelancer. You browse jobs, apply for
work and get hired and earn money. Sign up for free.

Info Gain Consulting

(http://infogainconsulting.com/index.php/careers.html)

Hyperion Planning Developer

We are looking for a strong Hyperion Planning developer with the following
skills and qualifications;

RESPONSIBILITIES:

- Design and Develop Hyperion Planning application
- Develop the complex calculations and fine tune it. (Calc Manager,
  Member formula, Calculation Script)
- Work closely with the Hyperion team and understand the requirements.
- Develop SQL load rules, FR, SmartView templates
- Produce the Design & technical documentation.
- SQL development a plus

SKILL LEVEL:

- Minimum 3 complete life cycles implementations
- Minimum 7 years' experience designing and/or developing Hyperion
  Planning
- Strong optimization and fine tuning
- Strong Maxl and PowerShell scripting knowledge

- Expert in Financial Report development
- Excellent verbal and written communication skills
- Ability to travel without restrictions
- Ability to work well in a team environment
- Oracle Hyperion certification a plus

Workday HCM Business Systems Lead

JOB DESCRIPTION:

About Us:

Info Gain Consulting's Information Management practice helps clients with developing a technology strategy and integrating **technology, processes** and **people**.

We help our clients transform data into actionable information to help them gain an advantage in forecasting, budgeting, planning, compliance and business performance.

Our integrated solutions include Enterprise Resource Planning (ERP), Business Intelligence (BI) and Data Warehousing (DW), Enterprise Data Management (EDM), and Performance Management Technology (PMT).

Workday HCM Business Systems Lead

The HCM Business Systems Lead will be responsible for driving enhancements as well as providing full life cycle support for our client's implementation of Workday HCM. The business systems lead will also act as a subject matter expert and be a key resource for projects that include rolling out new functionality in Workday and other HCM systems.

RESPONSIBILITIES

- Manage projects end to end; ensure coverage of all facets of testing, and a successful end-user experience
- Manage system enhancement and modification to meet business needs within Workday
- Manage security administration including business process and security groups configuration

- Assist with Compensation Planning and Talent Management programs including configuration, documentation and testing
- Partner with cross-functional teams (People Operations, Payroll, Finance, IT) to troubleshoot and remedy system issues
- Partner with cross-functional teams (People Operations, Payroll, Finance, IT) to identify opportunities for improving the effectiveness of processes, systems, and reports
- Develop and maintain system and program administration documentation
- Testing of new system features and releases and evaluating the impact to users

REQUIRED SKILLS

- 5+ years of experience working with HCM systems in a professional, fast-paced environment
- 2+ years of experience as a system administrator and/or system implementation experience with Workday
- Experience and deep understanding with Workday HCM in at least 4 of these areas: Compensation, Talent, Benefits, Business Process & Security configuration, Creating Dashboards and Loading EIBs
- Experience administering and running performance/compensation programs
- Experience configuring Workday benefits including building benefits groups, plans and leading an open enrollment cycle
- Excellent verbal and written communication skills; ability to communicate with employees at all levels
- Analytical approach to solving system issues including understanding system interdependencies

Proven ability to successfully juggle multiple projects and priorities and able to shift direction quickly when priorities change

iTelesource   (http://www.telesource.com/)

Lead generation
Lead qualification

Sales outsourcing

iTelesource is looking for experienced professionals.

iTelesource is growing fast, and with this success comes the challenge of finding exceptional people with a passion for sales lead generation. iTelesource offers great perks such as the ability to work from home, flexible schedules, and excellent pay. If you are an outgoing professional with a take charge attitude please review the following positions.

Business Development Representative: Are you a sales professional with a passion for cold calling? Do you wish to spend more time at home and less on the road? iTelesource offers a great alternative to the road weary sales professional.

As a Business Development Representative for iTelesource you will make outbound calls from your home office pitching our client's solutions to their targeted accounts. You must be able to craft a solution from research and dialogue that generates interest in our clients. You will log all time and activities via CRM as well as participate in weekly client calls. You must display the utmost of professionalism in all activities representing iTelesource and our clients. Training will be provided on all client engagements.

Requirements: (Must Meet ALL)
- Home office with unlimited long distance plan
- Ability to work 20+ hours per week during business hours
- 5-10 years sales experience in a Complex Sales environment
- Experience calling on VP and C level
- Knowledge of various technologies and business industries a plus
- Experience in multiple CRMs

Telecom Software Developers

TeleSource is seeking developers with most or all of the following skills: SS7, ISUP, DCAP, Unix, C++, LDAP, SSL, PKI, XML, DHTML and JavaScript.

Unix System Administrators

TeleSource is seeking competent Unix system administrators to join the technical team at our Web site hosting center. Must have experience with BSD and

LINUX, as well as C, send mail, and PERL. Windows NT Server Administration, Internet Information Server, Netscape SuiteSpot, Site Server, SQL Server, Index Server, Performance Monitoring, Web Statistics. Responsibilities include driving the design and architecture of tools, recommend solutions from various off the shelf applications, on-call support/incident response, tuning capacity planning and security. Should have experience with the installation, modification, performance analysis and tuning of Solaris operating systems.

Live Person

(http://www.liveperson.com/lp/computer-programming-jobs.aspx)

Work for a client via Live Person. When you sign up as one of LivePerson's Technology Experts, you'll be asked to create an online profile where you list your qualifications, education, specialties and any other information you'd like people looking for tech support to know about you. You'll indicate how you want to connect (chat, voice, or email) and upload a photo so clients can get to know you. Then your profile will appear in the list of available technology experts, and people can search for you by your specialty or keyword. The more you're online, the more clients will find you!

Connect with people who need computer help via instant chat, email, or using LivePerson's Voice Connect feature. Set your own fees and accept freelance work at your own discretion. Best of all, LivePerson has a large member base and is a public company that can be trusted to pay on time and provide support.

Lunarpages

(http://www.lunarpages.com/information/employment/junior-system-administrator-I)

We are looking for people who want a career in systems administration. Varying shifts; Remote positions available

DESCRIPTION:

- Monitors servers including booting a machine when necessary
- Responds to server alerts as per instructions from supervisory staff
- Responsible for server stability
- Provides technical support for Level I escalation issues via helpdesk, chat, telephone and forums

- Assists Customer Service Representatives with technical support issues
- Transfers accounts between servers when necessary for load balancing or account upgrades
- Continues development of Lunarpages and systems knowledge to more effectively answer calls
- Performs miscellaneous job-related duties as assigned

SKILLS:

- Knowledge and understanding of operating principles, practices, and procedures within area of business specialty
- Knowledge of Linux required
- Previous server administration a plus
- Knowledge of relational databases including a database query language
- Understanding of PHP and HTML
- Understanding of ASP helpful
- Understanding of JSP helpful
- Ability to communicate effectively, both orally and written
- Ability to work well with the public
- Ability to troubleshoot and resolve customer and server issues
- Skilled in the use of personal computers and related software applications
- Ability to work productively and efficiently to meet deadlines and quotas
- Attention to detail
- Analytical skills
- Ability to work in a team environment
- Knowledge of customer service principles, techniques, systems, and standards

Outline Systems

(http://www.flexjobs.com/jobs/telecommuting-jobs-at-outline_systems)

Please note: Flex Jobs charges a membership fee to see the job description and apply for the job.

Since 1997, Outline Systems has been providing IT and consulting services to its clients in the insurance industry. The management team at Outline Systems has years of experience in multiple areas with the ability to meet the business needs of each client. The services offered by Outline Systems consist of application development, application maintenance, testing, professional services, infrastructure management, and ITIL process consulting. Outline Systems has developed several web-based products that add overall value for their clients as well as business partnerships with well-known companies such as IBM, Microsoft, Oracle, Cisco, and Sun Microsystems. Outline Systems is a growing company that has been recognized by Inc., Deloitte, CRN, and Software Magazine for their growth. With this continued growth Outline Systems is continually looking for qualified professionals to join their team.

Rent A Coder (http://www.rent-acoder.com/allProjects.php)

Work for clients via the website. Sign up for free.

Smart Office Solutions
(http://www.smartofficesolutions.com/join_our_team/)

Director of Software Development / Enterprise Architect / CTO

To remain an industry leader, Smart Office Solutions, Inc. is continuing to enhance services through its latest strategic plans and growth. SOS is focused on developing its global messaging system, SMS, mobile technologies and other telecommunication services for companies with a remote sales force.

Until recently, our development has been done with an 'on the fly' mentality but the time has come to formalize the development processes and procedures. The Director of Software Development role will define, prioritize, and lead the daily software development operations as well as oversee systems operations. The Director of Software Development must be creative, a great problem solver, and be focused on ingenuity and performance. This position is responsible for the future hiring, management, and motivation of a first-class software engineering team.

The position requires the candidate be extremely comfortable in growing a department and preferably has taken a smaller organization and delivered measurable growth and success. The Director of Software Development will work with and report directly to the President and CEO to strategically grow the company. We value new ideas and make it our practice to candidly share and actively listen to new ideas. As an expanding company, this position provides the possible opportunity to grow into a CTO position.

JOB RESPONSIBILITIES

- Establishing the company's technical vision while leading all aspects of the company's software development.
- Improve all aspects of the technical development cycle, including functional and technical product specifications, testing, and quality assurance, documentation, production and installation, and configuration management.
- Playing an integral role in the company's strategic direction.
- Building our services and systems to scale to millions of users.
- Manage ongoing list of priorities; managing projects and developers.
- Interaction with customer's technical developers and occasionally directly to a customer.

SKILLS REQUIRED

- Strong technical competence in technology, site architecture, and the latest tools and techniques.
- Experience in technology implementation, program and project management.
- Extremely proficient in C#.net.
- Strong understanding of Oracle.
- Strong knowledge of system hardware, networking, TCP/IP, VoIP SIP.
- Proficient in software architecture /engineering.
- High level of telephony experience & knowledge of technology.
- Self-motivated, ability to adapt, create solutions, and learn quickly.
- Experience in high-level systems architecture.
- Strong business / technology / telephony understanding.
- Aggressive and creative problem solver.
- Ability to manage projects and developers.

- Excellent people and organizational skills.
- Effective communicator; both verbally and written.

ADDITIONAL DESIRED SKILLS

- Strong DBA skills a plus.
- Experience in CT/ADE programming a plus.
- Mobile phone development skills a plus (Microsoft Mobile / J2ME).
- Strong business experience is a plus.

EDUCATION

Earned a Bachelor's degree in software engineering, computer science, or similar (an advanced business degree desirable).

RELOCATION: As the company offices grow in Longwood and Charlotte, candidate may be required to relocate to the Longwood, FL or Charlotte, NC area (not immediate).

Snag A Job
(http://www.snagajob.com/job-search/q-part+time+ computer+technology)

A Part time job board for people trained in computer technology.

Toptal (http://www.toptal.com/#snag-effective-devs-now)

Toptal is an exclusive network of the top freelancers for software development and designers. Sign up for free and work with clients to do tasks related to developing and designing computer software and programs.

The Work Site (http://www.theworksite.com/)

The worksite offers computer job listings, work from home employment opportunities solutions and employment law information. Find IT Employment Opportunities. We provide an easy to use information technology job search for finding an open position in your field of expertise. Your new, higher paying IT job could be posted on our site. Register for free to begin.

Xerox
(http://www.xerox.com/jobs/work-from-home/enus.html)

Careers at home

Over the past 30 years we've recognized the benefits of working from home. We currently have more than 8000 home-based employees performing a wide range of functions, including:

- Customer Care
- Tech Support
- Data Entry/Verification
- Image Tagging
- Quality Control
- Systems Development
- Software Programming
- Administrative/Business Support

We're actively seeking high-quality individuals for work at home opportunities.

CUSTOMER CARE REPRESENTATIVE

Accolade Support
(http://www.accoladesupport.com/remote-agents.html)

We are looking for bright and energetic people to work from home.

Accolade Support utilizes agents that work from their home office. Each call center agent must pass several tests including an intensive nationwide background check, before they are able to take our calls. Every call is recorded, and calls are regularly checked for quality, accuracy, and friendliness. Utilizing remote call center agents has a lot of benefits to each of our valued client members.

Position Title: Call Center Agent
Position Type: Contract - Part Time
Compensation: $7.25 to $9.00 per hour

Start Date: Immediately

DESCRIPTION:

Accolade Support is a rapidly growing division of Tier 3 Support, Inc. We are looking for remote agents to join our team, working from home on an on-call basis. We'll get a schedule of your available hours and when our call volume rises during your available hours, we'll contact you to take calls from your home. This is the ideal position for someone who is around his or her home on a regular basis and is looking to make a little extra money in their spare time.

We're looking for bright, energetic individuals who enjoy speaking with people on the phone, and possess the in-depth understanding and the diverse skills to provide callers with the highest quality of service. Our clients demand the highest service level possible.   In turn, we are constantly working to build a team of friendly and efficient support professionals to meet our current clients growing call volumes, as well as the numerous new clients we begin services for each month.

SKILLS: Applicants should possess the following skill set:

Technical skills - A technical skill set with the ability to provide desktop troubleshooting, resolve Internet connectivity issues, and support software applications (with training).

Sales skills: The ability to sell products and services to a wide variety of markets to inbound callers.

Customer service skills - Working with callers who may be frustrated or upset that something hasn't gone as expected. A key component of this is assuring the customer that you will help them, calming them down, and resolving the situation for them when possible. Patience and a genuine desire to assist our customers is a must.

Attention to detail - Callers will regularly relate information including phone numbers, email addresses, product numbers, messages, and details about their particular reason for calling. Accurately relaying this information to our clients is crucial to your success in this position.

QUALIFICATIONS: To qualify for this position you must have, or obtain the following:

1. A U.S. based home telephone number. (No cell phones or VOIP phones)
2. A corded telephone set with a headset. (No cordless phones)
3. A PC with Windows 98, or 2000, or XP
4. Your PC wired to a cable modem, DSL modem, or broadband connection. (No wireless connections)
5. A quiet environment where you can take calls without being disrupted or callers hearing any noise or sounds in the background.

You must meet the following criteria to qualify for this position:

1. You must be geographically located in The United States,
2. You must be able to provide proof of having the legal right to work in the United States.
3. You must be willing to submit to a criminal background check.

To apply for this position please emails your resume in Microsoft Word Format, or Adobe Acrobat PDF format to us at: hr@tier3support.com. No telephone calls please.

ABC Financial

(https://www2.appone.com/Search/Search.aspx?ServerVar=abcfinancialser vicesinc.appone.com)

ABC Financial is a company that offers health club software solutions. They offer positions in customer service, marketing, sales, accounting or information technology; however, it is not clear whether all of the positions are available as remote positions. From the link above, if you scroll down you will see the search functions and if you search by "Remote – National" you will be able to see the positions available. At the time of this writing, there was an IT-type position available and also three customer service call center positions. Two of the customer service positions were for specific states, so it is recommended that you check with the site to see if there is a position open in your state. The third customer service was bilingual (English/Spanish) and did not have a specific state requirement.

Of note is that is that job description indicates that ABC Financial provides the computer equipment for you to work at home. For the customer service position, a high school diploma or equivalent was required, as well as 1-2 years of customer service experience. Calls would be mainly inbound assisting health club associates, as well as some outbound "soft collections calls." See their website for complete job description and complete list of qualifications.

Advanis (http://www.advanis.net/available-positions)

Home Based Telephone Research Interviewer Locations: Your home

Salary: Hourly wage as advertised, please call or email for more detail

Start Date: Immediately Hours of Operation: Monday through Friday 3-10 pm MST (5-12 pm EST) and Saturdays 10-5pm MST (12-7 pm EST)

Advanis is a Market and Policy Research company that has been doing surveys since 1997 and we are looking for telephone interviewers. We offer fully paid training and a set wage.

You need:

- A good command of the English language
- Excellent customer service skills
- A typing speed of 30 wpm
- A quiet, private place in your home • a computer with high speed Internet service
- A phone line in the office space – if you wish to leave your phone line available for people to call in on ,you would need to have a second (separate) phone line
- A landline phone. No cellphones.
- A corded headset with a noise cancelling microphone. No cordless phones or speaker phones.
- A personal computer (PC or Mac)

Bilingualism (French, Spanish, or other) is an asset, but not essential.

As a remote agent, you would receive additional benefits such as:

- The ability to claim a portion of household expenses such as Internet, power, rent, or mortgage
- No transportation cost to come to work and no parking costs
- Great web community to provide you with the support you need to do a great job
- Flexible scheduling that works with your home life

Application Procedure Applications will only be accepted through our online application form available on our website. We thank all applicants for their interest; however, only candidates under consideration will be contacted.

Advise Tech (http://advisetech.com/company-2/career-opportunities/)

Advise Tech is looking for a few people, preferably retired or college students who can devote 2-6 hours per week to start. Need to have professional phone skill and be friendly, exciting and enthusiastic. No travel necessary.

American Express
(https://jobs.americanexpress.com/jobs?   keywords=virtual%20home%20based%20work%20from%20home& page=1)

American Express has a large number of home based workers; their website is definitely worth checking out. College degreed will be a plus and preferred, but experience counts also, according to their job application, so don't let a lack of degree keep you from applying. To search for work at home jobs, from this link, click on the icon in the lower left-hand side of the page that says "Careers Worldwide," and from the next page that comes up, scroll down a bit to the dropdown menu on the right side that says "search jobs," and for the location, either choose your country or else the option for "all countries" at the bottom of the list. You don't have to choose a category. From the next screen, in the search box at the top, type in "work at home" and the work at home openings will be filtered for you to review. The American Express application is somewhat lengthy, either allows sufficient time to complete it at one sitting or you can save it and come back and finish it later, but it's a good idea to complete in one sitting. They hire travel agents and also customer care reps, as well as other positions. Check out their website, you can also be notified by email when new positions are added.

Apple

(https://jobs.apple.com/us/search?searchString=At%20Home%20 Advisor#location&ss=At%20Home%20Advisor&t=0&so=&lo=0*USA&p N=11&openJobId=39025008)

JOB SUMMARY:

You're a problem-solver and amazing with customers! You know what it takes to inspire a team to create an incredible customer experience with every interaction. You are able to coach, mentor and lead a group of remote team managers providing help when they need it and bringing out their very best. You know how to provide feedback and manage performance. You have a knack for strategic planning, program development and forecasting business needs. Because you'll work independently from home, you'll need the discipline and ability to work remotely from coworkers and management as well as the ability to effectively prioritize and manage your time. If this sounds like you, you could be the next At Home Area Manager for our Phone teams. This role requires you to work between the hours of 7:00 am CST - 10:30 pm CST and operated 7 days a week. This is a work from home position and we can consider candidates from cities across the US - you do not need to live in the city this is posted in to be considered.

KEY QUALIFICATIONS:

- 4+ years in a management capacity in a large or multi-site inbound call/contact/e-care center supervising managers
- Strong knowledge of Technical Support processes and procedures
- Experience managing a technical support team in a contact center
- Experience managing cross functional or cross site groups
- Experience managing home-based employees
- Strong and Effective written and verbal communication skills, ability to tailor your message to your audience
- Creative & Curious Solution Finder

- Flexible Schedule
- Knowledge of call center management tools such as Network Queue call routing, ACDs, call tracking systems, internet technology and reporting, IVRs, and core call center metrics
- Discipline to work remotely from home
- A quiet workspace, ergonomic chair, and desk
- High-speed Internet service (5 megabits download and 1 megabit upload) from a reliable provider

COMPANY DESCRIPTION:

At Apple, we believe in hard work, a fun environment, and the kind of creativity and innovation that only comes about when talented people from diverse backgrounds approach problems from varying perspectives. We believe each customer interaction is an opportunity to delight, impress, engage and inspire. We focus on all the small details to have the biggest impact! The At Home Area Manager is responsible for managing a set of team managers who directly manage our At Home Advisors. Must be a customer-focused person who is self-motivated, friendly, and has a passion to solve client issues in an efficient and effective manner. Must be effective in managing performance and developing remote managers through regular 1:1s, team meetings, coaching sessions, and setting expectations. Must be able to execute according to business requirements and provide business level consulting.

Education: Bachelor degree preferred

Arise.com (http://www.arise.com/) (click on "Become an Agent")

Arise works with a list of large, brand name, well known established companies and provides customer service, sales, and tech support via phone, online chat, and email interfaces. Arise has a business model that requires a business-to-business agreement with all agents, which requires either 1) Forming a corporation and becoming an Independent Business Owner contracted directly with Arise; or 2) Join an existing Independent Business already contracted with Arise, which will eliminate the need for setting up your own business. You can choose your own hours as they are available, available hours are not guaranteed, many clients offer a minimum hourly pay (but not all).

ACD Direct (http://www.acddirect.com/becomeanagent.cfm)

ACD Direct hires work at home agents primarily to take inbound calls for people calling in to make pledges for public radio and TV stations, occasionally other projects are available. The bulk of their available hours to work is during pledge drives, although they do have a large list of clients, but there will be significant periods of time when there is no or very little available work. There is no selling involved, hours are flexible. This is a good company for someone who can work a lot of hours during a busy period (such as pledge drives) and understand you will also have occasional slow times without much work.

ACD Direct seeks experienced customer service professionals to process calls in our virtual call center! Turn your experience into $$$ while starting a fun and rewarding opportunity!

You schedule when you want, what times you want and what days you wish to work!

Alorica (http://www.alorica.com/join-our-team/)

Alorica at Home is an award-winning service from Alorica, the nation's leading provider of outsourced communication solutions. We employ thousands of home-based agents located across the country as well as the industry's most robust and advanced infrastructure to deliver superior service to our clients' customers.

When you're an at-home agent, the flexibility is there for your schedule and life priorities, but the expectation of professionalism, loyalty and drive to take care of employee's remains. Alorica at Home is different from other work-at-home opportunities in that it is run as a business, employees are treated as professionals and support is available—the only difference between Alorica at Home and other successful businesses is that over half of its employees work from home.

The Alorica at Home training environment provides our agents the opportunity to drain at home through Instructor Led Training (ILT) where agents have a set training schedule in a real-time virtual classroom setting that offers more socialization with their peers and the opportunity to develop relationships with those they work with! In addition - and depending on the project, we also offer a self-paced, computer-aided training opportunity to our agents!

What You Do

Our agents support multiple client needs. However, depending on the project you may be:

1. Obtaining, entering and verifying customer information
2. Answering customer questions and resolving issues
3. Explaining sales features or offering additional products or services

Amazon *Work-From-Home CSA*

(http://www.amazonfulfillmentcareers.com/opportunities/customer-service/work-home-csa/)

Are you interested in eliminating your commute, reducing your carbon footprint, and working for an amazing company? Seeking more time to spend with your family and friends? Amazon's VCC (Virtual Contact Center) has an amazing opportunity for those who said yes!

You may have seen and heard those ads on the internet, in the paper, and on the radio, promising great *work from home* jobs, but wondered if they were too good to be true. Well this one is good, it's true, and we think you'll really enjoy it.

Full time and part time opportunities are available in Arizona, Kentucky, Texas, West Virginia, Delaware, Minnesota, Florida, Georgia, Kansas, North Carolina, Tennessee, Wisconsin, and Virginia for our seasonal customer service associate position.

- 3-4 weeks of paid training
- Seasonal and referral bonus opportunities $$
- Base compensation is $10/hour with the potential bonus opportunities
- Part-time and full-time positions available

REQUIREMENTS:

- In order to be considered for this position, your home residence must be in one of the following states; Arizona, Kentucky, Texas, West Virginia, Wisconsin, Delaware, Minnesota, Florida, Georgia, Kansas, North Carolina, Tennessee and Virginia

- High School Diploma or equivalent

- Basic typing, phone, and computer navigation skills

- Ability to navigate the Internet, email, and Instant Messenger tools

- 1+ years in a service environment dealing with the public

- Distraction free workspace

Technical Requirements:

- High speed hard wired internet (5 MB/second, no WiFi)

- Landline phone line for work only

- For PC, Windows 7 or 8, Windows Auto Update, & 64-bit Operating system

- Microsoft Security Essentials (Windows 7): http://windows.microsoft.com/en-us/windows/security-essentials-downloadWindows Defender (Windows 8): http://windows.microsoft.com/en-us/windows/turn-windows-defender-on-off

Blooms Today

(https://www.bloomstoday.com/apply/contractor.php)

Blooms Today is a flower and gift company that offers same-day delivery by a florist located in the same community as each customer. In order to expand its business worldwide, Blooms Today partners with 1-800Flowers, FTD, and Teleflora, and it is a member of the Society of American Florists. Though headquartered in Haymarket, Virginia, Blooms Today reaches worldwide and has a strong customer service focus with a satisfaction guarantee. Blooms Today offers a wide array of floral arrangements and gifts for all major holidays, and for a variety of life's moments, with gifts including gourmet baskets and sweets. As an employer, Blooms Today often seeks full-time and part-time talent, and hires additional talent around major flower-related holidays like Mother's Day.

BSG: Billing Services Group

(http://www.bsgclearing.com/contact_us/careers/live-operator-independent-contractor)

Live Operator Independent Contractor

Earn a guaranteed minimum $8.50 per hour, with the benefits of flexible work hours and working from home! VoiceLog is looking for English, Spanish or bi-lingual independent contractor live operators with flexible hours.

VoiceLog is the #1 provider of third party verification services in the US. Our operators receive live verification calls for telephone companies and other service industries looking to help combat sales fraud. All calls are recorded for quality assurance and compliance purposes.

Work at home as an independent contractor during the hours of 2pm CST to 11pm CST Monday-Friday and every other weekend. You can choose to work shifts of 2, 3, 4, 5, or 6 hours. As an inbound live operator verification agent, you will earn a guaranteed minimum $8.50 per hour

MINIMUM REQUIREMENTS:

- Quiet home office setting
- Personal computer running Windows Vista or Higher (Preferably Windows 7) or MAC OS X
- At least 2 Gigabytes of RAM is required (Preferred 4 Gigabytes of RAM)
- CPU (processor) Multi-core @ 2.2 GHz or above or Single-core @ 3.0 GHz or above
- Internet Explorer 7.0 or higher
- Microsoft Word, Excel and a working printer
- E-mail provider that allows enough space to receive fairly large documents

- Reliable DSL or Cable HIGH SPEED Internet access (dialup or satellite not acceptable)
- Current anti-virus software and Ad-Ware software
- AOL Instant Messenger account
- A second phone line (already installed) dedicated to accepting inbound calls, with no features (no VOIP, no digital phone, no call waiting, voicemail etc.)
- At least 1 year of customer service experience (inbound or outbound call center)
- Requires a Headset
- Required to work at least 20 hours per week

Applicants are contacted on an as needed basis and only if the applicant meets all requirements. If we do not contact you, please do not contact our Human Resources or Customer Service departments as they do not have access to the Independent Contractor application information.

Call Center International

(http://www.ccicompany.us/index.aspx)

CCI is a third-party call center company with clients in the telecom industry, that specializes in offering multilingual agents and the ability for its clients to reach potential customers in many different languages and a key feature they offer is that the agents speaking in those languages are familiar with the cultures of that particular community. Their at-home call center positions are sales agents, selling marketed services, with compensation on a commission basis. Per the CCI website, the average earnings are $20-30 per every active sale. There is no up-front fee mentioned on their website, or charge for training. Sales training classes and e-learning and communication software is provided to provide additional training, coaching, and company news. *Of note: It is indicated that "Calling lists to help you get started in making contacts."* I would recommend that you carefully research with CCI how contacts and leads are provided, not just at the beginning, but on a regular basis. If you are interested in applying with CCI, their website has clear links to follow, and it will indicate what languages they are currently hiring for.

Capital Typing

(http://www.capitaltyping.com/employment-application)

> Professional Customer Service Representatives are experienced in Email Response Management, Live Customer Support, Live Chat, and virtually every element of good customer care.

Cruise.com

(http://www.cruise.com/cruise-information/employment.asp?skin=001)

To be considered, email your resume to jobs@cruise.com indicating your job objective. If you are applying for one of our home-based career opportunities, please detail your recent cruise industry customer service or cruise sales experience in your email or on your resume. Without this information, consideration for an interview will not be given.

CURRENT HOME-BASED JOB OPPORTUNITIES (MULTI-STATE)

Cruise.com is now recruiting home-based cruise sales and customer service specialists for our January 2014 training classes. Each class will be held from Monday through Friday, 10 a.m. to 7 p.m. (EST), for three consecutive weeks. Training is web-based and accessed from your home office computer/internet provider (no travel required). Only candidates whose initial resumes or job applications reflect prior cruise industry experience will be considered. Phone interviews will be scheduled based on an analysis of the candidates' qualifications for the position. Training is paid, and all positions offer a base salary plus commission or incentive plan and an attractive employee benefits package including eligibility for travel agent benefits through IATAN membership.

Cruise Sales Agents (Home-Based) - Requires at least 2 years of recent cruise sales work experience, preferably in a call center environment selling all of the major cruise lines. Language fluency in English/Spanish or English/French or English/Russian is required for some openings. Purpose: To sell cruise vacations, insurance, and other product options to potential customers through inbound/outbound telephone calls/e-mail leads. To close the sale of a cruise booking, up selling cruise packages to maximize revenue. To meet or exceed minimum monthly sales productivity goals there are incentives. Base pay plus commission plan.

Online Support Agents (Home-Based) - Requires at least 1 year of recent cruise sales experience, preferably in a call center environment selling all of the major cruise lines. Purpose: To answer incoming calls from customers for the purposes of resolving problems, providing information, converting inquiries into invoices, selling travel insurance and answering questions while providing high level service to our customers. To meet or exceed minimum monthly productivity goals there are incentives.
Base pay plus incentive plan.

Customer Service Agent (Home-Based) - Requires at least 1 year of recent cruise industry call center experience in either sales or customer service. Related cruise industry experience is required. Purpose: To answer incoming calls from customers for the purposes of resolving problems, providing information, and answering questions while providing high level service to our customers. Base pay plus incentive plan.

DeRosa Communications (http://derosa.com/gigs/)

Appointment setting
Lead generation and qualifying
Sales pipeline management

Although there are no positions to immediately fill, the nature of the business is dynamic and needs do frequently surface. We also get inquiries from prospective clients with business models that are not a fit for us and we would be happy to put you in touch with them with both of your permissions. We try our best to match specific requirements with the appropriate skill and experience sets. To that end, there is a form to complete to tell about your special attributes. The information provided is kept private and not shared with anyone or any entity without your written permission.

EBI: Employee Background Investigations Solutions
(http://www.ebiinc.com/about/careers)

As a leader in our industry, EBI offers background check jobs in a fun, rewarding and motivating workplace. Team members at EBI love their work environment: relaxed yet high energy, fun yet productive. Our staff gains tremendous satisfaction and work experience from being part of a team that provides outstanding service.

At EBI we seek out individuals that are self-motivated, creative, have the ability to easily adapt and are team spirited. We are also looking for groups and individuals alike that provide best-in-class goods and services to enhance the EBI brand through mutual partnerships.

EGS: Expert Global Solutions

(https://jobs.egscorp.com/job/united-states/corporate-recruiter-temporary/2020/561419)

DESCRIPTION:

Who is Expert Global Solutions?

Have you ever had a great experience when calling, emailing or chatting with a customer service, technical support or financial care representative? If so, there is a good chance you were speaking to a member of the Expert Global Solutions (EGS) team.

At EGS, we provide world-class customer care, financial care, sales, technical support and back-office services to many of the best known brands in the world. With 40,000 employees around the globe, we strive to provide an amazing experience for every customer, every time. While our primary focus is delivering exceptional service to our clients' customers, we're pleased to offer exciting opportunities which enable the success of our operations, including roles in IT, Finance, Human Resources, Training, Legal and more.

Throughout our team, we are committed to fulfilling our vision of "Delighting our Customers as the #1 Rated BPO Partner in the World" through:

- Relentless customer focus;
- Demonstrated respect for others;
- Success through teamwork and collaboration;
- Passion for excellence; and,

- Personal and business integrity.

We want you to join our winning team. Let us show you what the new EGS can do for you!

SUMMARY:

Selects, interviews, and recommends placement of candidates for professional, management, executive and niche specialty positions.

ESSENTIAL DUTIES & RESPONSIBILITIES:

- Consults with management to identify and recommend the most qualified candidates and to deliver a comprehensive, compelling, and balanced offer.
- Extends offers to selected candidates and arranges for relocation when necessary.
- Develops effective working relationships with executive search firms and placement agencies.
- Selects recruiting sources and techniques to fulfill organizational needs by attractive qualified candidates.
- Partners with hiring managers and Human Resource Business Partners to develop and drive recruiting strategies for open executive and management level positions.
- Regularly communicates with key stakeholders on updates and recruiting status details.
- Ensures alignment of recruiting activities with business goals and objectives.
- Proactively recommend corporate-driven projects, communicate issues, concerns and questions, and understand changing project requirements and best practices.
- Ensure compliance with Corporate Global Recruitment Programs.
- Provide feedback to management concerning possible problems or areas of improvement.
- Make recommendations to implement improved processes.
- Responsible for understanding and complying with all policies, procedures, and regulations relating to job duties.
- Perform other duties as assigned by management.

QUALIFICATIONS:

Education

- Bachelor's Degree or equivalent relevant work experience.

Experience

- Four or more years of related experience required.
- Experience with recruiting professional and executive level talent for an international BPO or professional services organization.
- Prior experience with applicant tracking systems preferred.
- Knowledge, Skills, Abilities & Other Characteristics
- Exceptional verbal and written communication skills.
- Extremely well developed planning and organization skills with the ability to handle multiple priorities.
- Knowledge and experience in best practices related to candidate process management, behavioral interviewing, and other assessment techniques.
- Ability to adapt to changing business priorities.
- Proficient personal computer skills including Microsoft Office.
- Ability to prioritize and organize work in a multitasked environment.
- Ability to adapt to a flexible schedule.
- Ability to maintain the highest level of confidentiality.

    Work Environment
- Office environment.
- Ability to lift and/or move 20 pounds with or without accommodation.

Enterprise Car Rental

(http://careers.enterprise.com/careers/work-from-home-jobs)

By being hired into one of our Work from Home jobs at Enterprise Holdings, you'll be a key member of the Enterprise Holdings team. Professionals in Work from Home careers come from a variety of backgrounds, bringing an assortment of knowledge and skills to every area of our business. Please click on your desired Work from Home job below to learn more about the exact qualifications.

A job in Work from Home at Enterprise Holdings may be waiting for you!

Grindstone (http://www.grindstone.com/work-with-us/)

REQUIREMENTS - We are seeking Talented "Outbound" Telemarkers only

- 3 years of successful Business to Business Lead Generation and/or Appointment Setting Skills
- Experience speaking with Business Owners, CEO's, Presidents and decision makers
- Professional upbeat sounding telephone voice
- An ability to interact with prospective customers with a friendly consultative approach
- Ability to take direction and follow through
- Available to work from home at least 20 hours per week during business hours
- Have High-Speed Internet
- Have Skype
- Have Microsoft Outlook
- Have good Anti-virus protection and internet security
- Must subscribe to www.line2.com soft phone service for calling

Recruiting and retaining the best talent is one of the keys to Grindstone's success. Our highest priority is to find and keep the best people, no matter where they may be!

We are always looking for talented professionals to join our team. Work from your remote office, If you have a great phone voice, are organized and experienced in the services we provide our clients, then we want to talk to you. The majority of our clients need assistance in the Technology and Business Services sector, although we are successful with clients in other industries as well.

Our clients demand that we hire the best. Those who pass our thorough screening process will have the opportunity to flourish with a growing company. We are on the cutting edge of a new trend, and we believe in promoting from within.

Not afraid to pick up the phone? Ready to join a fantastic company? This work at home career maybe just the thing for you!

Intelichek (http://intelichek.simplicant.com/job/detail/10859)

Would you like to work from home?

Do you like to set your own hours?

Are you looking to work 10-20-30 hours a week?

If you answered "yes" to these 3 questions, then this opportunity might be for you.

Summary: To gather competitive intelligence by contacting providers of services to gain valuable information and capture data accurately in company's database.

InteliChek is a market research company specializing in collecting data to analyze what is happening in different markets and different industries. We do this by calling businesses across the North America and gathering information about the products and services they offer and the price of those products and services. Some of the data we have gathered include the cost of an oil change, the price of a specific tire, warranty information, hours of operation, etc.

We are always looking for great people that want to work on their terms and their schedule, who are reliable and have good communication skills.

JOB FUNCTIONS:

- Contact providers to inquire about services and pricing offered while posing as a household consumer.
- Accurate and timely Input of data received in to company database.

- Quick and thorough follow through on tasks assigned.
- Other tasks as assigned.

REQUIREMENTS:

- High School Diploma or GED equivalent, college degree a plus.
- Must be at least 18 years old.
- We are looking specifically for candidates who can work 15-25 hours a week between the hours between 8am and 7pm Monday-Friday and 9am-6pm on Saturday.
- Mystery Shoppers must have excellent attention to detail including proper grammar and spelling.
- Must be disciplined enough to follow directions and work productively at home with limited supervision.
- Excellent communication skills (written and verbal); must have strong grammar skills and articulate telephone voice. Must speak fluent English.
- We prefer candidates with an upbeat telephone personality that is able to play the role of a consumer without the provider knowing that they are a mystery shopper.
- Accurate typing or keyboarding skills of at least 35 wpm.
- Must have computer skills using MS Office, MS Windows, email, and performing internet searches.
- Excellent follow-up and follow-through with tasks assigned as well as timely communication with all InteliChek team members.

Intrep (http://www.intrep.com/people.html)

Intrep is a telesales company based out of Franklin Park, New Jersey that has been providing superior inside sales support since 1999. Intrep is owned by its founders, Mark Winwood and Dan Greenberg who have spent a combined 55 years working in sales, marketing and operations management in a variety of business-to-business industries. Since the majority of their sales associates work from home, Intrep puts candidates through a very in-depth screening process because they hire only the best of the best in sales and marketing professionals. However, Intrep rewards all its home based agents with higher than average wages, benefits, and opportunities for additional training and bonus programs.

Jet Blue

(http://work-here.jetblue.com/category/careers/customer-support/)

Customer Support crewmembers assist customers calling 1-800-JETBLUE. Across a range of situations, they are natural problem-solvers who offer helpful solutions and products to customers in a 24/7 operation, where working some weekends and holidays is an important part of the role.

Most Customer Support crewmembers are based out of our Salt Lake City Support Center (SSC). Upon hire, new Reservations Crewmembers attend orientation and training at SSC before starting work from home.

GETTING HIRED:

- Review the job description and be sure you meet the minimum qualifications of the role.
- Submit your application online.
- You may be selected to take a 45-minute online assessment.
- You may be selected to participate in a brief phone interview.
- If that goes well, you will be asked to attend Blue Review to learn more about the job and interview in a group setting.
- If selected, you must pass a background screening before receiving a formal job offer.
- Once cleared, new crewmembers are scheduled to attend an orientation and training at either the Salt Lake City Support Center or Jet-Blue University in Orlando

Kelly Services

(http://www.kellyservices.us/US/KellyConnect-WorkAtHome/)

Stable company. Steady work. As a highly regarded and reputable employer with more than 60 years of experience employing people like you, we offer professional and credible work at home opportunities. We're committed to providing our employees with the resources necessary to work at home successfully, including paid training and a dedicated support staff that's only a phone call away. There are no start-up fees, and you'll be paid for the hours you work, not just your call time.

Our work at home hiring process is simple and convenient! Most steps are automated and can be completed in the comfort of your own home.

1. Complete our online prequalification questions.
   The online prequalification is a brief questionnaire that asks basic questions to ensure you have the critical skills and appropriate work environment necessary for working at home.

2. Participate in a telephone interview with a Kelly recruiter.
   A Kelly recruiter will assess your qualifications to make certain you possess the minimum requirements and ensure you will be placed on an assignment that best suits your skills, abilities, and desires.

3. Complete online testing.
   Our online testing will assess your technical contact center skills to help determine the types of positions for which you are best suited.

4. Complete online on boarding.
   From the convenience of your own home, you will access our innovative on boarding application and submit all necessary hiring information.

5. Visit your local Kelly branch to complete the necessary I-9 paperwork.
   You are required to complete your I-9 documents in the presence of a Kelly staff member.

6. The Kelly Services team will work with you to identify positions that match your qualifications and provide support and guidance while you are working.

Maritz Researchers (http://www.maritzcx.com/about/careers/)

We are looking for professional, loyal, self-motivated employees to conduct customer satisfaction surveys. These part time positions offer quality employment, flexible scheduling, and an opportunity to learn about market research.

This position conducts market research/customer satisfaction surveys. Absolutely no sales or solicitation involved.

BASIC JOB REQUIREMENTS:

- Friendly Personality
- Proficient in general computer usage
- Ability to read verbatim and follow instructions

Virtual Call Center – Work from Home

- Requirements include: a good infrastructure to include a landline, computer and good internet provider, and a quiet work environment

QUALIFICATION REQUIREMENTS:

1. Good basic reading skills
2. Good command of the English language to ensure customer understanding
3. Explicitly follow verbal and written instructions
4. Friendly and professional in all situations
5. High tolerance for repetitive tasks
6. Self-motivation to achieve production and quality goals
7. Excellent Attendance

EQUIPMENT and WORK STATION REQUIREMENTS:

1. Broadband connection to the internet – Reliable and high speed
2. Desktop or Laptop with Microsoft Windows Operating System
3. PC with Microsoft 2000 & Internet Explorer Version 5.0 or better
4. Telephone with clear and reliable reception
5. Active e-mail account
6. Secure and private workspace
7. Workspace quiet and free of background noise
8. Workspace safe and free of hazards

Micah Tek (http://www.micahtek.com/jobs.shtml.)

MicahTek, Inc. is known globally as a full turn-key service center that provides a broad spectrum of information management and distribution services. Call Center, Live Agents, Interactive Voice Recognition, Website Design and Development, Registration and Events, Database Management and Hosting, and Product Fulfillment and Warehousing. The company is experiencing a period of rapid growth and therefore has multiple opportunities to work from home as a home based contract customer service agents. These positions are full time, with some degree of flexibility available. Training is provided to qualified candidates who are then allowed to work from the comfort of their home as virtual professionals. To find out more about the telecommuting opportunities that MicahTek can offer you, be sure to check out the links here on Flex jobs for great jobs.

This is a hi-tech progressive corporation offering over fifty job classifications. The Human Resource Department is continuously searching for qualified applicants who can work with integrity, fairness and confidentiality. MicahTek, Inc. offers competitive benefits for part-time as well as full-time employees. Optional benefits include health, dental, visual, life insurance and 401-K Retirement Plan.

Transfers and promotions from within the company are typical; however, oftentimes supervisory and managerial positions as well as entry level positions are filled from new applicants. Technical experience is a benefit, but not necessarily a requirement.

There is a great demand for data entry operators and phone operators to serve the 24-hour, 7-day a week call center. MicahTek provides on-site training and cross-training. Phone operators take product orders from incoming calls for multiple clients, provide customer service, and capture call record details. Basically, phone agents must love to type and talk on phones following clients' scripts.

My Favorite Mouse (http://www.myfavoritemouse.com/join.html)

Join Our Team:

As an " EARMARKED "Authorized Disney Vacation Planning Company, GalaxSea Cruises and Tours is seeking a very elite group of passionate Disney fans to sell Disney Destination vacations.

If you are the kind of magical person who:
Is answering questions now, for family and friends, to help them plan their Disney Destination vacations
Has an extended knowledge of Disney Theme Parks and Resort Hotels
Schedules character dining, behind the scenes tours, parade times, fireworks viewing times and more . . . . .
Has personal Disney travel experiences that you enjoy sharing with contacts so you have become the " GO TO PERSON " for magical answers ... always thinks of how much fun it would be to sell Disney vacations and make others " Dreams Come True "
Then . . . you may have the qualities we are searching for to become part of our Authorized Disney Vacation Planning Sales Team!
To be considered for the position, please email your resume and list of Disney Travel experiences to: info@myfavoritemouse.com

Neiman Markus

(http://www.neimanmarcuscareers.com/wfh/index.shtml)

The Neiman Marcus Direct Work From Home (WFH) program offers you a unique opportunity to provide exceptional customer service from the comfort of your own home to our distinguished web and catalog customers. With the advancement of technology, you will enjoy this job and still have time to do the things that are important to you. Every day our Work from Home Associates transform their home into a virtual customer support center. Through phone calls, live chats and email, associates manage all our customers' contacts with diligence and an unwavering commitment to excellence. The Neiman Marcus Direct Marketing segment conducts both print catalog and online operations under the Neiman Marcus, Horchow and Bergdorf Goodman brands.

Our Work from Home program will allow you to:

Work without a dress code
Cut down on transportation costs and commute time (*)
Have flexibility with personal and family priorities

At Neiman Marcus Direct, our employees are the "Cornerstone" of our business. We care about your growth and are committed to providing you with the necessary tools to be successful. You will attend a three-week-long training which includes time allotted for on-the-job practice, after which you will join "Cornerstone," our production mentoring program. For two additional weeks you will be guided by a group of high performers to ensure you have a successful transition after you have graduated from training.

As an employee of Neiman Marcus Direct, you will join a company that has been operating since 1907. We are a modern company that is still very much based on the principles of our founders. That is why we remain dedicated to exceptional customer service and superior merchandising. If you are looking for a home-based career opportunity, then consider Neiman Marcus Direct.

NewCorp (http://careers.asurion.com/careers/customer-service-jobs)

Are you a professional, dynamic individual with basic computer skills and a knack for helping others and looking for a unique opportunity to work from home?
Do you want to work for a company that has been named one of the "Best Places to Work "for two years in a row?
If the answer is yes—we want to talk to you!

NEW is hiring Home-Based Customer Care Representatives (CCRs) to take inbound customer service and support calls. As a Home-Based CCR, you help customers from the comforts of your home—answering their questions, troubleshooting problems with their product and arranging service or replacement as needed. It's a fulfilling job that gives you a variety of schedules, hourly pay and the opportunity to work from home.

Be Part of Our Virtual Team NEW's Home-Based CCRs span across the country. Through a variety of technologies and a supportive management team, we bring together our diverse group of employees to create a "virtual" team environment similar to our brick and mortar sites. We have virtual chat rooms that allow CCRs to access support, 24/7, should they need assistance. It provides a forum for supervisors and CCRs to communicate about issues and training opportunities.

Newton Group

(https://www.newtonelitesalesassociates.com/~newto7/employment.
php?pos=1)

The *Elite Sales Associate* (ESA)
We only hire experienced professionals who have a proven track record of elite professionalism. Because our model is virtual, we can hire from anywhere in the country. Therefore, we only bring on associates that truly represent the level of professionalism that our clients have grown to expect. As a matter of fact, our clients turn to us because our associates act as an extension of their own sales force.

The Main Objective
As an associate, you will represent our clients to initiate and develop relationships with their potential business prospects. During this process, you will manage the process of collecting valuable market data, understanding the needs of potential prospects, flagging warm leads, and setting appointments. Our software is designed to help you efficiently manage this process, so you can spend less time typing and more time carrying on high quality conversations with the right people. Although our clients request that our associates mention certain key points over the phone, we leave our associates with the autonomy to carry on the conversation. We understand that the ability to have high level conversations is a talent; therefore, we specifically seek out professionals who have displayed these talents through previous work experiences and who can display these talents through the interview process. We are willing to pay more than our competitors because we realize that those individuals with the greatest training and skills get the best results.

The Approval
Because our organization is growing very rapidly, we are always interviewing. Your objective through the interview process is to become an approved Elite Sales Associate. This means that you will be considered for all future campaigns unless your performance proves otherwise.

The Expectations
Must display core values (see mission statement)
Experience in telemarketing, customer service, lead generation, and appointment setting

High level of professionalism
Confidence on the phone with a strong phone presence
Initially work 4 hours per day (Approximately 150 dials)
Reliability and consistency
Discipline to work from home
Able to lead a conversation to extract the desired information
Effective and concise note-taking ability
Ability to type at least 40 WPM
Results that meet client expectations
Positive attitude
Experience using CRM software
Fully-equipped home office with no distractions (more details to follow)

Our Support
We arm our associates with the tools they need to successfully complete each campaign. We work with our associates on a regular basis to help them get the most out of their interactions with these business contacts. Also, we are extremely responsive and strive to keep a healthy and knowledgeable relationship with all of our associates.

Our CRM Software
We developed our own web-based CRM software that manages the process of initiating and developing relationships. As an associate, all you have to do is log in from your home computer to use it. This allows you to spend a very large percentage of your time having high quality conversations with the right people. Prior to working on your first campaign, you will be trained to use the software. The software was designed to be intuitive and easy-to-use. The software also has help screens to answer any questions that you might have. Our system also keeps track of the amount of hours worked, so you know exactly how long you worked, what the results were, and what you can expect to be paid.

Hours
Typically, our associates work four hours a day, Monday thru Friday, and optionally Saturday. For Business to Consumer campaigns, the hours are typically 4:00pm - 9:00pm, and for Business to Business campaigns, 10:00am - 4:45pm, all within the respective time zones. We do require a minimum of 20 hours per associate.

Reliability
We track the number of hours our associates work compared to the number of hours that they commit to working. If our associates fall below a predetermined level, then the relationship can be severely jeopardized or severed. We prefer associates who have a proven track record of working consistently and reliably from their home office. We look for sales associates who are comfortable working at their own residence, and do not see this opportunity as a "work at home, work whenever" situation. We are very understanding of occasional changes in one's schedule. However, all that we ask is that one works 4 solid hours each of the days they are scheduled to work.

"Work-at-Home" Requirements
Comfortable, quiet home office with no distractions
Capable computer system and printer
Reliable high-speed internet (cable or DSL required)
Phone purchased through TNG
Phone headset

Computer System Requirements
Computer: Intel or AMD Processor of 1.8Ghz or faster, with 512MB or more RAM
Operating System: Windows XP SP2 or higher; Mac OS X v10.5 or higher; Linux v2.6 or higher
Firewall installed & operating
Current anti-virus protection & spyware/malware detection
Router (minimum of 4 ports); Recommended: D-Link DIR-655

Internet Requirements
Reliable high-speed Internet (No satellite, wireless ISP, or dial-up)
Wireless connection within your home is acceptable, as long as your DSL or Cable connection is hard wired
Web Browser: Internet Explorer 7 or higher; Mozilla Firefox 3.5 or higher; Google Chrome 6+

Contact Us
If you are interested in completing the necessary steps in becoming an Elite Sales Associate, please e-mail your resume to the human resources manager

at jobs@newtonesa.com and request the Agent Qualifications - Basic Requirements document. All applicants must submit a resume before they will be considered for an interview.

* Note: Applicants must reside in and be a citizen of the United States

Nex Rep (http://www.nexrep.com/opportunities.html#opportunities)

Are you looking for work-from-home opportunity that allows time flexibility, growth, and the autonomy to be your own boss?

Are you friendly, outgoing, and passionate about being the best at what you do?

If you are, join hundreds of other independent contractor sales and tech support professionals at NexRep who are providing excellent customer service on behalf of our clients through inbound calls, outbound calls, or email.

Next Level Solutions
(http://www.dial-nls.com/content.php?link=Careers_ind)

Job Title: Virtual Independent Agents
Salary: Varies based on project

JOB DESCRIPTION:

The Virtual Independent Agent (VIA) are in charge to service outbound customers make sales calls from home, using a computer, a telephone line and a broadband access connection. VIA's qualifies lead eligibility, communicate features/benefits of account, overcomes objections.

We are looking for highly motivated and goal oriented individuals who are interested and enjoy:

The convenience of working from home
Being their own boss
Flexibility; Setting their own schedule
Balancing business and family
Starting your own business

QUALIFICATIONS:

Minimum of 20 Hrs per week availability
1+ year of telephone sales/customer service preferred
Ability to learn in a fast-paced environment
Excellent organizational skills with the ability to multitask
Excellent attendance records a MAJOR plus!
Solid PC skills
Bilingual (Spanish) a plus – not mandatory
Friendly and outgoing individuals willing to give our customers A+
Customer Service.

OPK Telemarketing
(http://www.opktelemarketing.com/jobs.html)

You can work from your home office as an independent contractor for
OPK— join OPK Telemarketing Services' team of elite business professionals. OPK is seeking callers who already have several years of sales
and/or telemarketing experience. Please tell us more about yourself by
submitting a resume and cover letter.

Pleio Good Start (http://www.goodstartu.info/)

We are looking for caring, motivated individuals who want to assist others with getting into a good routine with their medication. If you are a
self-sufficient, self-starter with a home office, a dedicated phone line,
and have a desire to help people, apply now!

Prospect Image (http://www.prospectimage.com/careers.php)

Production Assistant Contractor

We are looking for someone who is a quick learner. Position requires 2-4
hours per day depending on account. Training will be provided. Independent Contractor will be paid $10 per hour plus bonuses. Hourly rate
will increase with experience.

DUTIES:

Cold Calling Businesses

Appointment Setting
Data Entry
Database Management
Sending Faxes and/or Mailings
Filling out Daily Worksheet

REQUIREMENTS:

Separate business phone line
Basic computer skills
Microsoft Excel
2-4 hours per day of uninterrupted quiet time
Excellent organization skills
Good articulation and pleasant phone voice
DBA License (if necessary in your county)
To apply, please send resume to jobs@prospectimage.com

Service 800 (http://www.service800inc.com/careers/)

SERVICE 800 is looking for motivated individuals who are willing to work from home. You must be bright, personable and can articulate well verbally and in written form. You would be conducting interviews with customers who have recently had a service experience. Previous customer service experience, computer knowledge and telephone skills are mandatory.

PLEASE NOTE: In the United States, SERVICE 800 is only accepting applications from the following states: **FLORIDA, MINNESOTA, TEXAS, and WISCONSIN**. We hope to add to this list so check back frequently for changes to eligible states.

Successful Calling Rep Applicants must provide the following:

1. A personal home computer with Microsoft Windows XP or more current Operating System

2. Microsoft Office Suite (Excel, Word and PowerPoint)

3. A virus protection program and a firewall

4. High-speed internet connection (DSL, Broadband, Cable, etc.)

5. A separate, dedicated voice phone land line

6. A long-distance calling provider with an approved long-distance rate as a back up to the SERVICE 800 dialing process.

7. Quiet work space with no background noise

8. South America, Europe and Asia applicants must be fluent in English (reading and writing ability).

9. In **NORTH AMERICA**, you must have the ability to work 20 to 30 hours per week on consecutive days.

Sitel (http://www.sitel.com/careers/work-home/)

Calls may involve billing inquiries, account or product inquiries, product or service orders, installation scheduling

Home office environment allowing you to work free from distractions and interruptions during your shift. Sitel Work@Home Solutions™ is looking for qualified candidates to join our team of associates. We hire talented people who share our passion for providing exceptional customer service. As a Work@ Home associate, customer calls will be routed to your home office.

> Calls may involve billing inquiries, account or product inquiries, product or service orders, installation scheduling or technical product trouble shooting. Our clients come from various industries such as financial services, telecommunications, retail, hospitality, and health care. The Sitel Work@Home Solutions™ team is vital to our company's service offerings. As a member of this team of dedicated professionals, you will build a career working for a global leader and enjoy the benefits of working from home. - See more at: http://www.sitel.com/careers/work-home/workhome-agent-job-description/#sthash.8w3KHgJC.dpu

Starwood Hotels
(http://www.starwoodhotels.com/corporate/careers/paths/description.html?category=920060)

Starwood Hotels Reservation at home agent

> *Work @Home*
> Our @home Program gives Associates the opportunity to work in the most comfortable environment possible – home! Perks include:

- The ability to connect to a network of colleagues working at home around the world through chat and online learning sessions.
- Support from nearby Starwood contact centers. We encourage Associates to visit as often as they like.

Our @home Associates perform the same fun, rewarding duties as their on-site counterparts. And they get the same great benefits.

We offer a comprehensive package that includes:

- Savings plans
- Premiums
- Pay bonuses: annual, monthly, promotional, seasonal
- Employee assistance plan
- Emergency child/elder care
- Promotion from within
- Attractive hotel discounts
- Center events
- Hotel visits and events
- Unlimited training opportunities
- Career opportunities throughout the world -Substantial referral bonuses
- Corporate discounts
- Employee appreciation events

As a key touch point for our guests, Customer Contact Center Associates have the ability to directly influence how they feel about our brands and our company. The experience gained in this valuable role often leads to promotion within the Austin center, to one of our other global centers or one of our hotels located anywhere in the world!

Sykes (formerly Alpine Express) (https://jobs.alpineaccess.com/)

SYKES Home Powered by Alpine Access is a leader in the virtual contact center industry, specializing in SaaS-based talent management, cloud-based security and consulting services. With a workforce of 6,700 customer care professionals dispersed throughout the U.S. and Canada, this home-based customer contact solution supports more than 30 brands across 50 programs. Our industry-leading clients include Fortune 1000 companies in retail, financial services, telecommunications, healthcare, technology, travel and hospitality, media and entertainment. But whatever the industry, we are dedicated to working side-by-side with each of our clients to create customized, versatile solutions that generate high value for their business.

> Our Employees are delivering consistent quality and superior performance, our experienced customer care professionals work as expert extensions of our clients' brands. Comprised of people from diverse demographics – including those with impaired mobility, retirees, parents,adult students, veterans and military spouse – the success of SYKES Home is a direct result of the "passion to serve" and positive attitude of all our employees.

Talk2Rep.com

(http://chk.tbe.taleo.net/chk05/ats/careers/jobSearch.jsp?org=TALK2REP& cws=1&org=TALK2REP)

Talk2Rep Call Centers are currently hiring over 500 representatives for opportunities in both their Florida facilities and nationally for work at home positions. Positions include customer service, telemarketing, and on-line chat support for Talk2Rep's healthcare, telecommunications and utility clients.

"We are both fortunate and pleased to be afforded the opportunity to contribute to both the Florida and national economy by hiring only US citizens to work at home and in our call centers. We find that we can compete effectively against offshore companies by offering superior skills and services with US based employees," said Talk2Rep CEO Jim Ryan.

Talk2Rep invests heavily in recruiting and "highest quality call center agent" modeling to target and select the best US based employees possible. That's followed up with extensive, client specific training and education that result in superior service for our clients. "Our goal is to service our clients customers so that we get it right the first time and we strive to reduce repetitive calls to solve a problem or close a sale.

Initial job requirements for all positions include basic computer skills, good typing and internet skills along with a great attitude and a focus on assisting people. Talk2Rep's Florida call center based employees also require strong selling skills while work at home agents must have access to a high speed internet connection. All agents must pass various assessment tests and background checks.

Tele Reach (http://www.telereachjobs.com/4-0.cfm)

TeleReach Corporate, based in Houston, is a business development, appointment setting, lead generation and information gathering company. Since 1996 TeleReach has helped privately held and Fortune 100 client businesses:

- Dramatically Increase Their Sales Revenue;
- Improve Their Marketing Programs; and
- Efficiently Systematize The Sales/Marketing Process

Tracie Chancellor, the Founder, Owner and CEO, is an MBA graduate with 21 years of hands-on sales, marketing and business-to-business telemarketing experience. Chancellor's team is "a cut way above" the telephone marketing standard. Our staff, including managers and motivated producers, have excellent communication skills and in depth knowledge, from low tech to high tech, business experience. They are mature, often college educated and many are retired business veterans.

Teletech (http://www.teletechjobs.com/athome-en-US/search-home-jobs/)
Customer service

TeleTech offers a world of opportunities—literally. With service delivery centers in 17 countries worldwide, TeleTech provides a great opportunity for you to gain valuable experience working with diverse clients, customers, and cultures every day. In fact, our associates interact daily with more than 3.5 million customers in nearly 30 different languages around the world via phone, Internet, email, and other media.

U-Haul Customer Service
(http://jobs.uhaul.com/contact_center.aspx?jobtype=workfromhome)

If you are looking for a part-time job that allows you to work flexible hours, work from home from anywhere in North America, the Contact Center Work from Home Program might just be what you are looking for.

The following technical requirements must be met to be able to work from home.

- Have your own USB headset
- Upload and Download internet speeds of 2MB or greater. (Can be tested on http://www.speedtest.net/)
- PC or laptop that meets the following requirements:
- Windows XP, Vista 32-bit or 64-bit, Windows 7 or 8 32-bit or 64-bit operating system
- 5gb hard disc space available (or greater)
- Pentium 4 or higher processor
- Network card
- 2G RAM (minimum)
- Anti-virus software. (free recommended version is AVG)
- Job Titles (available at the time this book is being written)
- E-Storage Sales Representative

DESCRIPTION:

Storage Specialists receive incoming calls from customers calling regarding the different types of storage that we offer. Storage specialists answer general storage/rental inquiries, accept tenant payments and make reservations for storage rooms, U-Haul trucks, trailers, towing devices, and U-Box portable storage. Storage Specialists answer calls for both company owned stores and our affiliates.

- Part-time positions available

The following technical requirements MUST be met to be able to work from home:

- A minimum up load and down load speed: 2 Mbps or greater is REQUIRED to work from home. Run a speed test NOW to check your system, click here www.speedtest.net and click on "Begin Test", you will be required to provide speed test results for interview.
- You must have your own USB headset PC or laptop that meets the following requirements:

- Windows 7 32-bit or 64-bit , Windows 8 operating system 5gb hard disc space available (or greater)
- Pentium 4 or higher processor
- Network card
- 2G RAM (minimum)
- Anti-virus software.

REQUIREMENTS:

- Basic keyboarding and computer skills
- Excellent verbal communication and listening skills
- Clear speaking voice
- General knowledge of U.S. geography
- Positive business attitude
- Enjoy working with people
- Applicants must be at least 16 years of age, either currently in school and/or have a high school diploma or GED

EDUCATION/TRAINING:

Paid Training.

Work Environment: This is a work from home position.

Work Status: Moonlighter/Part-Time

Hours Needed:
(These hours may change based on business needs)

- Sun - 6am to 9pm
- Mon - 6am to 9pm
- Tue - 6am to 9pm
- Wed - 6am to 9pm
- Thu - 6am to 9pm
- Fri - 6am to 9pm
- Sat - 6am to 9pm

Roadside Assistance Agent

DESCRIPTION:

The responsibility of a U-Haul Roadside Assistance Agent is to provide exceptional customer service with a sense of urgency when assisting our customers. This includes identifying the problem, selecting and dispatching appropriate repair services to assist the customer, adding essential documentation to contracts, as well as handling and determining a resolution to escalated calls.

Candidates are required to have attention to detail, the ability to take incoming calls back to back, patience and a positive attitude. All candidates must be able to rationalize certain situations and make decisions based on reason and best judgment. Comprehension of policy and procedures will play a critical role in performance of these expectations. The primary job responsibility is to diagnose mechanical issues and arrange service for the customer that will be time sensitive. This will include walking the customer through mechanical complications over the phone, and explaining technical assistance in a way the customer will understand.

This is a great place to start being a part of the U-Haul team, to learn and have the opportunity for growth and advancement.

We offer 24 hours Roadside Assistance, 7 days a week, 365 days a year.

Exemplary attendance, written and verbal communication is expected. Flexible schedules are available, with paid training. Availability to work weekends is required for consideration.

REQUIREMENTS:

- Previous call center experience is preferred
- Dispatching experience is preferred but not required
- The ability to provide consistent positive experience for the customer in any given circumstance.
- Possess good reasoning and decision making skills to properly address Customer needs.

- Compose detailed documentation of events using the customer's verbiage to ensure their concerns are addressed accordingly.
- Communication with U-Haul associated service providers and reporting personnel.
- Mechanically inclined individual with a general knowledge of mechanical and automotive skills.
- Must be availability to work weekends and holidays.

This is a work from home (WFH) position, when you telecommute from home you MUST have:

- High-speed internet - Download and upload of 2MB or higher and ping speed below 70ms
- Processor - 1 GHz Intel Pentium P4 processor or better
- Memory - minimum of 2 GB of RAM Memory
- Operating System – Windows 7 or 8
- Browser - Internet Explorer or Chrome
- 5GB hard disc space available or greater
- Network card
- Anti-virus software (AVG - free recommended version / *McAfee, Comodo and Kaspersky are not compatible)
- USB Headset with noise-cancelling – a headset that plugs into your computer for use during calls.
- Your computer needs to be physically connected to the modem by a cable. Wireless connectivity, such as connectivity via a wireless router, is not acceptable.

EDUCATION/TRAINING:

- 100% commitment during training is required for a successful career with U-Haul.
- Paid 4 week training

Work Status: Moonlighter

Center Sales-Reservations Agents

DESCRIPTION:

Looking for a competitive and challenging position that rewards you for your efforts?

Want a part-time job working from home?

Help us by making a difference and enriching our customer's experience during stressful moving times. With over 16,000 locations around the nation, we are looking for exciting/motivated and enthusiastic Center Sales Agents to assist our customers with rental inquiries and making reservations for our trucks, trailers, hitches, towing devices, storage & U-Box units. Enjoy working from the comfort of your home office!

This job might be for you if:

- You enjoy helping people and love being rewarded for your performance
- You thrive in a fast paced sales environment with a focus on quality and attention to detail
- You are enthusiastic and empathetic and love creating an enjoyable experience
- You live for a challenge, are goal oriented, be willing to learn different systems, and easily navigate between multiple screens
- You communicate efficiently through Instant Messenger
- You can work independently delivering practical solutions and you thrive in a collaborative team environment
- You have the perfect home-office free of distractions and background noise
- You have a good understanding of U.S. geography
- You are willing to commit to our successful 4 week remote training
- Join our team today and embark on your home career with ample room for growth and exciting opportunities.
- Status:
- Part-time - hours vary during slow and busy seasons

- $8.25 per hour + bonus

REQUIREMENTS:

Qualified applicants will also need to meet the following technical requirements:

- High-speed internet - Download and upload of 2MB or higher and ping speed below 70ms
- Processor - 1 GHz Intel Pentium P4 processor or better
- Memory - minimum of 2 GB of RAM Memory
- Operating System – Windows 7 or 8
- Browser - Internet Explorer or Chrome
- 5GB hard disc space available or greater
- Network card
- Anti-virus software (AVG - free recommended version / *McAfee, Comodo and Kaspersky are not compatible)
- USB Headset with noise-cancelling – a headset that plugs into your computer for use during calls.
- Your computer needs to be physically connected to the modem by a cable. Wireless connectivity, such as connectivity via a wireless router, is not acceptable.

EDUCATION:

Applicants must be at least 16 years of age, either currently in school and/or have a high school diploma or GED

TRAINING:

The competition for this role is fierce, 100% commitment during training is required for a successful career with U-Haul.

- Paid 4 week training from home

Work Status: Moonlighter
Hours Needed:
(These hours may change based on business needs)

- Sun - 6am to 12am
- Mon - 7am to 10pm
- Tue - 7am to 10pm
- Wed - 7am to 10pm

E-Customer Service Agent

DESCRIPTION:

Looking for work-life balance?

Do you want to avoid traffic jams and work in a comfortable environment?

Help us by making a difference and enriching our customer's experience during stressful moving times. With over 16,000 locations around the nation, we are looking for exciting, self-motivated and enthusiastic Customer Service Agents to assist our customers with rental equipment issues.

Enjoy working from the comfort of your home office!

This job might be for you if:

- You enjoy helping people during stressful times
- You thrive in a fast paced virtual environment with a focus on quality and attention to detail
- You are enthusiastic and empathetic and love creating an enjoyable experience
- You live for a challenge, are goal oriented, be willing to learn different systems, and easily navigate between multiple screens
- You communicate efficiently through Instant Messenger
- You can work independently delivering practical solutions and you thrive in a collaborative team environment
- You have the perfect home-office free of distractions and background noise
- You like U.S. geography and finding different locations on the map
- You are willing to commit to our successful 4 week remote training
- Join our team today and embark on your home career with ample room for growth and exciting opportunities!

This is a moonlighter position, must be available to work at least 32 + hours a week. Ideal candidates will have an open availability.

(32 hour availability does not mean you will work 32 hours a week)

REQUIREMENTS:

- Experience in Windows-based computer programs with excellent navigational skills is preferred
- At least 6 months of customer service experience is preferred
- Must be motivated with strong work ethic
- Excellent communication and customer service skills
- No selling required.

This is a work from home (WFH) position, when you telecommute from home you must have:

- Processor - 1 GHz Intel Pentium P4 processor or better
- Memory - minimum of 2 GB of RAM Memory
- You must be able to download software, a VOIP (Voice over Internet Protocol) phone system will be used, and a landline or cell phone is NOT needed for this position.
- Broadband or High Speed Internet is required. (must be hardwired). Cricket, Air card, satellite or other non-wired ISP connections are not allowed
- Operating System – Windows 7 or 8
- Browser - Internet Explorer or Chrome
- 5GB hard disc space available or greater
- Network card
- Anti-virus software (AVG - free recommended version / * Avas, Comodo, McAfee, Microsoft Security Essentials II and Kaspersky are not compatible.)
- USB Headset with noise-cancelling – a headset that plugs into your computer for use during calls. Your computer needs to be physically connected to the modem by a cable.

EDUCATION/TRAINING:

The competition for this role is fierce, 100% commitment during training is required for a successful career with U-Haul.

- Paid 4 week training from home

Work Environment:

This is a work at home position that requires a quiet, private, work area, and an individual who is self-motivated and able to work independently.

Work Status: Moonlighter
Hours Needed:
(These hours may change based on business needs)

- Sun - 7am to 5pm
- Mon - 8am to 5pm
- Tue - 8am to 5pm
- Wed - 8am to 5pm
- Thu - 8am to 5pm
- Fri - 8am to 5pm
- Sat - NA

Vera Fast (http://www.verafast.net/job_opportunities.htm)

How would you like to work from the comfort of your own home; enjoy convenient hours; use your personal computer to help us meet our client's needs? Sound too good to be true? Think there's a catch? Well there isn't. As you can see from our home page, we work primarily with the newspaper industry. Our customer service representatives work from their homes making customer service calls for our newspaper clients. In many instances, we are checking on the customer's service and reporting back to the newspaper so they can take appropriate action.

If you are currently employed full time, you will need to be realistic about your availability for this opportunity. To juggle home and work responsibilities, you need self-discipline, a schedule, and cooperation from your family. The nice thing about working for us is that child-care, wardrobe and transportation are virtually non-existent.

Are you…

- A self-starter with good communication skills?
- Well-disciplined and able to work on your own?
- Dependable?
- Organized?
- Able to commit to working 16 or more flexible hours per week, mostly in the evening and on the weekend?

Do you have…

- A Pentium Class 4 or better PC running Windows Vista, Windows 7 or Windows 8? (no Macintosh)
- A reliable, fast, broadband internet connection using DSL or Cable? (no Satellite) * for optimal performance, a wired internet connection is highly recommended
- An email address?
- A working printer with ink and paper attached to your computer?
- A landline with phone, or a cellphone with unlimited minutes, or a VoIP connection?

* Please note that you cannot use a "majicjack" or any similar device.

You also need...

- Basic typing and personal computer skills.
- A quiet work area without interruptions.
- A social security card and current state issued photo ID.

* A USB headset may be needed in the future.

Working Solutions (www.workingsolutions.com/)

Industry:

Business Process Outsourcing (BPO) that provides inbound technical support, sales and customer service as well as data entry and editing services.

COMPANY DESCRIPTION:

Based in Plano, TX, Working Solutions bills itself as "the first company to utilize an entire workforce of home-based customer sales and service agents." Founded in 1996, the company utilizes independent contractor virtual call center agents, which it calls "Agents On Demand," to services clients' call center needs. Additionally it also hires contractors for data entry work.

Qualifications:

Applicants must be 18 years old. Working Solutions "looks for skilled, educated, and motivated people" to fill its ranks. Agents are required to provide their own computer equipment (with Windows Vista or higher) and Internet service (DSL or cable).

TYPES OF WORK AT HOME POSITIONS:

Working Solutions hires independent contractors to work on a project basis in home call centers and on data entry.

Virtual call center agents handle inbound and outbound customer service, sales, market research and/or technical support. These positions could include enrollments, retail sales, reservations, account support and technical assistance on electronics, websites, software and telephony. Agents work with customers over the phone, through online chat and email.

The company also seeks bilingual agents with fluency in Arabic, Bengali, Cantonese, Creole, Filipino, French, French-Canadian, German, Hindi, Italian, Japanese, Korean, Mandarin, Portuguese, Russian, Samoan, Spanish and Vietnamese. Company also hires travel agents with knowledge of Apollo, Amadeus, Galileo, Sabre or WorldSpan and corporate booking experience.

PAY AND BENEFITS:

Because Working Solutions hires independent contractors there is no guarantee of minimum wage or any number of hours per week. However, the position is likely a part-time call center job. The company says its projects, which all compensate differently, pay anywhere from $7.50 to $30 an hour. However, they may not necessarily calculate pay on an hourly rate. Agents invoice Working Solutions, based on their projects' pay instructions, and are paid every two weeks.

Again because it hires independent contractors, the company does not offer benefits of any kind. Agents are able to choose their own hours online. However, the availability of hours can vary making it difficult to earn a full-time living at Working Solutions. Despite their status as independent contractors, agents aren't charged any fees by the company.

GEOGRAPHIC RESTRICTIONS:

The company hires Agents OnDemand in all U.S. states and from across the world. However the number of projects, particularly call center jobs, for residents outside the U.S. is more limited.

APPLYING TO WORKING SOLUTIONS:

Submit an application online through the company's website. You may paste a resume into the comments field of the application. At the end of the online application, you will be asked to answer a few questions in part one of an assessment. Multiple choice and written-answer questions will test your knowledge of customer service as well as assess your grammar and writing skills.

After submitting this, you will be able to complete the second part of the assessment. For this you will call in and record answers regarding customer service scenarios. After this your application will be evaluated and you will be notified if your application will be placed in the "pending pool," meaning that you will be considered for opportunities that match your qualifications. If there is a match you will be contacted by email. It can take several weeks to months to be matched with the first project.

If you've thought about working from home and being your own boss, the Agents On Demand program might be the right fit for you. Working Solutions looks for skilled, educated, and motivated people to assist customers with sales, service and technical support transactions. Agents work directly with customers over the phone, through online chat sessions, and email.

Retail Sales/Customer Service

Working Solutions is partnering with retail and consumer goods companies to provide top of the line sales and service solutions.

As a sales and service specialist you will assist buyers with their transactions. It takes a love of customers to be the best sales and service agent. You will work online and over the phone with customers.

A strong sales background is important for this program. Agents must be able to upsell while answering customer questions.

We ensure quality service through the best agents—which could be you. Know that Working Solutions receives an over four star rating from agents on Glassdoor. It's what clients expect.

Still interested? Please keep reading.

PROGRAM REQUIREMENTS:

Excellent customer service – Agents need strong verbal communication and rapport-building skills to help callers with questions about products and options.

SALES SKILLS – Agents must be comfortable working to upsell on most calls.

MULTI-TASKING – Agents must be able to operate multiple systems simultaneously while maintaining constant communication with customers.

BACKGROUND CHECK: Agents must successfully pass a background check that includes a Social Security number verification and a criminal history check.

Sporting Goods/Outdoor Sales/Service

Working Solutions is partnering with a premier sports, outdoor and lifestyle retailer. It offers a broad assortment of quality hunting, fishing and camping equipment—along with sports and leisure products, footwear, apparel and much more. You will work online and over the phone with this retailer's customers.

Our client's philosophy is to deliver an unparalleled shopping experience by:

- Providing convenience
- Offering a broad selection of quality products

- Delivering exceptional customer service
- Selling the right merchandise at everyday low prices

Agents will provide sporting goods expertise to help callers place orders from the client's catalog or website, as well as assisting them with any existing order. Agents will use a variety of systems and sites to retrieve product information, place orders and clearly document those calls as they occur.

A strong sales background is important for this program. Agents must be able to recommend complementary products to customers. For example, a customer ordering running shoes would be offered socks and other running apparel as well.

We ensure quality service through the best agents—which could be you. Know that Working Solutions receives a 90% recommend rate from agents on Glassdoor. It's what clients expect.

Still interested? Please keep reading.

Program hours: The client's current operating hours are 7 a.m. – midnight (Central Time), seven days a week. Agents need to commit to a minimum of 20 hours a week during those hours to remain proficient and on active status for this contract.

Background check: Agents on this program must successfully pass a background check. It includes a Social Security number verification and a criminal history check.

Program requirements:

Sporting/outdoor expertise – Agents must be sporting or outdoor enthusiasts to guide customers through the order and add-on sale process. Academy customers expect to speak to an expert on each call.

Excellent customer service – Agents need strong verbal communication and rapport-building skills to help callers with orders, tracking and product information.

Sales skills – Agents must be comfortable offering additional sporting and outdoor products as complements to the items being ordered on each call.

Multi-tasking – Agents must be able to operate multiple systems simultaneously while maintaining constant communication with customers.

Event Ticketing –Sales/Service

Do you love sporting events, concerts or the arts? Working Solutions has a place for you as an online ticket agent. Our agents strive to knock it out of the park with stellar service to keep customers coming back as ticket buyers and sellers.

We ensure quality service through the best agents—which could be you. Know that Working Solutions receives an over four star rating from agents on Glassdoor. It's what clients expect.

Still interested? Please keep reading.

Program hours: We assist with customer interactions from 6:30 a.m. to 11:00 p.m. (Central Time), seven days a week. Agents need to commit to a minimum of 20 hours a week during those hours to remain proficient and on active status for this contract. We ask agents plan to work some weekend hours each week. There are high-volume weeks in March when agents will need to be able to work increase their hours to cover customer demands.

Program requirements:

Excellent customer service – Agents need strong verbal communication and rapport-building skills to ensure that sellers and buyers will be return customers.

Multi-tasking – Agents must be able to simultaneously operate multiple systems, while maintaining constant communication with customers.

Technical ability – Agents should have a strong technical background and be computer literate. They need to feel comfortable learning new systems and be able and willing to make minor adjustments to their computers to work with the client's program technology. Experience in Seibel is a bonus.

Be a fan – Agents should be knowledgeable about events—sports, concerts and/or the arts.

Flexibility – This program has peak weeks in March. Agents will need to work additional hours beyond the program's typical operating hours.

Compensation – Agents are paid based on each minute spent working with a customer. This translates to an equivalent of $12 - $18/ hour (USD).

Xerox

(http://xerox-virtual.jobs/virtual-usa/customer-care-assistant/EE3403B0D 34547D890B01577F7075E71/job/)

Customer Care Assistant in United States

Xerox is the world's leading enterprise for business process and document management. Its services, technology, and expertise enable workplaces - from small businesses to large global enterprises - to simplify the way work gets done so they operate more effectively and focus more on what matters most: their real business. Xerox offers business process outsourcing and IT outsourcing services, including data processing, healthcare solutions, HR benefits management, finance support, transportation solutions, and customer relationship management services for commercial and government organizations worldwide. The company also provides extensive leading-edge document technology, services, software and genuine Xerox supplies for graphic communication and office printing environments of any size. Xerox serves clients in more than 160 countries.

If you meet the requirements of this position and want to work for a world-class company with a great marketplace reputation, apply today.

Using a computerized system, responds to customer inquiries in a call center environment. May perform one or more of the following: Respond to telephone inquiries and complaints using standard scripts and procedures; Gather information, researches/resolves inquiries and logs customer calls. Communicates appropriate options for resolution in a timely manner. Informs customers about services available and assesses customer needs.

All other duties as assigned.

Xerox is an Equal Opportunity Employer and considers applicants for all positions without regard to race, color, creed, religion, ancestry, national origin, age, gender identity, sex, marital status, sexual orientation, physical or mental disability, use of a guide dog or service animal, military/veteran status, citizenship status, basis of genetic information, or any other group protected by law. People with disabilities who need a reasonable accommodation to apply or compete for employment with Xerox may request such accommodation(s) by sending an e-mail to//accommodations@xerox.com//.

DATA ENTRY

Axion Data Services *(www.axiondata.com)*

Pennsylvania-based data outsourcing firm Axion Data Services hires independent contractors to perform data entry for its clients. These jobs are performed off-site and usually from home.

Data entry jobs at this company pay independent contractors on a per-piece basis. The company accepts applications when it has jobs available.

Types of Work-at-Home Opportunities at Axion Data Services: The data entry work that Axion offers is entering data from scanned images. Some of the types of data entry projects that Axion contractors work on are loyalty program applications, contest entries, advertising insertions, customer response cards, student records, product registrations and questionnaires.

Most of its operators work part time, 20-25 hours per week, but the amount of work available may vary. However, when an agent works those hours is usually flexible. Agents log on to Axion's system, review available projects and choose which ones to do.

QUALIFICATIONS AND REQUIREMENTS:

Basic computer skills, such as installing and removing software, creating new folders, sending email and using the Internet, are absolutely required.

Additionally, accurate data entry skills and following instructions are important qualifications. Operators must provide and maintain their own computer—either a Windows PC or Mac system—or a high speed Internet connection. Contractors must have either a telephone answering machine or voice mail. Contractors will have to download some free software and may be required to purchase software.

Successful applicants will have a clean criminal and must sign a confidentiality agreement.

Pay and Benefits: All data entry agents are hired as independent contractors. This means there are no benefits and no guarantee of minimum wage.

Axion Data pays its data entry operators on a per-piece basis, which varies based on the complexity of the project. For example in some projects, the data entered is small, and agents can input 2 to 4 forms per minute at a compensation rate ranging from 4 to 8 cents per form. This works out to a potential range of $4.80 to $19.20 per hour; though, keep in mind that earning the top number is unlikely because faster jobs likely have a lower rate. Other projects require 30 to 60 minutes per document, with compensation ranging from $5-9 per document (potentially $5 to $18 per hour). Agents submit invoices for their work every two weeks and are paid 28 days later.

Capital Typing (http://www.capitaltyping.com/data-entry-careers)

Data entry operators play an important role in the increasingly important process of handling information. Data entry typists work on computer keyboards to input data into computers and complete forms on data entry screens (computer monitors). Data entry work also includes scanning documents.

The most important qualifications for entry-level computer data entry positions are high keyboarding speeds, and some employers will administer data entry typing tests. A data entry clerk with some data entry training or experience usually acquires his / her data entry skills on the job.

Data entry outsourcing and remote data entry have made it possible for freelance data entry workers to get work-at-home data entry jobs. Virtual data entry and internet data entry have also resulted in many online data entry positions being outsourced by data entry companies to off-shore data entry clerks.

This trend in the data entry business is threatening U.S. data entry operators because offshore data entry persons are normally paid less than U.S. data entry clerks. Data entry companies are thus able to increase their profit margins by outsourcing data entry projects overseas.

As data capturing technologies become more widely available, data entry clerks may suffer and the demand for data entry key operators will diminish. However, because data capturing technologies cost more than data entry clerks the need for data entry personnel is not expected to drop immediately.

Capital Typing is a major outsourcing data entry and market research company that will employ skilled data entry personnel who have experience and are willing to work hard and learn to improve their data entry skills. Our Data Entry and Market Research Services Department already has an experienced staff of data entry clerks, some of whom are well trained and tested offshore data entry clerks. If you would are seeking a legitimate data entry job, contact Capital Typing.

Cass Information Systems

(http://www.cassinfo.com/Corporate/Careers/Job-Openings/COL-Offsite-Invoice-Payment-Specialist.aspx)

Job position: Offsite Invoice Payment Specialist
Primary position responsibilities:
Operate and maintain a PC in a work-at-home environment

Accurately enter data to pay utility invoices and prepare customized reports

Perform required steps dictated by online programs and procedures

Knowledge and minimum requirements

Must be able to key a minimum of 9,000 KSPH, both alpha and numeric combined

Candidates must have good analytical and problem-solving skills and be dependable and quality minded

Training will be done in the office Monday through Friday 9:00 AM – 2:00 PM for approximately 90 days. The home schedule is a minimum of 20-25 hours over Saturday/Sunday, Monday, Tuesday and Friday.

Location: Columbus, Ohio-working at home

DionData Solutions (http://www.diondatasolutions.net/opportunities.htm)

COMPANY DESCRIPTION:

Missouri-based data management firm DionData Solutions uses independent contractors to perform data entry from home, making it one of a fairly small number of legitimate work-at-home data entry companies in an industry filled with data entry scams.

Types of Work-at-Home Opportunities at DionData Solutions:

Data entry independent contractors at DionData enter data from images of documents, often handwritten ones such as applications. The work is compensated on a per-piece basis.

Applying to DionData Solutions:

The DionData Solutions website says it is accepting applications. However, that doesn't necessarily mean it is hiring. This message has not changed for years. Applications are accepted via email only. Though it says it can't respond to all applicants, the company encourages applicants to resubmit after 30 days. Like Axion Data, another legit home data entry company, Dion Data likely keeps a list of possible contractors and hires as needed.

There are no fees to apply or for training.

Qualifications and Requirements:

DionData requires of its home data entry operators: 60 WPM accurate typing skills; basic computer skills, such as sending and receiving email with attachments, using the Internet, uploading and downloading files; the ability to work independently on multiple projects simultaneously; excellent communication skills--written and verbal.

Operators must provide and maintain their own desktop computer (dual monitors is a plus) and a high speed Internet connection (DSL or cable). U.S. citizenship and residency is required.

PAY AND BENEFITS:

All data entry agents are hired as independent contractors which mean there are no benefits and no guarantee of minimum wage. In fact, home data entry jobs very often play less than the minimum wage, especially at the beginning before the data entry worker has developed enough familiarity with the process to work quickly. DionData pays its data entry operators on a per-piece basis, which is typical.

Driver Guide
(http://www.flexjobs.com/jobs/telecommuting-jobs-at-driverguide.com)
(Flex Jobs charges a membership fee to see the entire job description and apply for the job position)

Driver Guide is an award winning database of thousands of product software drivers, firmware and support documents (manuals) for hundreds of technology products available on the current and past markets. Often hard to find drivers for computer peripherals can be found on Driver Guide thanks to their tireless search and the talents of their IT team. The company continues to experience growth and therefore has multiple opportunities to work from home as a database helper, PHP Developer or Graphic Designer. These positions are part time, with some degree of flexibility available. Training is provided to qualified candidates who are then allowed to work from the comfort of their home as virtual professionals. To find out more about the telecommuting opportunities that Driver Guide can offer you. Apply for Driver Guide jobs using Flex jobs.

Quicktate (iDictate) (http://www.quicktate.com/)

Industry: Data entry, general transcription, medical transcription
Company Description:
Quicktate supports a variety of services and apps that convert short bits of recorded speech into the written word. These include Evernote apps (voice-mail messages and audio notes), TweetCall (dictated tweets), CallTroops (phoned letters to military personnel), and Voice on the Go (dictated texts). However, Quicktate and its partner iDictate also offer services for longer transcription projects, which include medical reports, conference calls, and legal files.

Types of Work-at-Home Opportunities at Quicktate or iDictate:
In these micro jobs, data entry operators listen to audio files and transcribe them. The voicemail message files average 1-2 minutes in length, while the other recordings are longer. Hours are flexible and operators can work as many or as few hours as they can handle and/or obtain. In this type of crowd-sourcing platform operators log on to the company's system and claim files to transcribe.

Data entry operators begin at Quicktate and may be promoted to iDictate, which pays more. Quicktate also does medical transcription, which also pays more. Most Quicktate transcription is done in English or Spanish. However, the company also seeks transcribers with skills in French, Italian, German, Chinese, Farsi, Portuguese and Japanese for iDictate projects.

PAY AND BENEFITS:

All Quicktate and iDictate's data entry agents are hired as independent con-tractors. This means there are no benefits and no guarantee of minimum wage.

Quicktate and iDictate pay its data entry operators on a per-word basis. The rate of pay for Quicktate general transcription is $.0025 per word or 4 words for 1 cent, while the rate for Quicktate medical transcription and iDictate work is $.0050 per word or 2 words for 1 cent. This might work out to $5-7/hour at Quicktate, but keep in mind there is not likely enough work to make this a full-time pursuit.

Payment, which is weekly, is through PayPal account only.

QUALIFICATIONS AND REQUIREMENTS:

Quicktate seeks professional transcriptionists that follows directions well, have a strong grammar and typing skills, accurate spelling and punctuation and can listen to voice files and accurately type what they hear.

Typists must supply their own equipment, supplies, work space and Internet connection. Computers may be Windows-based or Macs and must have a Firefox, Safari, or Google Chrome browser. Additionally, typists must have a Yahoo IM account and download and install QuickTime. Express Scribe is a free software application that may be useful. A headset, and possibly a foot pedal, may be needed.

All contractors for Quicktate must fill out an electronic W-9 tax form even if they are not located in the United States.

APPLYING to QUICKTATE:

To apply, create a typist account by filling out an application on the Quicktate website. Two non-family references are required, and you must answer two short essay questions. (Be sure to use correct grammar and spelling.)

Next, applicants should read through the Help Desk FAQ and other postings to become familiar with the procedures. Applicants must then take a quiz that will cover both Quicktate procedures and include an audio file to transcribe. If you wish to be considered for transcription in other languages than English or medical transcription jobs you must complete those audio files.

Expect to wait at least two weeks to hear back from Quicktate. If your application is approved, you will receive a letter. Until then, you will not be able to log in to your account and accept assignments.

Virtual Bee (https://www.virtualbee.com/)

Industry: Data entry

COMPANY DESCRIPTION:

Lionbridge Technology, Inc., acquired *crowd sourcing* company Virtual Solutions, the parent company of VirtualBee (which changed its name from KeyForCash), in 2012. Virtual Bee uses a workforce of home-based independent contractors to securely enter its client's data, using technology that only allows each of the data entry keyers to see a portion of the confidential original data.

Types of Work-at-Home Opportunities at Virtual Bee:

Home-based data entry operators log on to the Virtual Bee system and choose data entry tasks. They see an image of the data and then must enter it with accuracy. See this video to learn more: ***www.youtube.com/ watch?v=EAA9IKuvXSM***

PAY AND BENEFITS:

All data-entry keyers are hired as independent contractors. This means there are no benefits and no guarantee of minimum wage. Payment is on a per piece basis, and different types of data entry pay at different rates. Expect the per-piece rate to work out to about $5-6 per hour.

Pays weekly by check, but the minimum amount paid out is $30. Hours are flexible but there may be certain days of the week or periods during the year when work is not available.

QUALIFICATIONS AND REQUIREMENTS:

You also must be at least 18 years old to work for Virtual Bee. A score of 97 to 100 percent on the evaluation test is the main qualification of this job.

The company hires worldwide. However, the company divides its workers into two groups--one is for those who reside in the continental 48 United States and the second is for all international individuals (as long as they have maintained a physical presence outside of the United States for the previous 3 consecutive calendar years).

Technical requirements are a computer with an Internet connection and a web browser with JavaScript enabled.

Applying to Virtual Bee:

Click on "Sign Up" on the Virtual Bee website, and then fill in the short form with basic information about yourself. You will then receive an email with a link to a three-part evaluation. This is a test of your data-entry keying ability. It is important that you follow the directions carefully. You will need a score in the high 90s (on a 100-point scale) to become registered at Virtual Bee. However, you can retake the evaluation once a day until you achieve that score.

It may take 6 to 8 weeks to hear back from Virtual Bee. There are no fees of any kind to work here. However, you may see advertised offers on its website. Participating in these is not required and will not improve your chances of being hired.

Working Solutions (www.workingsolutions.com/)

Business Process Outsourcing (BPO) that provides inbound technical support, sales and customer service as well as data entry and editing services.

Company Description:

Based in Plano, TX, Working Solutions bills itself as "the first company to utilize an entire workforce of home-based customer sales and service agents." Founded in 1996, the company utilizes independent contractor virtual call center agents, which it calls "Agents On Demand," to services clients' call center needs. Additionally it also hires contractors for data entry work.

QUALIIFICATIONS:

Applicants must be 18 years old. Working Solutions "looks for skilled, educated, and motivated people" to fill its ranks. Agents are required to provide their own computer equipment (with Windows Vista or higher) and Internet service (DSL or cable).

TYPES OF WORK-AT-HOME POSITIONS:

Working Solutions hires independent contractors to work on a project basis in home call centers and on data entry.

Virtual call center agents handle inbound and outbound customer service, sales, market research and/or technical support. These positions could include enrollments, retail sales, reservations, account support and technical assistance on electronics, websites, software and telephony. Agents work with customers over the phone, through online chat and email.

The company also seeks bilingual agents with fluency in Arabic, Bengali, Cantonese, Creole, Filipino, French, French-Canadian, German, Hindi,

Italian, Japanese, Korean, Mandarin, Portuguese, Russian, Samoan, Spanish and Vietnamese. Company also hires travel agents with knowledge of Apollo, Amadeus, Galileo, Sabre or WorldSpan and corporate booking experience.

In addition to call center agents Working Solutions hires for *data entry jobs*, which don't involve phone time.

PAY AND BENEFITS:

Because Working Solutions hires independent contractors there is no guarantee of minimum wage or any number of hours per week. However, the position is likely a *part-time call center job*. The company says its projects, which all compensate differently, pay anywhere from $7.50 to $30 an hour. However, they may not necessarily calculate pay on an hourly rate. Agents invoice Working Solutions, based on their projects' pay instructions, and are paid every two weeks.

Again because it hires independent contractors, the company does not offer benefits of any kind. For more information on the distinction between employees and contractors, Agents are able to choose their own hours online. However, the availability of hours can vary making it difficult to earn a full-time living at Working Solutions. Despite their status as independent contractors, agents aren't charged any fees by the company.

GEOGRAPHIC RESTRICTIONS:

The company hires Agents OnDemand in all U.S. states and from across the world. However the number of projects, particularly call center jobs, for residents outside the U.S. is more limited.

APPLYING TO WORKING SOLUTIONS:

Submit an application online through the company's website. You may paste a resume into the comments field of the application. At the end of the online application, you will be asked to answer a few questions in part one of an assessment. Multiple choice and written-answer questions will test your knowledge of customer service as well as assess your grammar and writing skills.

After submitting this, you will be able to complete the second part of the assessment. For this you will call in and record answers regarding customer service scenarios. After this your application will be evaluated and you will be notified if your application will be placed in the "pending pool," meaning that you will be considered for opportunities that match your qualifications. If there is a match you will be contacted by email. It can take several weeks to months to be matched with the first project.

Writers Research Group (http://www.writersresearchgroup.com/company/jobs.html)

We are always in search of talented, self-motivated, detail-oriented professionals capable of meeting strict client specifications and tight deadlines.

We offer a range of exciting opportunities:

Data Entry Specialists input a variety of data for a wide range of projects. Quick, accurate typing and attention-to-detail are a must for this position.

EDUCATION

AdmissionsConsultants
(http://www.admissionsconsultants.com/employment.asp)

Type of Job: admissions
Based in Vienna, VA, AdmissionsConsultants hires candidates with admissions committee experience and good interpersonal skills as consultants for its work at home jobs.

Aim-for-A Tutoring (http://www.aim4a.com/tutors.php)

Type of Job: Online Tutoring
Online tutors teach a variety of subjects, including math, science and English, as well as test preparations for GED, PSAT, SAT, GRE, GMAT and AP for students from around the world who range in age from elementary school to college. Teaching experience and a college
degree in a subject taught is required.

American Public University System (http://apus.jobs/)

Type of Job: Online Adjunct Faculty

Encompassing American Public University (APU) and American Military University (AMU), this online Higher education institution hires adjunct faculty members as well as a few administrative positions as Work at home jobs. Master's degree in subject matter is required.
Experience in college-level teaching And/or PhD is preferred.

Argosy Public University System

(http://online.argosy.edu/about/employment.aspx)

Type of Job: Online Adjunct Faculty
This college with online education and brick-and-mortar campuses hires online adjunct Faculty to teach graduate and undergraduate courses. Master's or doctoral degree required for these online teaching jobs.

Auralog (http://www.homejobsformom.com/job/auralog)

Type of Job: Adult Education, Language
Offers online teaching jobs for language tutors to work in conjunction with its "TeLL me More" language software.

Brainmass (https://brainmass.com/join-expert)

Type of Job: Online Expert
Register as an Expert (master's degree or PhD required) in a subject, then answer questions posted by students. The Expert earns a percentage of the fee paid by the questioner and can earn more if the answer is downloaded by other students. Also, the Expert can earn more money writing an e-book, making a quiz, and submitting a reference solution to the Brainmass Library. Pay is in Canadian dollars and is monthly when the Expert has earned at least $50 CAD.

California Virtual Academies

(http://cava.k12.com/who-we-are/career-opportunities)

Type of Job: K-12, Special Education, Language
A network of public charter schools that provides education for students in the state of California. California Virtual Academies hires certified K-12 teachers in California to work from home. In-person meetings in county of employment are required.

Capella University

(http://www.capellaeducation.com/careers/?ref=driverlayer.com%2Fweb)

Type of Job: Online Faculty and Instructors
Typical work-at-home at this online college including faculty chairs, core faculty, adjunct faculty, dissertation mentors and channel partner.
Search for positions with an "offsite" location.

Classof1 (http://www.lilystone.org/classof1.html)

Type of Job: Online Tutoring
Indian company offers online tutoring, homework assistance, test prep, content development and e-learning courses aimed at college and K-12 students in the U.S., U.K. and Australia.
Subjects include math, science, English, social studies, technology, accounting, journalism medicine, engineering, business, economics and more.

Connections Academy

(https://www.connectionsacademy.com/careers/home.aspx)

Types of Education-Related Jobs: K-12 Tutoring
Connections Academy, a ""school without walls," is a virtual educational program serving K-12 students throughout various states in a non-classroom-based environment. It hires certified teachers for online teaching jobs.

Creative English Solutions (CES)
(http://www.englishsolutions.ca/ces_jobs.php)

Types of Education-Related Jobs: Test Writing
Canadian company CES develops practice tests for TOEFL and TOEIC. It hires experienced test writers and voice actors from Canada.

Eduwizards (http://www.eduwizards.com/careers.php)

Types of Education-Related Jobs: Online Tutoring at K-12 and College Level
Company hires freelance tutors and salaried tutors. K-12 tutors in math, science English/reading in the Supplemental Education Services (SES) and No

Child Left Behind (NCLB) program are paid an hourly rate of around $20. U.S. residency and state teaching certification required. Freelance tutors pay a fee to be listed.

Edu Writers (http://eduwriters.com/index.html)

Who We Are:
In business since 1998, we have provided thousands of people with the help that they need for school and for their professional lives.

What We Do:
We provide custom research, writing and editing services to students and professionals.

The Benefits of Working For Us:
Working from home, our freelance writers earn from $7 to $15 per page and receive a substantial income. We give our writers the freedom to choose what and when they want to write, allowing writers to set their own schedule based on the deadlines they choose.

What We Are Looking For:
Customer service and repeat clientele are our company's priorities. We are looking for writers who understand the requirements of our priorities by showing us that they can be extremely accurate and always meet deadlines. A college degree is required. All majors are welcomed and encouraged to apply. Our writers research, write and edit papers on a variety of topics from business and agriculture to computer science and biology. Knowledge of various writing styles and documentation is not required, but will be taken into high consideration during the application process. We also hire internationally; however, all applicants must have an impeccable command of English.

What We Are Not Looking For:
Many people start to work for us and for some reason; they think that they can plagiarize their assignments. They cut and paste sections or even whole pages of websites. And we are forced to do the same thing: get rid of them. We have developed software that checks all writing for plagiarism. If we find it, we will notify the writer that he or she does not work for us any

longer. We are an employer and we expect our independent contractors to work. So, if you are thinking, "What an easy gig. I can just take stuff off the Net," please do not waste our or your time.

Employment:
If offered a writing position, you will be considered as an independent contractor of the company and will be responsible for reporting any taxes to the Federal Government. You also will be required to sign a contract with the company regarding company policies. All employees residing within the United States of America are required to complete Internal Revenue Service form W-9, Request for Taxpayer Identification Number and Certification. Information provided within this form is checked for accuracy.

E-Tutor World (http://www.etutorworld.net/careers.html)

Types of Education-Related Jobs: Sales, Tutoring
Sales associates for eTutorWorld choose work their work schedules for these work from home jobs, promoting online tutoring services in math and science for school students in grades 5 to 12.
No financial investment required. Free training.

Gofluent (http://www.gofluent.com/web/us/jobs-in-the-north-america)

Types of Education-Related Jobs: Business English Trainer
Teaching English by phone, Gofluent seeks home-based trainers who are native English speakers who are Bilingual in French, Italian, German, Russian and Korean.
They are hired only from Kansas, Missouri, New York, Oregon, Pennsylvania and Canada.

Homework Tutoring
(http://www.homeworkhelp.com/tutorjoinus.php)

Types of Education-Related Jobs: Online Tutoring for High School and College
Online tutoring service offers homework help for high school and college students in a variety of subjects.
Emails resume to be considered for these home-based jobs.

Herzing University

(https://www.herzing.edu/about/employment-opportunities)

Types of Education-Related Jobs: Online Adjunct Faculty
At this online college based in Wisconsin, most of the positions listed as "remote" are for online adjunct Faculty. However, other positions allow tele-commuting, but many require time in the office as well.

Instructional Connections

(http://www.instructionalconnections.org/employment/)

Types of Education-Related Jobs: Online Coach/Teaching Assistants, Course Development
Company provides instructional support to colleges. Online coaches, who are part-time, independent contractors, work with students and faculty, monitoring engagement, grading assignments and facilitating course discussions. Pay is based on a per-student, per-course
formula. Master's degree or higher required. Subjects include nursing, education (literacy, reading specialization, special education, bilingual education, educational law, educational administration and mathematics or science education), mathematics, chemistry and biology.

ITT Technical Institute

(http://www.itt-tech.edu/employment.cfm)

Types of Education-Related Jobs: Online Instructors/Online Admissions Representative
Indiana-based technical school offers online as well as on-campus learning in technology, criminal justice, business, and nursing. Online instructors follow an approved curriculum, rather than developing the courses. Use "online" as the keyword searching all locations.

Johns Hopkins Center for Talented Youth (CTY)

(http://cty.jhu.edu/jobs/)

Types of Education-Related Jobs: K-12 Online Tutoring
Instructors critique student writing, make assignments, compose progress reports and evaluations for students in grades 3 to 12. Requirements include

BA in appropriate field and at least one year teaching experience. Search CTY or "work at home" in JHU Jobs database.

Kaplan (http://www.kaplan.com/careers-at-kaplan/career-areas)

Types of Education-Related Jobs: Online Tutoring, College Instructors, ISDs, Sales Reps Education company Kaplan has work at home openings for college-level online instructors, instructional designers and SAT tutors. Use "virtual" as the keyword in the job search database.

Laureate Education, Inc.
(http://www.laureate.net/AboutLaureate/Careers)

Types of Educated-related Jobs: College-Level Course Development, Instructional Design, Management
Laureate Education Inc. is the developer of online education at Walden University, Kendall College, NewSchool of Architecture & Design, College of Santa Fe, and Laureate Higher Education Group.
Most jobs require at least a master's. Choose "Virtual" as job location.

Manhattan GMAT (https://www.manhattanprep.com/jobs/)

Types of Education-Related Jobs: Test prep tutoring
Company offers tutors "live courses, online courses and private tutoring students" and pays them $100 an hour for teaching (less during training). The focus of this company which has locations nationwide in the United States as well as in Canada, England and France, is on-site, but there are online jobs as well.

Online/Remote University jobs
(https://www.higheredjobs.com/search/remote.cfm)

This website lists all the current online/remote university education jobs. Most of these positions are adjunct instructor/online course facilitation and require a Masters or Doctorate degree.

Parliment Tutors (http://www.parliamenttutors.com/career.php)

Types of Education-Related Jobs: K-12 Online Tutoring Including SAT, GRE Prep and AP subjects New York company hires both in-home and online tutors in the United States.

Pearson (http://jobs.pearson.com/go/All-Jobs/329643/)

Types of Education-Related Jobs: High School Level Essay Scoring, Test Development Scorers must have a bachelor's degree or higher, experience teaching high school English, reside and be authorized to work in the U.S. and have access to a private, secure computer with Internet connection. In test development, Pearson hires freelancers to write, do graphic design and review tests.

Quarasan (http://workathomemomrevolution.com/writing-and-editing-gigs/work-home-k-12-assessment-writingediting-quarasan/)

Types of Education-Related Jobs: Writing/Editing
Educational publisher hires writers and editors for work at home jobs. Many jobs require teaching experience and/or certification.

ScholarlyHires.com (http://www.scholarlyhires.com/Search/Job/10028-7?utm_source=Indeed&utm_medium=cpc&utm_campaign=Indeed)

Online Part-Time Faculty - Health Information Management (Grad Program) - American Public University System in Virtual Online

Detailed Job Description

Synopsis of Role:

Part-time and full-time teaching faculty share our commitment to learning, teaching, interaction with students and faculty, service to our communities of practice, and scholarship. They are united by the common goal of inspiring academic excellence in students with a broad range of interests and experiences consistent with the Community of Inquiry Framework as adopted by APUS for cognitive presence, teaching presence, and social presence. They are key to creating a rewarding online learning experience for students by engaging them, challenging them, and supporting them. They contribute to and participate in a range of activities related to effectiveness and excellence in teaching and student retention. Faculty members remain aware of discipline content intent for the courses they teach. They follow APUS guidelines, processes, and methods and are responsive to mentoring and coaching.

Academic Responsibilities and Essential Functions:
- Teaching excellence
  - Deliver online lessons to undergraduate and/or graduate students.
  - Initiate, facilitate, interact and moderate online classroom forums.
  - Be a faculty leader in your classes embracing fully the Community of Inquiry Framework of Teaching Presence, Cognitive Presence, and Social Presence.
  - Evaluate and grade students' class work, assignments, and papers within the timeframe set forth by APUS policy providing effective feedback to guide student learning and success.
  - Comply with APUS guidelines and expectations for quality faculty engagement online.
  - Engage in the classroom and reply to emails, etc. at least every other day, including one day during the weekend.
  - Remain aware of classroom procedures and use of instructional materials.
  - Participate in professional development to enhance teaching skills.
- Attend discipline specific and administrative meetings as scheduled.
- Maintain 'discipline' knowledge by participating in one's own discipline-related professional communities.
- Support APUS initiatives and departments.

REQUIRED SKILLS:

- Adaptability/Flexibility — Open to change (positive or negative) and to considerable variety in the workplace.
- Communication – Ability to communicate information and ideas in writing and speaking so others will understand.

- Cooperation – Pleasant with others on the job and displaying a good-natured, cooperative attitude.
- Critical Thinking – Using logic and reasoning to identify the strengths and weaknesses of alternative solutions, conclusions or approaches to problems.
- Education — Knowledge of principles and methods for teaching and instruction for individuals and groups, and the assessment measures.
- Initiative – Willing and able to take on responsibilities and challenges.
- Learning Strategies — Selecting and using training/instructional methods and procedures appropriate for the situation when learning or teaching new things.
- Monitoring — Monitoring/assessing performance of yourself to make improvements or take corrective action.
- Self-Control – Maintain composure, keep emotions in check, control anger, and avoid aggressive behavior, even in very difficult situations.
- Stress Tolerance —Ability to accept criticism and deal calmly and effectively with high stress situations.

REQUIRED EXPERIENCE:

- Terminal degree in Health Information Management or a closely related field from a regionally accredited institution is required.
- Registered Health Information Administrator (RHIA) certification is preferred.
- One or more years of experience in Health Information Management is required.
- College-level teaching experience is preferred.
- Online teaching experience is preferred.
- Proficient in Microsoft Office Suite programs required.
- Record of excellence in teaching.

PREFERRED AREAS OF EXPERTISE AND EXPERIENCE:

- Electronic Health Records (EHRs)
- Medical Billing and Coding

Smarthinking.com
(https://careers-smarthinking.icims.com/jobs/intro?hashed=0)

Types of Education-Related Jobs: Online Tutoring
The Washington, D.C.-based education organization hires part-time (usually 9-20 hours per week), work at home tutors for students of varying abilities and ages. Tutors may work from anywhere in the world as long as they have computer and Internet access (and a U. S. bank account).
Peak season for hiring is May-August and November-December every year. Most tutors are paid on an hourly basis. Paid training. Hires graduate and undergraduate students, high school teachers and other experienced tutors.

Southern New Hampshire University
(http://www.snhu.edu/about-us/employment)

Types of Education-Related Jobs: Online Adjunct Faculty
Private university in New Hampshire hires online adjunct faculty for undergraduate and graduate courses.
Most courses are already designed and faculty members facilitate learning. However, some courses are instructor-designed. These courses pay $2,200 to $2,500 for 8-and-11-week classes. Online training is provided.

Sylvan Learning Centers
(http://workathomemoms.about.com/od/education/p/Sylvan-Learning-Center.htm)

Types of Education-Related Jobs: Online Tutoring K-12
While many of the opportunities for certified teachers at Sylvan are based in offices, there is some   work from home opportunities for tutors once established at a center as well as some corporate home-based positions as well.

Teach for America (http://www.teachforamerica.org/join-our-staff)

Types of Education-Related Jobs: Online Tutoring Management
This non-profit values the virtual workplaces, though obviously its classroom teaching jobs are not work at home. However many of the management jobs

can be telecommuted from anywhere in the United States. Management jobs often require teaching experience.

TutaPoint.com (http://www.tutapoint.com/info/tutor)

Types of Education-Related Jobs: Online Tutoring
High school level online tutors in Math, science and Spanish must be enrolled in (or have graduated) from an American or Canadian college or university and be available to work from 2 p.m. to 1 a.m., Eastern Standard Time. Pay begins at $12 per hour in addition to incentives. Tutors, who are independent contractors must
commit to at least 5 hours per week. U.S. residents only

Tutor.com
(http://www.tutor.com/apply/what-our-tutors-do)
(http://www.homeworkhelp.com/tutorjoinus.php)

Types of Education-Related Jobs: K-12 Online Tutoring
This online ter, school, after school program, or from home. To become certified as an online tutor. You must have a degree from or be enrolled in a U.S. or Canadian college, and then you must pass a test in your areas teaching service connects students to tutors from computers in their local library, Community cenof specialty and submit a writing sample. The process takes 1-3 weeks.

Tutors tutor students from computers in their local library, Community center, school, after school program, or from home. To become certified as an online tutor. you must have a degree from or be enrolled in a U.S. or Canadian college, and then you must pass a test in your areas of specialty and submit a writing sample. The process takes 1-3 weeks.

Tutorvista.com (http://www.tutorvista.com/howitworks.php)

Types of Education-Related Jobs: K-12 Tutoring, College-Level Tutoring
Hires experienced teachers with graduate degrees usually from outside the U.S. for part-time and full-time openings.

UniversalClass   (http://teachonline.universalclass.com/index.htm)

Types of Education-Related Jobs: Adult Education Course Writing, *Online Instructors*

Company provides online continuing education courses to schools, libraries, companies, educators and individuals. It hires instructional writers to author courses on a variety of subjects.

Pays $.04-$.07 per word for writing of course material. Online instructors need a 4-year degree and 4-6 years of work experience in field, and teaching certification and online teaching experience is preferred.

University of California Berkeley Online Extension
(http://extension.berkeley.edu/static/about/jobs/teaching/)

Types of Education-Related Jobs: Adult Education, Online Course Instructors, College-Level minimum of master's degree is required but for some courses a doctorate is required.

Experience with Online education is preferred.

University of Phoenix
(http://www.phoenix.edu/faculty/become-a-faculty-member.html)

Types of Education-Related Jobs: Online faculty, instructional design

Faculty for this online college needs a master's degree or doctorate in teaching subject as well as working experience in the subject. Jobs are part time (10-20 hours/week). Company also has corporate jobs in instructional design and other education-related fields, but many of these are on-site positions.

Western Governors University
(http://www.wgu.edu/about_WGU/employment/online_faculty_jobs)

Types of Education-Related Jobs: Distance Learning Mentors

Online college hires mentors to oversee distance-learning students' progress. Minimum requirement is a bachelor's degree, but master's or doctoral degree and relevant industry experience are preferred.

FINANCE/ACCOUNTING
AND BOOKKEEPING

Acounting Department
(http://www.accountingdepartment.com/careers)

Virtual CPA/Controller

ESSENTIAL DUTIES AND RESPONSIBILITIES:

- Develop policies and procedures as they relate to client service
- Develop the role of the Controller function to our client base
- Ongoing phone consultations with client base
- Enhance reporting and analysis to our client base
- Support and train our bookkeeping staff in performance of their daily responsibilities
- Month-end closing and issuance of financial reports to all clients every month
- Implementation and start-up of new clients
- Special client projects
- Tax preparation and planning for clients
- Experience building a team/department (in growth mode)
- Other duties as assigned

ESSENTIAL SKILLS AND EXPERIENCE (candidates must satisfy all of the following to be considered:

- Extensive knowledge in accounting and tax for businesses in the under $20M market
- 7-10 years public accounting experience
- 5-7 years supervisory experience
- Ability to multitask and set daily, weekly and monthly priorities
- High degree of computer literacy, including extensive knowledge in Microsoft Office, and specifically Outlook
- Excellent written and oral communication skills

MINIMUM EDUCATION & TRAINING REQUIRED:

- Certified Public Accountant - must be current
- Strong experience with QuickBooks and/or other accounting software packages
- Minimum Bachelor's Degree preferred

Virtual Full Charge Bookkeeper

Your Role

We're looking for a self-motivated, high energy full charge bookkeeper. Position responsibilities include A/P, A/R, payroll and month-end closing services, as well as other accounting related functions as requested by the client. The right individual for this position will be able to successfully prioritize and manage multiple client needs, while maintaining a high level of accounting services and professionalism.

How you will contribute

Here's what we are seeking in our Full Charge Bookkeeper and the minimum requirements you must have to qualify for the position:

- Must be a US Citizen who resides in the US. Candidates outside of the U.S will not be considered.
- 3+ years performing full charge bookkeeping
- 2+ years using Quickbooks Software – most recent experience on resume
- Demonstrated ability to handle multiple accounts simultaneously
- Exceptional attention to detail with excellent written and verbal communications skills
- Strong work ethic – "whatever it takes" attitude
- Must be decisive and work well under pressure
- Confident in one's abilities and able to work independently, with minimal direction

Virtual Monthly Bookkeeper

Your Role

We're looking for a self-motivated, high energy Monthly Bookkeeper who will be responsible for managing monthly bookkeeping services (aka 'after the fact bookkeeping') for multiple clients. The right individual for this position will be able to successfully prioritize and manage multiple client needs, while maintaining a high level of accounting services and professionalism. This is a 100% work from home position.

How you will contribute

Here's what we are seeking in our Virtual Monthly Bookkeeper and the minimum requirements you must have to qualify for the position:

- Monthly bookkeeping for 30+ clients simultaneously
- Processing sales tax and payroll tax
- Process payrolls for various clients
- Financial Statement Preparation
- Monthly bank account and general ledger reconciliations
- 1099 Processing
- Provide quality customer service; frequent interaction with clients via telephone and webcam

ESSENTIAL SKILLS AND EXPERIENCE:

- 5+ years performing full charge bookkeeping, including monthly bookkeeping (after the fact bookkeeping)
- Must have experience working in Accounting Services or CPA firm - minimum 3 years
- Familiar with sales and payroll tax
- Demonstrated ability to handle up to 30 clients simultaneously
- Ability to meet deadlines
- 3+ years using Quickbooks Software

- Exceptional attention to detail with excellent written and verbal communications skills
- Strong work ethic – "whatever it takes" attitude
- Must be decisive and work well under pressure
- Confident in one's abilities and able to work independently, with minimal direction
- Comfort level using webcam as means of communication internally and with clients.

Balance Your Books

(http://www.accountingdepartment.com/careers)

Accounting outsourcing firm hires CPAs, bookkeepers with experience providing A/P, A/R, payroll and general and sales people offering the "opportunity to telecommute."

Bateman And Company (http://www.batemanhouston.com/)

Accounting firm hires work-at-home accountants on a permanent, part-time basis. Texas residents preferred.

Book Minders (http://www.bookminders.com/)

Accounting outsourcing firm hires home-based accountant and sales persons on a full- and part-time basis, offering benefits for some positions.

Click Accounts

(http://www.clickaccounts.com/whoweare_careers.html)

Business process outsourcing (BPO) service provider accepts resumes from accounting and bookkeeping professionals to work at home.

E-Billing Solutions (http://e-billingsolutions.net/jobs/)

E-Billing Solutions is an equal opportunity employer. E-Billing Solutions has a "virtual" office, meaning each of our employees work from his/her home, determining their own hours. Employees must undergo a rigorous background check. Working knowledge of HIPAA is a prerequisite for employment.

E-Billing Solutions is always interested in adding qualified individuals for data entry, coding and receivables. Complete our online application below if you wish to be considered for any of these positions.

First Data (https://www.firstdata.com/en_us/home.html)

Transaction processing company hires management and sales professionals to work from home. Use "remote" in keyword field.

Intuit (http://www.intuitatwork2012.com/)

Industry: Financial services and software

COMPANY DESCRIPTION:

Based in Mountain View, CA, this financial software giant owns Quicken, QuickBooks, TurboTax, GoPayment, Mint.com and Intuit Healthcare Solutions. The company has 8,000 employees worldwide.

TYPES OF WORK-AT-HOME OPPORTUNITIES AT INTUIT:

CPAs and enrolled agents can apply for Intuit jobs as work-at-home tax advisors for TurboTax

Intuit has a variety of remote positions in software engineering, sales, marketing and finance in the U.S. and Canada.

Qualifications, salaries and requirements will vary widely. However, its work-at-home, online tax advisor jobs, which support its TurboTax product, are a new part of its operations with the release of TurboTax 2011 and are in the U.S.

ONLINE TAX ADVISOR QUALIFICATIONS AND REQUIREMENTS:

These 500 to 1,000 tax advisor positions are for certified public accountants (CPA), enrolled agents (EA) and tax attorneys, who will support TurboTax products via phone, chat and email (with no required up selling) and provide written summaries of tax solutions to customers. Unlike a typical tax preparer job, these experts will give advice but won't actually do tax preparation.

Full- and part-time, seasonal positions are available. Some seasonal agents are promoted to permanent managerial positions. During tax season expect 30 to 40 hours per week of work. The season begins with paid training, which consists of training sessions taking place from November to January, and the season ends in late April. A variety of established schedules that cover the hours of 5 a.m. to 9 p.m. Pacific Time, seven days a week are available. However flexibility to take extra work during peak hours may be required.

Successful applicants for the online tax advisor must have active credentials as an enrolled agent or CPA and a preparer tax identification number (PTIN). Additionally tax advisors need a minimum of 5 years of experience preparing federal and state returns, extensive knowledge of tax laws, experience using tax preparation software, excellent verbal and written communication skills and the ability to work with minimal supervision and to research IRS and state publications, regulations, and GAAP publications. Bilingual ability and experience with electronic filing and software troubleshooting are considered a plus.

Advisors need a distraction-free space with a computer and phone and should be willing to commit to work 30 to 40 hours a week. Intuit has a made a point to promote these positions as military spouse jobs.

PAY AND BENEFITS:

These tax advisor jobs are employment positions--not independent contractors--with benefits such as medical, dental, and 401K, as well as product discounts.

Intuit has not released the hourly salaries it will pay online tax advisors, but it says its agents who work the whole season can earn a bonus of $8,000. For context on the possible hourly wage, according to the Bureau of Labor Statistics, the average salary of a tax preparer is about $15.50 per hour. However, many tax preparers are not as experienced at Inuit's tax advisors and are not enrolled agents or CPAs, as required by Intuit. On the other hand, work-at-home jobs sometimes pay less than their on-site counterparts.

APPLYING FOR INTUIT JOBS:

Apply at Intuit jobs website. Use the keyword "remote" to find all the telecommuting jobs including the online tax advisor positions.

GAME TESTER

Become A Game Tester (http://www.becomeagametester.com/)

Test video games and get paid $30 - $50 per game.

Game-Testers.net (http://www.game-testers.net/)

- Part-time job,
  everyone is welcome
- Earn from *$50 to $150 per hour*
- Play from anywhere and *get paid to play*!

Global Beta test Network
(https://www.surveymonkey.com/r/?sm=gZhLTC5g5j8GIlWw1eXzizJCB
%2fnSvpKowrxuxQB3UNE%3d)

This company uses "Survey Monkey" as an application process.

"The information you provide to us will only be used for the purpose of recruiting you for Beta Testing and possible future employment opportunities.

Indeed: Video Game Tester (remote)
(http://www.indeed.com/q-Gaming-l-Remote-jobs.html)

This website gives you a list of job openings and how to apply for them.

Upwork: Video Game Tester Needed
(https://www.upwork.com/o/jobs/browse/skill/game-testing/)

There is a list of Game Tester jobs on this website. Select the job and submit a proposal. You will be notified when the proposal has been accepted.

VMC   (https://www.vmc.com/games/GBTN_Testers/)

At-home game testers don't ordinarily get to test AAA titles before they're released, but some games are going to be so big they need to be stress-tested by players all over the world. These aren't MMOs—they're AAA multiplayer console games everyone will be playing and talking about once they're released.

VMC Games is giving qualified gamers the rare opportunity to play those games now. These paid game testing jobs run on a weekly basis across all continents, where testers are working from their own home throughout those sessions.

We're constantly growing with new opportunities! Look out for our testing sessions featuring multimedia streaming platforms, mobile applications, and more!

We need game testers who:

- Are at least 18 years old and will sign a non-disclosure agreement
- Can focus well and follow instructions in a timely manner
- Will maintain professional behavior at all times

INSURANCE

Aetna

(http://www.aetna.com/about-aetna-insurance/aetna-careers/working-at-aetna/why_flexible.html)

The company's careers website helps jobseekers find telecommuting jobs by allowing a specific search for potential telework positions. To search for telecommuting jobs at Aetna, first choose "Yes" in the drop-down menu under "Potential Telework Position." As mentioned above, these jobs only have the potential for telework in the future. To further refine these jobs to ones that are actually being hired as work-at-home jobs or to ones that have a definite plan to become telecommuting, use "telework" as your keyword. Next do a new search with "work at home" as a keyword as these will bring up different jobs.

This major insurance company hires nurses, physicians and managers to work from home. While some positions are specifically designed for telework, in others telework opportunities will be considered. Search jobs database with keyword "telework."

ARO Contact Center   (http://www.callcenteroptions.com/shell.asp?p=hr)

Though mostly a virtual call center, this BPO hires also has telecommuting jobs for insurance auditors--phone auditors and physical auditors. Both types of auditors conduct premium audits for general liability and workman's compensation, but the physical audits, though they complete most of audit by phone, include a final physical walk-through. Additionally, it has home-based positions for LPNs and RNs doing telehealth work. See more work-at-home jobs for LPNs.

Based in Kansas City, MO, ARO, Inc., utilizes an at-home workforce based inside the United States as it offers business process outsourcing (BPO) for companies in industries such as insurance, healthcare, pharmaceutical and energy.

TYPES OF WORK-AT-HOME POSITIONS:

ARO hires only employees and not independent contractors. ARO offers both full- and part-time employees set schedules.

Some of the people ARO hires to service its clients include call center agents (customer services and B2B), insurance agents and auditors, and nurses (RN and LPN). More specifically, the positions for which it hires are:

Call center agents - Some positions are customer service only, e.g., medical history interviewers who take both inbound and outbound calls from applicants. These jobs require customer service skills, good listening and ability to document conversations using computer applications. Knowledge of medical terminology is a plus. Other call center jobs are for inbound and outbound sales. Experience in sales and a minimum commitment of 25 hours per week is required in these jobs.

Premium insurance auditor - Company hires both phone auditors and physical auditors. Phone auditors only use the phone and the computer to conduct premium audits for property and casualty insurance, i.e., general liability and workman's compensation. Physical auditors do the same but must do a final physical walk-through at the company being audited.

Licensed insurance agents - Company has work-at-home jobs for both life insurance and property and casualty agents making both inbound and outbound calls.

REQUIREMENTS:

While ARO hires in all U.S. states, it is not always hiring in every state. Applicants must have a dedicated work space with a door. No noise background noise from pets, children or other sources is tolerated. Also the agent must supply a computer, a high speed Internet (cable or DSL), a dedicated phone line with no call waiting features (VoIP services may be acceptable), and a basic telephone with amplifier and headset. Cordless and cell phones are not acceptable.

APPLYING TO ARO:

To apply for any of these positions, go to ARO's website and click "Apply to Be a Remote Employee Today!" Fill out the contact information, choose which type of job for which you are applying and upload your resume. You should then receive a confirmation email. If the company is hiring in your area and you meet the requirements, you may receive another email inviting you to complete a full application and to interview by phone.

TRAINING:

Training varies based on the position and can be done remotely or at a corporate location. Training is paid at the same as the regular hourly rate and lasts 6 to 10 weeks for 3 to 8 hours per day.

FARA
(https://yorkrsgcareers.silkroad.com/yorkext/EmploymentListings.html)

Types of work at home insurance jobs: auditors

Insurance services provider hires premium auditors, as independent contractors, for work at home positions. However, these insurance jobs require local travel.

The Hartford
(https://thehartford.taleo.net/careersection/2/moresearch.ftl?lang=en)
Types of work at home insurance jobs: nurses, adjusters, sales people, attorneys and claims consultants

Use the keyword "remote" to search the company's job listings...

Humana (https://www.humana.com/about/careers/)

Types of work at home insurance jobs: nurses (RN), medical coders, chart auditors, licensed insurance reps, accountants, physicians, writers and sales.

Headquartered in Louisville, Kentucky, Fortune 500 health insurance company, Humana Inc. hires for several types of telecommuting positions. Choose "Work at Home" in the drop down menu in the company's job database for location.

ING (http://ing.us/about-ing/careers)
Types of work at home insurance jobs: underwriting, sales, marketing

Insurance and financial services company offers work at home positions in underwriting as well as home-based sales and marketing positions in both its insurance and investment management divisions.

LiveOPs   (http://cloud.liveops.com/glp-liveops-multichannel-demo.html?gclid=CITD-8bxl7sCFbQWMgodTRkA1g)

Industry:
Call Center: at home insurance jobs: licensed insurance agents
Based in Santa Clara, CA, this privately held company provides call center outsourcing to clients using only U.S.-based home call center agents. Its more than 20,000 virtual call center agents are all independent contractors.

TYPES OF WORK-AT-HOME OPPORTUNITIES:

Most calls are inbound sales calls; however there are several types of center agent positions:

Advanced sales agent - According to LiveOPs web page, the average advanced sales agent can invoice $9.62 per 30 minute block.

Outbound agents - According to LiveOPs web page, the average Outbound Agent makes $5.25 per 30 minute block but incentives are available.

Licensed insurance agent

Applying to Become a LiveOPs Agent:
LiveOPs agents are not employees but independent contractors, who are paid mostly on a per minute basis. Agents may schedule their time in blocks as short as 30 minutes. Agents must be 18 years old and reside in the 48 contiguous United States. LiveOPs does not charge a fee for training, but it does not pay during training. LiveOPs does charge a $50 fee to new agents for a background and credit check.
To apply to be a LiveOPs agent you must:
Create a login with a valid email address and sign in.
Provide information on your background, including information about sales experience.
Take an assessment for comprehension and computer skills (optional).
Verify that you understand the requirements.
Audition your voice.

Based in Santa Clara, CA, this privately held company provides call center outsourcing to clients using only U.S.-based home call center agents. Its more than 20,000 virtual call center agents are all independent contractors. Among the call center agents it hires are licensed insurance agents.

MetLife
(https://www.metlife.com/careers/index.html?jobs=careers/job-search/sales-jobs/index.html)
Types of work at home insurance jobs: underwriters, analysts

Large insurance company hires underwriters and controls analysts for work from home positions. However, the company also has flexible workplace options (including telework) for other employees as well.

Parameds
(http://www.wahadventures.com/2012/01/working-at-home-with-parameds.html)

Parameds is a work at home company.

Parameds, a company more than a decade old, is a third-party company who works to collect information for insurance companies. Parameds hires remote workers for the Attending Physician Statement Retriever position as well as roles like underwriting.

The Attending Physician Statement Retriever job does not require a lot of specific background or skills, which is why I have chosen to focus on this role.

What do Attending Physician Statement Retrievers (also referred to as APSs) do for Parameds?

Paramed APS workers make outbound calls to retrieve data on a case by case basis. It seems to most commonly involve calling medical offices to retrieve patient information on behalf of insurance companies. However, Parameds deals with more than just medical insurance. From disability and life insurance to death claims, there is a large market to be cared for by Paramed.

Equipment Requirements for the Attending Physician Statement Retrievers at Parameds?

You will need to download Skype to make your calls. Any fees when you use Skype for your calls are reimbursed by Parameds. Or, you have the choice of using your own home land line or even your cell phone but those charges are not covered by Parameds.

If you use Skype or any other VoIP service like Gmail's Calling Service, you will need to buy a USB headset that can be plugged into your computer. This expense is not covered by Parameds but is generally inexpensive.

You will also need a working space with a quiet background. You do not want to sound like you work at home by having sounds of your dog barking, TV blasting and kids talking in the background. A good noise canceling microphone and an office with a door with a lock makes for a nice working environment!

Is the Schedule at Parameds Flexible?

Oh this is the part about Parameds that I love! There is a lot of flexibility! You are required to be available for at least 6 hours a day Monday through Friday. However, as far as I have read, you are not given a set schedule of hours. Your 6 hours can be broken up throughout the day. There will be some 'cases' you will receive that will require you to call before 4:30pm in their time zone. Also, some of the supervisors like to see you start around the same time each day. But that is something you will discuss with your supervisor at the appropriate time.

While you are required to be available for at least 6 hours a day, it does not mean you will work 6 hours a day. Some days will require less and some may require more. This brings us to the next subject of discussion- how you are paid.

How Much does Parameds Pay their Work at Home APSs?
Parameds, like many other companies, keep their pay rate hidden under a privacy agreement signed before being hired. But it is important to know they do not pay on an hourly rate. A Very helpful forum posting said this about the Parameds pay:
You are paid per completed case which is dependable on how quickly you can close out your cases (your turnaround time). How long to complete is really dependable on the facility you work with and how well you can tempt them into rushing this for you. Some you can complete out within the 1st day of receiving the case and others could take 60+ days to complete.

What is the Pay Schedule at Parameds?
Parameds MAILS a check on the 1st and the 15th of each month. If pay-day is on a weekend or holiday, they will pay the next business day.
Eeek. Parameds waits to pay out your first check until 30 days after you begin work! AND if you quit within that first 30 days, you forfeit your pay!!!

Parameds is simply not for everyone. It is a job that is filled with unknowns. You don't always know how much work you will have, how much your paycheck will be or if the next call you make will result in a screaming and attitude filled person you need to help you close out your case- so you can be paid for it!
So, How do you Apply for Parameds?
Send your resume to joinus@parameds.com It is not always known if they are currently hiring, but sending an inquiry to Parameds is the best way to find out.

Quest Diagnostics
(http://jobs.heart.org/j/t-Teleinterviewer-I-PartTime-Work-From-Home-e-Quest-Diagnostics-Incorporated--l-Lees-Summit,-MO-jobs-j2721462.html)

At Quest Diagnostics Incorporated, we understand urgency. But more than speed, we focus our energies on accuracy. Currently, we seek a Part-Time Work at Home TeleInterviewer 1:
Responsibilities

Basic Purpose:
-This position completes life insurance applications via telephone for a single client company.

Training Hours:
-The Part-Time Work at Home TeleInterviewer 1 opportunity requires working from the ExamOne Lee's Summit, MO (800 NW Chipman Road Ste 5900; Lee's Summit, MO 64063) office for 6-8 weeks for training before working from home
-Training hours are Monday - Friday 5pm to 9pm

WORK FROM HOME HOURS:

-Hours can vary, however, they are usually part-time evening hours

REQUIRED EQUIPMENT:

-DSL/Cable connection speed 1.0 Mbit down/256 Kb upload speed minimum
(Cannot be through aWiFi internet connection or satellite provider)
-Home telephone line with local Kansas City area number
Note: the position requires the applicant to reside in the Kansas City metro area
-Analog Phone
-Analog Headset
-Desk
-Chair
-Lighting
-Surge Protector
-Quiet Working Space
-The position may also require a router and multiple in home visits for setup and repair of equipment. The smart computer and all other necessary technical equipment will be provided by Quest Diagnostics

PRINCIPLE DUTIES AND RESPONSIBILITIES:

-Complete interviews with life insurance applicants via telephone. These interviews will include gathering medical, financial, occupational, and avocation histories. Review and edit information collected during the interview for quality assurance purposes.

-Manage the C4 Call Management System by making telephone calls, logging call attempts, documenting information within orders as necessary and recording call results.
-Responds to the needs and requests of clients and Quest Diagnostics management and staff in a professional and expedient manner.
-Observes all compliance policies and safety policies and procedures as outlined in the Quest Diagnostics
-Safety Manual or safety matters included in other special training

KNOWLEDGE AND EXPERIENCE:

-High School Diploma or Equivalent required, some college courses preferred.

MINIMUM SKILLS REQUIRED:

-Ability to type 25 wpm adjusted for accuracy
-Strong communication skills
-Accurate, detail oriented
-Proficient teamwork skills
-Good work attendance record
-Organizational skills
-Six (6) Months Customer service experience

MINIMUM SKILLS PREFERRED:

* Background in Medical Terminology
Want to be able to wear your fuzzy slippers to work? How about save over $1,800 on fuel expenses? Our Part-Time Work at Home TeleInterviewer 1 do both!

HOW TO APPLY:

Please Log In or Register to Upload a Resume and complete the online Application. Because of the large number of applicants to job openings, Quest Diagnostics will only contact candidates to be interviewed.

Sedgwick Claims Management Service

(https://www.sedgwick.com/careers/Pages/default.aspx)

Types of work at home insurance jobs: claims service assistants

Claims Management Company with call centers in Michigan and Ohio hire claims service assistants either as work at home or with an eventual transition to working from home.

United Health (http://careers.unitedhealthgroup.com/)

Industry:
Insurance, Health Care

Types of work at home insurance jobs: nurses, contract managers, Medicaid specialists, auditors, analysts and consultants

Based in Minnetonka, Minnesota health insurance company: United Healthcare Group is a Fortune 500 company that offers telecommuting positions in nursing and other fields. More than 20 percent of this large health insurance company's employees take advantage of its telecommuting opportunities.

Company Description:
Based in Minnetonka, Minnesota health insurance company: UnitedHealthcareGroup is a Fortune 500 company (#21 in 2009) with 75,000 employees.

Types of Work-at-Home Positions:
More than 20 percent of this large health insurance company's employees take advantage of its telecommuting opportunities. UnitedHealth Group hires registered nurses for telecommuting positions as well as others with experience in the insurance industry. Many of the "work at home" nurse positions involve seeing patients in their homes but some are telephone-based positions.
Non-nursing positions that may be telecommute jobs include contract managers, Medicaid specialists, auditors, analysts, consultants and medical coders.
Using United Healthcare's Employment Page: UnitedHealth Group Website Select "Yes" under the drop-down menu for "Telecommuter Positions" to find jobs eligible for telecommuting.

Well Point
(http://wellpoint.jobs.net/all-jobs/?cbsid=6ea5584cd2fb4145bff91f2e70339 3ce-337422253-VN-4)

Types of work at home insurance jobs: insurance sales

One of the nation's largest health care companies, WellPoint allows some positions both in nursing and in other fields to be telecommuted after a certain amount of time in the office.

Working Solutions

(http://www.workingsolutionsjobs.com/jobs/descriptions/ licensed-life-health-insurance-agents-work-at-home-all-us-dallas-texas-job-1-5704685?utm_source=Indeed&utm_medium=organic&utm_ campaign=Indeed)

> Working Solutions is partnering with a major insurance provider to enroll customers in a variety of insurance products. Licensed Life and Health Insurance Agents must be able to communicate effectively with customers by listening to their requests and suggesting suitable policies for their consideration. Agents will work online and over the phone to evaluate the characteristics of each client to determine the appropriate insurance policy in addition to providing product support.
>
> Agents must be actively licensed in Life and/or Health Insurance to work with this client. A strong sales background is important for this program.
>
> We ensure quality service through the best agents—which could be you. Know that Working Solutions is rated at four plus stars from agents on Glassdoor. It's what clients expect.
>
> Still interested? Please keep reading.
>
> **Background check:** Agents must successfully pass a background check that includes a Social Security number verification and a criminal history check.

PROGRAM REQUIREMENTS:

> **Active license** – Agents must hold a current Life and/or Health Insurance license for this program. Please specify the state(s) in which you are licensed.
>
> **Excellent customer service** – Agents need strong verbal communication and rapport-building skills to help callers with questions about products and options.

Sales skills – Agents must be able to generate new business by selling one or more types of insurance by explaining various policies and helping customers' to choose plan(s) best suited them.

Multi-tasking – Agents must be able to operate multiple systems simultaneously while maintaining constant communication with customers.

Zurich in North America (http://www.zurichna.com/zna/careers/careers.htm)

Types of work at home insurance jobs: insurance sales, account executives
Search "work at home" in this insurance company's jobs database. Most remote positions are for account executives and occasionally an attorney.

MEDIA AND ARTS

Avanti Press (http://www.avantipress.com/#/about/)

Photography, Writing
Pet-centric greeting card maker licenses photographs from freelancers. Occasionally accepts new verse writers

BC Virtual Tour (http://www.bcvirtualtour.com/opportunities.html)

Take pictures of homes on the real estate market in British Columbia for a commission and travel expenses.

The Bradford Group (http://www.thebradfordgroup.com/careers/)

Designers, Illustrators
Collectibles Company seeks freelance artists to work with its product Development teams
On products that include collector plates from The Bradford Exchange, ornaments and music boxes from Bradford Editions, cottages from Hawthorne Village, and figurines from The Hamilton Collection.

Cape Shore

(http://www.cape-shore.com/?page_id=13&PHPSESSID=2c807034f78021
45d86cf404427f765e)

Artists/Illustrators
Company hires freelance artists working in acrylic, gouache, watercolor, oil
paint, pastel and mixed media collage to create work in a variety of themes
(nautical, Christmas, regional, floral, etc.) for its line of paper products.

Cricket Magazine

(http://www.cricketmag.com/17-Illustration-Guidelines-for-Cobblestone-
Publishing-Companys-six-magazines-for-kids-ages-6-and-up)

Illustrators
A magazine accepts hand-drawn and computer-generated illustrations from
freelancers.
Send non-returnable samples for consideration for an assignment.

Excel Sportswear (http://exceltees.com/careers/artists/)

Illustrators, Cartoonists
Sportswear Company hires freelancers to supplement its in-house art staff in
creating original illustrations of mascots, cars and high school sports.

Look Better Online (http://www.lookbetteronline.com/)
Photographers

Portrait photographers take pictures of clients who need images for dating
sites. Home studios are OK, if they meet certain requirements.

Marion Health (http://www.marianheath.com/)

Artists/Illustrators
Greeting Card company accepts submissions for everyday greetings for
some humor.

Metaphor Studios (http://www.metaphor-studio.com/)

Writers, Graphic Designers, Illustrators, Marketing Professionals, and Web Designers Metaphor Studio are a creative consultancy that specializes in building brand communities.

Two years' experience required.

Nature Friend

(http://www.naturefriendmagazine.com/index.pl?linkid=11;class=gen)

Photography

Monthly magazine purchases nature photography freelancers.

Oatmeal Studios

(http://www.oatmealstudios.com/html5/pages/about_us.html)

Artists, Cartoonist

Artist's guidelines for greeting card company call for "fresh and fun-looking artwork in any media and style. Also, sophisticated, funky cartoony-type art (people and/or animals) with or without words. Color work is best."

Obeo (http://www.obeo.com/public/global/jobopportunities.aspx)

Photographers

Take pictures of homes on the real estate market. Amateurs accepted. Free-lance photographers are at the core of our business. We are looking for people with a photography background (amateur or professional) or for those who wish to be in the photography industry and have their own equipment. At Obeo we require external flash photography on all of our homes, so you need a little more than just a digital camera.

Photography orders are forwarded to you via e-mail and it will be your responsibility to:

Set appointments

Photograph the home

Process and upload photos to our website

It normally takes less than 30 min to photograph a home and less than 20 min to process the photos for each home. Payment is on a "per house" basis for each property that you photograph as a sub-contractor.

Payment amounts depend on what type of photography is requested and the general market conditions in which you live.

Opuzz Voice (http://www.opuzz.com/voice_submission.asp)

Voice actors doing recordings from home. They are not accepting submissions at the time this book is published. Check their website and be ready for when they do.

Papryus
(http://www.papyrusonline.com/category/about+papyrus/artist+submission+guidelines.do)

Artists, Illustrators, Photographers
Greeting card and stationary company purchases from freelance artists a range of materials from graphics, traditional, whimsical, humor and contemporary pieces to photography.

Recycled Paper Greeting (http://www.prgreetings.com/)

Artists
Freelance artists can submit artwork along with a message for consideration for Greeting Card Company.
Does not accept electronic submissions.

Studio D (http://talent.studiod.com//)

Video Producers, Writers
Demand Studios accepts applicants with writing, editing and filmmaking skills. They are assigned to produce made-for-the-Internet content that appear on sites like eHow.com, LIVESTRONG.COM and dozens more sites. Writers are paid both on a flat fee and revenue sharing basis.

The Sun Magazine
(http://thesunmagazine.org/about/submission_guidelines/writing)

Writers, Photographers Pay ranges for freelance writing assignments (essays, interviews, fiction and poetry) from $300 to $2,000. One-time use of photos pays $100-$500.

Tongal.com   (http://tongal.com/home)

An ideal opportunity to let your creativity soar --- it is a website that accepts your idea, pitch the idea and if the idea is accepted, you get more support and compensation follows after the project is completed.

MEDICAL TRANSCRIPTION

Accentus (http://www.accentusinc.com/careers/us.php)

Industry:
Medical document management firm, i.e., medical BPO specializing in transcription and medical coding.
Company hires experienced work-at-home medical transcriptionists for a variety of shifts as well as coders.

COMPANY DESCRIPTION:
Accentus, which was formerly called Transolutions and is now part of Nuance Healthcare, is headquartered in Ottawa, Ontario, but it offers services hires in both the United States and Canada. The company offers medical transcription services to doctors, clinics and hospitals and medical coding to his hospital clients.

TYPES OF WORK-AT-HOME OPPORTUNITIES AT ACCENTUS:
The company offers remote medical transcription jobs in the U.S. and Canada. In the U.S. some of these positions (acute division) are for employees, while the jobs in the U.S. ambulatory division and the Canadian jobs in both ambulatory and acute are for independent contractors.
In medical coding, it hires experienced, certified medical coders and coding quality assurance staff. These opportunities are for work-at-home and on-site (travel-to-client) coders.

More on these types of positions:
A medical transcriptionist practices a specialized form of transcription. He or she listen to a physician or medical practitioner's dictated notes regarding a patient and transcribes them for addition into the patient's medical file.

Typically a medical transcriptionist uses similar. Medical coding jobs can often be done from home. However, certification and experience (typically about three years) are usually required for work-at-home, medical coding jobs.

REQUIREMENTS FOR MEDICAL TRANSCRIPTION JOBS:
In the United States:
The acute division, which serves hospitals and multi-specialty clinics, hires part-time employees for 24-32 hours per week's week for shifts cover all hours in the day. Weekend work is required. One year of acute care transcription/editing experience is required.

Additionally experience on accounts with 40+ dictators and ESL dictators are needed. Windows-based computer with XP or Windows 7 is required.
These jobs offer medical/dental insurance, paid time off, Internet reimbursement and other benefits. The ambulatory division hires experienced, independent contractors for flexible schedules of mostly weekdays.

These jobs do not offer benefits.

In Canada
Both the ambulatory and acute division positions are for independent contractors only. In the acute division, transcriptionists should be certified or have two years training and a minimum of two years recent experience transcribing and editing in acute care. However, the recent completion of an accredited medical transcription course with an average of 90 percent or higher may be substituted for experience.

Transcribers must commit to produce a minimum of 250-300 audio minutes per week
(approximately 20-25 hours).
In the ambulatory division, most of the jobs are full-time contract positions for transcriptionists with a minimum of 3- to 5-years' experience within a specific specialty that can produce 80 audio minutes per day. Hours are typically weekdays.

REQUIREMENTS FOR MEDICAL CODING JOBS:
Coders in the U.S. must have certification, such as CCS or CCS-P and/or CPC or CPC-H, RHIT and RHIA, as well as 3- to 5-years coding experience. Those applying to remote coding positions should have experience working in a virtual office. (On-site coders must be available to travel.)

APPLYING TO ACCENTUS:
Choose either the Acctentus Career Canada page or Accentus Careers United States.

Then choose the type of work--coding or transcription--and apply through its online applications system.

Applied Medical Services
(http://www.fastchart.com/about/careers/)

Company hires independent contractors in as home-based medical transcription jobs as well as for medical billing and coding jobs.

Eight Crossing
(http://www.eightcrossings.com/career.php)

Sacramento-based Eight Crossings recruits for medical transcription jobs in its office and for working at home. Two years' experience required.

Medical Transcriptionist via Flex Jobs
(https://www.flexjobs.com/jobs/online-medical-transcription)

Please note: You will need to pay a membership fee to see and apply for this job on Flex Jobs

Careers are available in multiple arenas in this exciting, fast-paced, and rapidly growing organization. We are seeking US-based medical transcriptionists with a minimum of two years of experience in medical transcription or Certification in lieu of experience.

Due to the stat nature of the business, we are open 24 hours a day, 365 days a year. Employees are requested to work every other weekend or the equivalent of 32 hours of weekend time per month.

Both in-office and remote positions are available. Career advancement opportunities - including 3 levels for MTs, trainers, supervisors and quality assurance specialists - are available. For more information, please contact us.

REQUIREMENTS:

VOIP/PBX System
eFAX System
Virtual Resume
Resume
Recent Graduate from an approved Transcription program

M*Model (http://mmodal.com/about-us/careers/)

M*Modal telecommute jobs include professional, transcription, coding and support positions. Transcriptionists must have one Year of recent work experience as a medical transcriptionist or must be a recent graduate of an AAMT certified transcription program.

NetMed Transcription
(http://www.netmedtranscription.com/Employment.html)

If you're interested in working with NetMed Transcription Services or would like additional information about the company, please email Tami Gregg at tgregg@netmedtranscription.com.

Or send your resume to:
NetMed Transcription Services, L.L.C.
2604 Sunnyside Drive
Cadillac, MI 49601
ph. 1.800.981.6676

Nuance (http://www.nuance-nts.com/default.asp)

Medical documentation Services Company, formerly known as Webmedx, hires medical transcriptionists and quality assurance specialists.

Professional Medical Services

(http://www.professionalmedicalservices.org/mt_requirements.html)

Hires medical transcriptionists with at least 4 years of experience in hospital transcription for acute care accounts. Part-time and full-time positions are for independent contractors.

Portal Healthcare Solutions/Ascend

(http://www.ascendhealthcare.com/Contact_Employment.html)

Company has opportunities for medical transcriptionists and quality assurance specialists as well as sales and operations.

Spectra Medi

(http://www.spectramedi.com/medical-transcription-services-jobopening.htm)

Spectrum Health offers a wide range of healthcare services to individuals in communities throughout the state of Michigan with headquarters in Grand Rapids, Michigan. Spectrum Health is a not-for-profit healthcare system that provides services for its patients through a variety of facilities that includes a medical center, community hospitals, a children's hospital, medical groups, physician groups, and its own health plan. Spectrum Health has been the recipient of numerous awards including the "101 Best and Brightest Companies to Work For" and Thomson Reuters' "Top 10 Health Systems in the Nation." In addition, Spectrum Health is one of the largest employers in Michigan with over 21,000 staff and physician employees and a network of more than 2,000 volunteers. With its network of facilities, Spectrum Health typically offers a variety of employment opportunities to start or continue a career in the healthcare industry

Ubiqus (http://www.ubiqus.com/GB/recruitment.htm)

Ubiqus is an Equal Opportunity Employer. It considers all positions without regard to race, religion, color, sex, national origin, age, disability or other categories as proscribed by federal, state or local law.

Fill out our online application. If we are interested in your credentials, we will contact you by email or telephone:

Note: Transcriptionist Applicants, please read our disclaimer before beginning your application

Verbatim Transcriptionist

Medical Transcriptionist

Summary Writer

Medical Summary Writer

NURSES

About.com Health Channel (http://www.about.com/health/)

Medical work-at-home jobs include: Nurses, physicians, medical writers About.com contracts with more than 1,000 guides and topic writers who are experts in their many different fields including many medical professions. Pay starts at $675 per month but compensation increases with page view growth. Nurses and physicians are often hired in the Health Channel.

Aetna (http://www.aetna.com/about-aetna-insurance/aetna-careers/)

Medical work-at-home jobs include: Nurses and physicians are among the Medical Professions who work from home at the insurance company.

After-Hrs Triage (www.intellatriage.com)

RN Based triage Service for Hospice and Home Health – IntellaTriage

American International Group (AIG)
(http://www.aig.com/careers_3171_437777.html)

Medical work-at-home jobs include: Nurses
After a specific amount of time working on-site, this company allows some nursing positions, such as case managers and medical reviewers to be telecommuted. Try keywords "telecommuting" or "work-from-home" in jobs database.

ARO (http://www.aroptions.com/about-us/careers.php)

While most of the home-based jobs at this BPO are for customer service, sales and 2B telemarketing agents, it also serves patients with nurse's telehealth.

Telehealth – at ARO

Company hires nurses, both RNs and LPNs, for inbound and outbound calling positions.

Carenet (https://www.care-net.org/aboutus/employment.php)

Medical work-at-home jobs include: Nurses

Based in San Antonio, this medical Business Process Outsourcing (BPO) provides support to insurance Companies and health care systems. Virtual call center agents who are registered nurses (RNs) answer Questions or perform telephone triage. Pay sis $25 per hour.

Industry:

Health Care, Medical Call Center

Company Description:

Headquartered in San Antonio, Texas, Carenet is health care services company that offers its clients—which include employers, insurance companies, hospitals and other medical providers, and government--the services of a medical call center staffed by registered nurses working from home.

Types of Work-at-Home Positions:

For its work-at-home jobs, Carenet hires registered nurses as "Care Advisors." (It does have customer service call center jobs for non-nurses, but these are not work-at-home jobs.) The types of services these RNs provide include telephone triage, medical decision support, medical device monitoring services, member engagement and health care support. This is a 24-hour service, so overnight shifts may be available and/or required.

Requirements and Qualifications:

Successful applicants must have a two-year nursing degree at minimum, an unrestricted, current Texas RN license (or a current state license as a RN with the ability to become licensed in Texas), three years of clinical experience in acute, ambulatory area or telehealth. Carenet hires in Nurse Licensure Compact (NCL) states in the U.S. Currently these include Colorado, Iowa, Maryland, Mississippi, Missouri, Nebraska, New Hampshire, North

Carolina, South Carolina, South Dakota, Tennessee, Texas, Virginia, Wisconsin. Onsite training in Texas may be required.

Compensation and Benefits:
Pay is approximately $25 per hour*. Employees receive options for medical, dental, vision insurance, 401(k), life insurance, paid time off and holidays.
Using Carenet's Employment Page: Carenet Employment website
Click on above link then choose "Clinical Services (RN)." Choose Care Advisor, and then follow the link to submit an online application.

Cigna (http://careers.cigna.com/CIGNAPage.aspx?page=14)

Types of work at home insurance jobs: nurses (RN), providers relations analysts, contract managers, claims coordinators

Cigna hires several types of work at home insurance jobs including registered nurses to work-at-home as disability and workers comp clinical case managers. Try "work from home" and "work at home" as keywords to search Cigna's job openings.

COMPANY DESCRIPTION:
Cigna Corporation is a global health insurance and services company with more than 30,000 employees worldwide. Based in Bloomfield, CT, it was formed in 1982 with the merger of the Connecticut General Corporation and INA Corporation.
The company offers health insurance and a variety related products and services such as medical, dental and supplemental insurance; behavioral health, pharmacy and vision care; benefits management; health coaching; condition management; and group life, accident and disability insurance. Cigna is named one of my as one of my top major corporations for telecommuting.
In 2002 the company began a pilot work-at-home employment program mostly aimed at claims workers and field health care workers. Today more than 3,000 workers telecommute.* On the company's website it touts its "results-driven environment." Such environments are usually conducive to telecommuting.

TYPES OF WORK-AT-HOME OPPORTUNITIES:
Cigna hires several types of work at home jobs including registered nurses to work-at-home as disability and workers comp clinical case managers as well as data and providers-relations analysts, contract managers and claims coordinators.
Pay and Benefits:
Pay varies with position.
Cigna offers a number of benefits for full-time employees, which include health, dental, vision, life and long-term care insurance; educational assistance, elder, adoption and child care assistance, flexible work arrangements and 401(k).

The company's jobs database has no specific selection for finding telecommuting jobs postings.
Use the keyword field to narrow the search. Try both "work from home" and "work at home" as keywords to search job openings.

Insurance company Cigna's division Intracorp hires RNs to work at home as disability and workers' comp Case manager. Use "work from home" as keywords to search Cigna's job openings. Hiring is done from a NY location.

Conifer Health Solutions (http://coniferhealth.com/careers/)

Medical work-at-home jobs include: Nurses, Medical coding

Covance (http://jobsearch.covance.com/)

This U.S.-based biopharmaceutical development services company, or a contract research organization, or a contract research organization, has pre-clinical and clinical research operations in more than 25 Countries and more than 10,000 employees worldwide. It hires clinical research associates to work from home and physicians as medical directors in specific locations in the U.S., Canada and Europe.
Use "home-based" to search its jobs database.

Fonemed (http://fonemed.com/employment)

Medical work-at-home jobs include: Nurses Company hires registered nurses from the United States and Canada to work from home to provide Telephone triage and health care advice to callers from
across North America. Also hires on-site customer Service reps, based in Newfoundland, Canada; need a minimum of a high school diploma.

The Hartford
(https://thehartford.taleo.net/careersection/2/moresearch.ftl?lang=en)

Medical work-at-home jobs include: Nurses
Type "remote" in the address for at-home positions.

Healthfirst
(https://healthfirst.taleo.net/careersection/hf_ext_cs/jobsearch.ftl?lang=en)

Medical work-at-home jobs include: Nurses New York based health insurance company hires nurses as case managers to work from home.

Health Net (http://careersathealthnet.com/)

Medical work-at-home jobs include: Nurses
Health insurance company operating in 27 states hire nurses as case managers, care coordinators and care Managers with the option to telecommute. Use "telecommuting" as search keyword of company's job database.

Humana (https://www.humana.com/about/careers/)

Types of work at home insurance jobs: nurses (RN), medical coders, chart auditors, licensed insurance reps, accountants, physicians, writers and sales.

Inland Empire Health Plan
(https://ww3.iehp.org/en/about-iehp/careers/)

Medical work-at-home jobs include: Nurses
The nation's largest health care services company, McKesson specializes in pharmaceutical distribution and health care IT systems and software.

Nemours (http://careers.nemours.org/)

Pediatric health system with locations in Delaware, New Jersey, Pennsylvania, Washington, DC, and Florida hires work from home telephone triage nurses.

Nurse Telephone Triage (http://www.nursetriage.org/)

Medical work-at-home jobs include: Nurses
Company hires RNs with five years of nursing experience (preferably in pediatrics), telephone Triage experience and knowledge of and experience in using Barton Schmitt protocols.

Paradigm Health Services
(http://www.paradigmhealth.org/General%20Pages/Employment%20 Pages/employment%20opportunities.htm)

Medical work-at-home jobs include: Nurses
Company hires licensed nursing professionals in Tennessee, Mississippi, North Carolina, Virginia, Kentucky and Georgia for full and part-time positions. Some telehealth positions available.

Pathway Medical Staffing (http://www.pathway-medical.com/)

Medical work-at-home jobs include: Nurses
Medical recruiting firm, in the New York City metro area
Specializes in non-clinical nursing positions.
Search using keyword "telecommute."

PPD (http://www.ppdi.com/Careers.aspx)
Medical work-at-home jobs include: Clinical research associates (BS in science field or RN certification required), medical writers. This global contract research organization (CRO) provides drug discovery, development and life-cycle management services within the health care industry.
It hires medical writers and clinical research associates (CRA) for work-at-home positions.

Professional Dynamics

(http://www.pdimcs.com/professional-dynamics-careers.aspx)

Medical work-at-home jobs include: Nurses, physicians
California-based company provides service in the workers compensation industry and to first party medical and employee benefit sectors. Some nurse case manager and physician peer review positions are telecommuting.

Remote Medical International

(http://www.remotemedical.com/About-Us/employment)

Medical work-at-home jobs include: Nurses, physicians
The "remote" in the name of Seattle-area Company refers to faraway places not working at home.
However, the company does have a telemedicine department and some other telecommuting jobs.

SironaHealth (http://www.sironahealth.com/careers)

Medical work-at-home jobs include: Nurses

Triage 4 Pediatrics

(http://www.triage4pediatrics.com/employment.shtml)

Medical work-at-home jobs include: Nurses
Based in Plano Texas this company hires RNs in the DFW are to work at home in afterhours telephone triage. Requirements include 3-5 years in pediatrics, licensure in Texas, carrying malpractice insurance and drug test. Weekends and evenings are required but part-and full-time
schedules are available.

United Health Group (http://careers.unitedhealthgroup.com/)

Medical work-at-home jobs include: Nurses, LPNs, medical coders
More than 20 percent of this large health insurance company's employees take advantage of its telecommuting opportunities. UnitedHealth Group hires registered nurses for telecommuting positions as well as others with experience in the insurance industry.

WellPoint

(http://wellpoint.jobs.net/AllJobs/?cbsid=6ea5584cd2fb4145bff91f2e70339
3ce-337422253-VN-4)

Medical work-at-home jobs include: Nurses
One of the nation's largest health care companies, WellPoint allows some positions, in nursing and in other fields, to be telecommuted after a certain amount of time in the office.

MEDICAL CODING

Accentus (http://www.accentusinc.com/careers/us.php)

Company, formerly known as Transolutions, hires as employees experienced work-at-home medical transcriptionists for a variety of shifts as well as medical coders in the U.S. and Canada.
Requires Certification as a CCS or CCS-P and/or as a CPC or CPC-H but RHIT and RHIA credentials will qualify as well.

Company hires RHIA, RHIT, CCA-P, CPC, CPC-H, or CCS with at least three years of recent multi-specialty coding experience for full-time and part-time positions.

Amphion Medical Services

(http://amphionmedical.com/careers/coders-coding-reviewers/)

Company hires RHIA, RHIT, CCA-P, CPC, CPC-H, or CCS with at least three years of recent multi-specialty coding experience for full-time and part-time positions.

Aviacode (https://aviacode.catsone.com/careers/)

Hires independent-contractor medical coders with three years of coding experience and at least one certification from either AAPC or AHIMA. According to its website, coders
could earn from $18-$30 per hour. Managers and quality assurance supervisors are employees often hired from the ranks of its independent contractors.

The Coding Network, LLC
(http://www.codingnetwork.com/medical-coding-jobs/)

Medical coders must have three years of coding experience in a particular clinical specialty and certification by one of the industry's credentialing bodies (AHIMA, AAPC, RCCB, ACMCS, etc.).

Conifer Health Solutions (http://coniferhealth.com/careers/)

Health care services firm that focuses on the financial and patient communication aspects of health care hires work from home employees in nursing and coding as well as sales.
AHIMA certification and three years of experience required. Use "telecommuting" as a keyword to find home-based positions.

Humana (https://www.humana.com/about/careers/)

Many of this major health care company's work-at-home positions have geographic requirements. Its medical coding jobs from home require coding certification (RHIT, RHIA, or CCS) and may require travel to its Louisville, KY headquarters. In addition to medical coding jobs from home it hires RN positions are for field healthcare and involve visiting patients at home. It also sometimes has opportunities for registered nurses, chart auditors, licensed insurance reps, accountants, physicians, writers and sales people for remote positions.

Maxim Health Information Services
(http://www.maximhealthinformationservices.com/remote-medical-coding-jobs.aspx)

A subsidiary of Maxim Healthcare Services, a healthcare staffing company, MHIS provides medical coding, auditing, and clinical documentation improvement services to clients.
It offers both on-site and remote medical coding jobs.

Precyse
(http://careers.precyse.com/(X(1)S(aiezulrorat5tmzezzmwe4wz))/default.aspx?AspxAutoDetectCookieSupport=1)

Healthcare information management outsourcing company hired medical coders, transcriptionists, quality assurance specialists, registrars and auditors to work from home. Choose "All Remote
Locations" for location in its jobs database. Coders must have active RHIA, RHIT, CCS, CCS-P, CPC or CPC-H certification and a minimum of three years' experience coding inpatient records in a hospital HIM department.

Pyramid Healthcare Solutions

(http://www.pyramidhs.com/healthcare-consultant-careers.html)

In addition to remote jobs for medical coders, this company also offers work at home jobs for coding managers, auditors and sales persons. Check "Nationwide Remote" for location in the jobs database.

United Health Group (http://careers.unitedhealthgroup.com/)

Search United Health Group's jobs database with the keyword "coder" and the "Telecommute" drop-
down menu to "Yes."

MEDICAL CALL CENTER

Aetna

(http://www.aetna.com/about-aetna-insurance/aetna-careers/find-a-career/)

Major insurance company offers telephone jobs for nurses, mental health professionals, and CSRs that are listed as "potential telework" positions. Unless the job posting specifically
says it will hire telecommuters, this likely means that telecommuting will be considered for an employee after a certain amount of time--perhaps a year.

ARO (http://www.callcenteroptions.com/shell.asp?p=hr)

While most of the home-based jobs at this BPO are for general customer service, sales and B2B telemarketing agents, it also has virtual positions for LPNs and RNs doing telehealth call center work as well as jobs for insurance auditors.

Carenet
(http://workathomemoms.about.com/od/medicalandnursingjob1/p/Carenet.htm)

Texas-based firm provides support to insurance companies and health care systems across the country. Its home-based medical call center of registered nurses (RN) answer questions
or perform telephone triage. It hires CS in San Antonio, but these are not work-at-home positions.

Fonemed
(http://www.flexjobs.com/jobs/telecommuting-jobs-at-fonemed)

Company hires registered nurses from the United States and Canada to work from home to provide telephone triage and health advice to callers from across North America. Also hires customer service reps that need a minimum of a high school diploma.

The Hartford
(http://www.careerbuilder.com/Jobs/Company/C8F1336GLZ3MC7LND99/The-Hartford/)

In addition to hiring RNs for remote telephone jobs as case managers, this insurance company hires others in non-medical WAH jobs, such as claims representatives. Check off the option for remote jobs in the company's job listings.

Health Net (http://careersathealthnet.com/)

Heath insurance company operating in 27 states hires nurses as case managers, care coordinators and care managers with the option to telecommute. While not exactly call center jobs, the care manager jobs have a significant amount of telephone contact with patients. Use "telecommuting "as a search keyword of company's job database.

Humana (https://www.humana.com/about/careers/)

The telephonic nursing jobs at Humana go beyond the basics of medical call centers (such as telephone triage) into field such as case management and

quality assurance, but many of them list call center experience as a requirement. Some of its work-at-home positions have geographic requirements. Check off "Virtual/Work at Home" in the company's
jobs database.

Medical Services Bureau

(http://www.medicalservicebureau.com/Jobs/Index.htm)

After on-site training in El Paso, TX, or Austin, TX, part-time medical call processors can work from home. The job duties include for answering inbound calls, taking short messages and confirming information.

Nurse Telephone Triage Service

(http://www.nursetriage.org/nowhiring.html)

Company hires RNs with five years nursing experience (preferably in pediatrics), telephone triage experience and knowledge of and experience in using Barton Schmitt protocols.

SironaHealth

(http://www.sironahealth.com/about-us/careers/open-positions)

Company hires nurse consultants (RNs) to practice telephone triage or computer-assisted nursing through Inbound and outbound telephone calls with patients whose physicians, hospitals, insurers or employers are SironaHealth clients. Company has customer service rep (CSR) and medical service rep (MSR) positions for non-nurses but these jobs are based in Maine.

Triage 4 Pediatrics

(http://www.triage4pediatrics.com/employment.shtml)

Based in Plano, TX, this company hires RNs in the DFW area to work at home in after-hours Telephone triage. Requirements include 3-5 years in pediatrics, licensure in Texas, carrying malpractice insurance and drug test. Weekends and evenings are required but part- and full-time
schedules are available.

UnitedHealth
(http://careers.unitedhealthgroup.com/search-jobs.aspx)

More than 20 percent of this large health insurance company's employees take advantage of its telecommuting opportunities. However, many of the telecommuting nursing jobs is for in-home care, but there are a few call center jobs for nurses.

Medco Health Solutions-Express Scripts
(http://careers.express-scripts.com/who-we-hire)

Headquartered in New Jersey, Medco Health Solutions, Inc. is a leading pharmacy benefit manager with the nation's largest mail order pharmacy operations. Through advanced pharmacy, Medco improves the health and lowers the total cost of care for clients and their members. If you would like to help improve pharmaceuticals for thousands of consumers around the world and want to join the Medco team as a home based professional, consider one of the telecommuting job leads posted here.

PHARMACISTS

Certified Epic Willow Analyst - Pharmacist

(http://www.indeed.com/cmp/G2-Works-LLC/jobs/Certified-Epic-Willow-Analyst-805cdcac20679713)

G2 Works is looking to bring top talent to our organization, based primarily on our mission to provide our customers with solutions, rooted in turning data into actionable information, paying our success forward and our commitment to respecting and valuing everyone we work with.

At the core of G2 is our personal commitment to our employees, it is our fervent interest to provide you with the ideal work environment, a workplace that improves the quality of our professional and personal lives.

ROLE DESCRIPTION:

A successful Candidate will have relevant clinical pharmacist experience and possess a current Epic Willow Certification. Candidate will also have previous Willow build and implementation experience. In this role the Candidate will be required to contribute to the build of the Client's Pharmacy System (Willow). They will leverage their clinical expertise to identify opportunities to optimize the medication use process and aid in delivery of quality patient care. The Candidate will be working on specialty builds which includes Beacon and infusion, which is why a Pharmacist is required for this position.

ROLE REQUIREMENTS:

- Epic Willow Certified
- Previous build and implementation experience working directly with Willow
- Knowledge of workflow validations and instructional design
- Clinical Pharmacist; Pharmacy Degree
- Ability to travel 50-75%
- Flexible and adaptable

- Excellent issue resolution skills
- Experience coordinating work with other teams across a program
- Excellent communication skills

DESIRED SKILLS:

Epic Beacon experience
Project Management Skills
Integration Skills

REQUIRED EXPERIENCE:

- Epic Willow Build and Implementation Experience: 2 years

Comprehensive Pharmacy Services (CPS)
(https://chk.tbe.taleo.net/chk05/ats/careers/requisition.jsp?org=COMPREH
ENSIVEPS&cws=1&rid=5383)

Corporate Pharmacy Data Management Assistant
Employment Duration: Full time
Region: Home-Based
Location: Home-Based
Department: CPS Clinical Services

DESCRIPTION:

Pharmacy Data Management Assistant-Full-Time
CPS Corporate Clinical Services Division
Home Based
A great opportunity to apply your hospital pharmacy technician and
pharmacy automation skills!
About the Job: This position requires experience as a Pharmacy Technician in a hospital pharmacy, experience with pharmacy automation, and
current Licensure as a Pharmacy Technician one or more states. The
position will work from a home office and does require some travel from
time to time.
The CPS Corporate Clinical Services Division provides CPS hospital
pharmacies with expert support in developing and maintaining standards of excellence in clinical services and purchasing. The Corporate

Data Assistant will report to a CPS Clinical Services Vice-President. Primary responsibilities include:

- Assisting CPS accounts with all implementation, maintenance and ongoing evaluation of drug spend trending reports (DST),Operational Metrics (OM), and the Rx Document Solutions databases

- Coordinating the setup of new accounts, training, and follow-up of data variances and verification of data elements. In addition, this position will be responsible for assisting accounts in pharmacy automation optimization to maximize patient safety, productivity and cost effectiveness.

- Assisting the Automation Manager with the development of automation optimization action plans for appropriate sites to improve and monitor applicable processes.

- Assisting with CPS development and communication of automation best practices.

The position is exempt and salaried and will work from a home office. Some travel is required (approx. 3 meetings per year).

REQUIRED EDUCATION/EXPERIENCE:

- Two-year Associates degree in business, information technology, healthcare or equivalent experience.
- Current or recent experience as a Hospital Pharmacy Technician
- Current licensure in good standing as a Pharmacy Technician by a state board of pharmacy.
- Hospital experience must include - Unit-based cabinet and robot experience or equivalent automation experience.
Highly desirable - Pharmacy information systems and programming experience highly desirable.

KNOWLEDGE/SKILLS:

-Demonstrated automation implementation and project coordination skills desired.
-Must have good knowledge of MS office software, especially Excel and Access.

-Strong written and verbal communication skills and strong analytical skills.

Rewards: A competitive compensation package and comprehensive benefits including:

Medical/Dental/Vision Insurance

401(k) with a match

Paid Time Off Program, including holidays

Company Paid Short and Long Term Disability

Basic and Supplemental Life Insurance

Medical Flex and Dependent Care Accounts

CVS Health

(http://jobs.cvshealth.com/us/work-from-home/pharmacist/jobid8786211-pharmacy-supvfld-mgmt)

Pharmacy SupvFld Mgmt

Location: MI - Work from home

Job Category: Pharmacist

Clinical Licensure Required : Pharmacist

Job Type: Full Time

POSITION SUMMARY:

Ensures that Pharmacists in area of responsibility comply with all federal, state and local laws as well as standards pertaining to the pharmacy. Provides professional, developmental and technical guidance and support to Pharmacists. Manages the company's pharmacy marketing, quality control and inventory optimization programs. Optimizes pharmacy sales and profit.

- Manages the pharmacy marketing program that includes but is not limited to patient counseling, doctor detailing, patient recruiting, identifying levels of generic substitutions and developing price structuring and in-store screening programs. Works with the District Manager to ensure standards are adhered to as they pertain to the practice of pharmacy within the stores

- Communicates corporate programs to Pharmacists (e.g. store bonus program, etc.). Provides status updates and keeps Pharmacists informed of personnel policies and procedures. Seeks out opportunities relative to the pharmacy acquisition program.

- Ensures professional quality control standards are maintained through control of misfills (identifying and correcting the causes), optimization of process flow and communication of professional pharmacy practices. Ensures Rx inventory optimization by monitoring store inventories and sales. Markets to Third Party Organizations.

- Participates in the recruitment of Pharmacists and assists with college recruiting. Establishes procedures to follow through and obtain feedback on the recruiting process from initial interview through placement. Implements training programs involving interns, extern's and newly hired Pharmacists. Selects trainers for the intern/extern programs and identifies stores to be used for training.

- Works with the HR Business Partner in the areas of performance appraisal, salary management, succession planning and training. Attends professional conferences as a participant and/or a speaker. Assumes additional responsibilities and performs special projects as needed or directed.

REQUIRED QUALIFICATIONS:

- B.S.or Pharm D degree in Pharmacy; state specific licensure or licensure eligibility
- Management and supervisory experience of pharmacy staff required
- Ability to interact with the health care profession, excellent communication skill

PREFERED QUALIFICATIONS:

- Management and supervisory experience of pharmacy staff across multiple business units preferred

EDUCATION:

- B.S.or Pharm D degree in Pharmacy; state specific licensure or licensure eligibility.

Evolent Health

(http://www.evolenthealth.com/join-us/current-opportunities/?nl=1&jvi=oq
d61fwu,Job&jvs=Indeed&jvk=Job)

Clinical Pharmacist -remote

Evolent Health is looking for a Clinical Pharmacist to join its population health team. As a member of a team of nurses, social workers, physicians, pharmacists, health economists, and program coordinators, you will have the opportunity to make a profound impact on the lives of people living with multiple chronic illnesses. You will connect with your patients in person, on the phone and through email, in the hospital, physician office, and patient's home - essentially however and wherever the patient needs your assistance to improve their health, better understand their illness and coordinate their care.

This is a remote position.

RESPONSIBILITIES:

Patient Care

- Assess the drug therapy needs of patients & monitor progress of therapy through consultations, patient education and clinical laboratory monitoring. Assess patients for medication adherence barriers and develop a plan to maximize patient's medication success through improving or maintaining adherence to medications.

- Based on this assessment and in conjunction with the patient, the patient's physician and other members of the population health team, create a care plan that will address the identified needs, remove barriers and improve the health of the patient.

- Provide patients with a personal medication record that can be shared with caregivers, with prescribers, and across care transitions.

- Interact with a wide range of patients but with a focus on providing care to patients enrolled in SNPs (special needs plans) to include C-SNP and D-SNP programs; therefore, providing pharmaceutical care to geriatric, disabled, medically needy and those needing financial assistance in a such a way to manage chronic diseases, avoid inappropriate hospitalizations and help patients move from high risk to lower risk on the care continuum.

PROVIDER SUPPORT

- Develop and deliver physician drug education plans & strategies (including pharmacy-specific benchmark reports) to promote cost-effective prescribing
- Serve as expert in clinical pharmacokinetics & pharmacodynamics and is knowledgeable in drug information including contraindications and dose adjustments

CARE MANAGEMENT COLLABORATION

- Serve as an accessible authority on drug usage, interactions, over-dosages, compliance and other pharmaceutical information including non-formulary and restricted drug determinations
- Develop and deliver pharmaceutical education to population health team
- Assist in development and execution of pharmacy-specific population health strategic and tactical plans including HEDIS measure and CMS Star rating improvement
- Function as liaison and subject matter expert related to client PBM systems and processes most specifically related to drug utilization management, drug prior authorization and pharmacy claim adjudication

PHARMACY PROGRAM SUPPORT

- Assist in development and lead the execution of clinical pharmacy programs & initiatives and other Pharmacy and Therapeutics activities
- May serve as preceptor for pharmacy students and pharmacy residents in accordance with established protocols

QUALIFICATIONS

Required (Specialist I)

- Pharmacy doctorate degree
- Completion of 1 year residency related to practice area or 3 years of equivalent clinical practice experience
- Current active pharmacy license in good standing in at least one state

Required (Specialist II)

- Pharmacy doctorate degree
- 3-5 years clinical practice experience
- Current active pharmacy license in good standing in at least one state

Preferred

- Board certification (Geriatrics (CGP), Pharmacotherapy (US-BCPS) or Ambulatory Care (US-BCACP)) – a plus
- Certified patient educator (e.g., Diabetes, Asthma)- preferred
- Health plan or PBM clinical pharmacy experience (1-2 years)
- Exceptional interpersonal, presentation, oral and written communication skills

Expert Global Solutions-(EGS)
(https://jobs.egscorp.com/job/united-states/registered-pharmacist-virtual/2020/586976)

Registered Pharmacist – Virtual

DESCRIPTION:

As a Pharmacist with Expert Global Solutions, you'll have the opportunity to help people every day while performing the work you love – all from a safe and comfortable environment.

What you'll be doing

You'll use your knowledge and experience to make an impact every day while supporting top industry-leading healthcare companies. Your work might include prior authorization, clinical appeals, mail order, prescriber education, patient counseling, drug information and customer service.

Your main responsibilities will include:

- Interpret/verify physicians' prescriptions, access and input prescription information and verify whether the order is within program guidelines

- Consult with customers and/or physicians regarding the use of medications and potential drug interactions
- Review and approve/deny requests for prescription prior authorizations
- Oversee the activities of pharmacy technicians, pharmacy clerks and customer service representatives, if applicable
- Organize workload, set priorities and complete assignments in a timely manner and utilize resources appropriately while complying with department program standards. This is a production role.
- Conform with and support department quality assurance and improvement guidelines
- Perform various duties related to the fulfillment of program deliverables

Why you'll want to join the EGS team

- We offer standard work hours with very limited weekend work
- No night shifts
- You'll work from a safe and comfortable environment
- No need to stand on your feet all day or ring up nail polish and milk at the store counter
- You won't have to interact in-person with "doctor shoppers" trying to fill prescriptions
- Competitive salary
- Health & dental benefits
- 401(k) with company match
- Paid time off
- A great team environment with supportive co-workers
- You'll work on behalf of some of the best-known healthcare companies in the world
- You'll feel empowered to do things the right way amid a culture of high personal and business integrity
- There's real opportunity to grow and advance your career
- We're a strong, global company that truly cares about our local communities

QUALIFICATIONS:

Who we're looking for
The best fit for this job is someone who:

- Has a current Pharmacist License (or must be acquired within 30 days of employment)
- Has a B.S. in Pharmacy and/or PharmD degree from accredited School of Pharmacy
- Has at least one year of experience working in a retail pharmacy setting (preferred)
- Understands and knows how to apply all state and federal laws and regulations related to the practice of pharmacy
- Adheres to safety rules and regulations and maintains the confidentiality of patient and department information
- Collaborates well with other health care professionals
- Has good computer skills, including Microsoft Office
- Possesses excellent communication skills
- Cares about helping
- Has the ability to multitask well
- Can adapt to a flexible schedule
- Can maintain the highest level of confidentiality

Who we are

Expert Global Solutions (EGS)is a global customer service organization, serving the world's leading companies and best-known brands. With more than 40,000 employees in locations around the world, our people deliver extraordinary service – via phone, email and chat, every day. Embracing a diverse workforce with a shared commitment to deliver outstanding customer service, EGS offers significant opportunity to build a rewarding career, in a dynamic and customer-oriented environment.

Work Environment

- Office environment.
- Ability to lift and/or move 20 pounds with or without accommodation.

Are you ready to help your customers every day while also strengthening yourself and your career? If so, apply now to join the EGS team!

We provide Equal Employment Opportunity for all individuals regardless of race, color, religion, gender, age, national origin, marital status, sexual orientation, gender identity, status as a protected veteran, genetic information, status as a qualified individual with a disability and any other basis protected by federal, state or local laws.

Indeed.com

(http://www.indeed.com/q-Virtual-Pharmacist-jobs.html)-- (*go to this website and see the up-to-date Pharmacist remote positions*)

Medco Health Solutions-Express Scripts

(http://careers.express-scripts.com/who-we-hire)

Headquartered in New Jersey, Medco Health Solutions, Inc. is a leading pharmacy benefit manager with the nation's largest mail order pharmacy operations. Through advanced pharmacy, Medco improves the health and lowers the total cost of care for clients and their members. If you would like to help improve pharmaceuticals for thousands of consumers around the world and want to join the Medco team as a home based professional, consider one of the telecommuting job leads posted here.

Planet Pharma

(http://jobs.planet-pharma.com/jobdetails//jobdetails/regional-cra-(bms)/
remote,-us/7247)

Regional CRA (BMS)

JOB DESCRIPTION:

- Expedites the pre-study and study initiation processes including the conduct of Pre-Study valuation and Site Initiation visits.
- Conducts Site Initiation visits in collaboration with RCO Site Managers and/or GCO&S Protocol Managers, where applicable, to orient and train site personnel regarding the protocol and applicable regulatory requirements.

- Identifies, evaluates, and recommends potential investigators/sites on an on-going to assist in the placement of planned clinical studies with qualified investigators.

- Critically reviews and analyzes site activities through frequent visits and contacts to monitor study sites following the monitoring plan and applicable COMPANY SOPs, to assure compliance with the protocol, ICH and/or FDA GCP Guidelines and other local regulations. This includes, but is not limited to: - Manages multiple protocols, across therapeutic areas, which may require travel, based upon assigned site location and/or geographic territory.

- Ensures quality of data submitted from study sites and assures timely submission of data.

- Ensures safety and protection of study subjects according to the monitoring plan, COMPANY SOPs, and ICH and/or FDA GCP Guidelines.

- Supervises overall activities of site personnel over whom there is no direct authority and motivates /influences them to meet study objectives.

- Anticipates and proactively solves study site problems/issues as they occur. Initiates, recommends and communicates corrective actions as needed.

- Ensures documented follow-up to all outstanding issues, within the scope of this position profile.

- Appropriately escalates serious or outstanding issues to line manager and project team members.

- Facilitates the Regulatory Compliance audit process, as needed.

- Provides monitoring assistance to site monitor colleagues, as requested, in addition to serving as mentors to other colleagues as assigned.

- Proactively communicates and escalates with all internal and external stakeholders any issues identified at study sites while developing the corresponding mitigation strategies and recommended approach.

- Prepares and submits written reports, both monitoring and administrative, in a timely, accurate, concise and objective manner.

- Interacts and builds professional and collaborative relationships with all study personnel (study coordinator, investigator, and pharmacist), peers, and COMPANY office-based personnel.
- Uses multiple technologies to foster, maintain, and enhance open communication.

REQUIRED QUALIFICATIONS:

- Minimum of a Bachelor of Science degree in a health related field with 5 or more years clinical research experience including at least 5 years CRO/sponsor monitoring.
- Exhibits a high level of flexibility and sets an example for the department when facing changes such as program priorities, protocol modifications, enrollment challenges, etc.
- Employs good fiscal management to conserve the costs of departmental operation and controls travel expenses.
- Previous large pharmaceutical experience preferred.
- Demonstrated success in working independently
- Strong communication and leadership skills

PHYSICIANS

About.com Health Channel
(http://workathomemoms.about.com/od/medicalandnursingjob1/tp/Work-At-Home-Physician-Jobs.htm)

About.com contracts with more than 600 guides who are experts in their fields to write online content from Home. They are paid a minimum of $675/month to start. However, compensation
increases with page view Growth. Nurses and physicians are often hired as Guides in Health Channel. Additionally, a medical review board that oversees content works remotely.

Aetna (http://www.aetna.com/about-aetna-insurance/aetna-careers/)

This major insurance company hires nurses and physicians to work from home. While some positions are specifically designed for telework, in others telework opportunities will be considered. Search jobs database with keyword "telework."

American Well (http://www.americanwell.com/careers.html)

Boston-based company, which offers telehealth consultations, online practices, clinical collaboration and medical mobile apps to patients, providers and employers, hires MDs and RNs.

Covance (http://jobsearch.covance.com/Physician-jobs.aspx)

This U.S.-based biopharmaceutical development services company, or a contract research organization, has preclinical and clinical research operations in more than 25 countries and more than 10,000 employees worldwide. It hires clinical research associates to work from home and
physicians as medical directors in specific locations in the U.S., Canada and Europe. Use "home-based" to search its jobs database.

Humana (https://www.humana.com/about/careers/)

Some of the work-at-home positions in this major health care company have geographic requirements. Most are for registered nurses but it sometimes has opportunities for medical coders, chart auditors, licensed insurance reps, accountants, physicians, writers and sales people.

Imaging On Call
(http://www.imagingoncall.com/about/teleradiology-jobs/)

BENEFITS OF TELERADIOLOGY CAREERS – FOR DOCTORS
Flexibility in scheduling and lifestyle
Freedom to travel
Competitive compensation and bonuses
Ability to work from the comfort of your own home, wherever you choose to live
Opportunity to learn from a wide variety of interesting cases not normally seen by radiologists at small facilities.

Imaging On Call is always seeking high quality radiologists. If you think a career in teleradiology job is right for you, we want to hear from you. Applicants must be certified by the American Board of Radiology and Fellowship training is preferred. State license(s) are required to practice teleradiology.

IMAGING ON CALL OFFERS EXCITING TELERADIOLOGY CAREERS – FOR DOCTORS
Professional team environment with a close, family atmosphere
Flexible schedules
Bonus system for accurate and productive radiologists
Company paid malpractice insurance
Full time, in-house credentialing staff to assist with medical staff appointments and licensing

McKesson (http://www.mckesson.com/careers/careers/)

The nation's largest health care services company, McKesson specializes in pharmaceutical distribution and health care IT systems and software. It hires nurses and physicians in nonclinical work-at-home jobs.

MedCases
(http://workathomemoms.about.com/od/medicalandnursingjob1/tp/Work-At-Home-Physician-Jobs.htm)

Providing continuing medical education (CME), this company develops peer-reviewed, case-based, medical education initiatives for physicians, students and other health care practitioners. Remote Medical International The "remote" in the name of Seattle-area company refers to faraway places, not necessarily working at home. However, the company does have a telemedicine department and some other telecommuting jobs.

Permedion (http://hmspermedion.com/careers/physician-reviewers/)

We seek qualified physicians of every specialty to be part of our physician reviewer panel. Requirements to join our panel include appropriate licensure, board certification in specialty, and at least five years of active practice in your specialty in the United States. Contracted as needed, our panel of independent and external medical review physicians performs a variety of reviews, including medical necessity, utilization review, and overall quality evaluation on a variety of cases. All documentation and material for review is sent directly to the physician reviewer.

Professional Dynamics
(http://workathomemoms.about.com/od/medicalandnursingjob1/tp/Work-At-Home-Physician-Jobs.htm)

Medical work at home jobs include: Nurses, physicians Case Management California-based Company provides service in the workers compensation industry, and to first- party medical and employee benefit sectors. Some nurse case manager and physician peer review positions are telecommuting.

Virtual Medical Group
(http://www.virtualmedicalgroup.com/join.html)

Board certified physicians connect with patients via videoconferencing, telephone, and Internet chat, consulting with and possibly writing prescriptions for patients in the states in which they are licensed.

Vrad (http://corporate.vrad.com/Careers.aspx)

This company, formerly known as Virtual Radiologic Teleradiology Services, is a provider of teleradiology services and solutions. It hires radiologists to work from home.

Requirements include ABR or ABOR certification; hold at least one state license, eligible for hospital credentialing and available high-speed internet access. Full medical liability insurance is provided.

SALES

American Express

(https://jobs.americanexpress.com/jobs/15018292/United-States-Mgr-Account-Development-Eastern-US-Healthcare-Vertical-Role?lang=en-US)

Mgr-Account Development, Eastern US (Healthcare Vertical Role)
Client Management & Sales

JOB DESCRIPTION:

American Express Global Corporate Payments solutions are preferred by the world's top businesses. We are innovators in the payments industry, at the forefront of creating solutions for mid-sized and large companies that help them leverage their purchasing power, eliminate many labor-intensive operations in expense management, and broaden the use of cards and electronic payments to take the place of cash and checks. We continue to expand the ways in which companies can maximize working capital, and provide world-class Card member benefits to their employees. The GCP US Large Market Client Group manages strategic corporate payment relationships with clients. This Manager, Healthcare Industry is responsible for growing and retaining the corporate payments spend in a portfolio of existing clients within the Healthcare Vertical segment.

- Serve as payments expert for all corporate payments solutions within portfolio to deliver on the GCP value proposition
- Leveraging industry knowledge and expertise in development of growth and retention strategies and delivery of insights to clients
- Achieve portfolio growth and retention targets
- Influence and innovate to overcome complex client barriers, resolve escalated issues, and manage internal stakeholders
- Lead development of proposals and pricing for client renewal and expansion, negotiate client contracts, and oversee implementation of solutions

- Use the Challenger Selling Model as a guide to teach clients, problem-solve, and tailor sophisticated commercial card solutions

- Identify portfolio growth opportunities and deliver on plan to achieve, collaborating with internal resources to maximize/expand supplier network and spend growth Proactively provide expertise on policies, benchmarking, and recommendations to optimize programs, reduce costs and drive efficiencies for clients

- Identify and develop relationships with decision-makers within client organizations to influence program management and growth

- Interface with various divisions of American Express to develop and implement customized and strategic account plans

Offer of employment with American Express is conditioned upon the successful completion of a background verification check, subject to applicable laws and regulations.

QUALIFICATIONS:

Seeking a minimum of 5 years prior strategic relationship management and/or sales experience, with experience in healthcare-related industry. Ideal skill set includes the following:

- Entrepreneurial approach to portfolio management; able to identify opportunities and manage through sales process

- Understanding of healthcare industry, key trends and payment processes

- Innovative and collaborative approach to solving problems and overcome barriers impacting client value or growth

- Demonstrate effective oral and written presentation and communication skills, with the ability to influence internal and external partners

- Ability to gain in-depth understanding of client needs, to develop and execute a client-focused account plan with limited support and guidance

- Proven relationship management skills demonstrating a comfort level and effectiveness in seeking out and establishing relationships at C-levels and within cross-functional areas within large companies

- Ability to effectively present products, technical solutions, and financials to clients in a strategic manner

- Must be able to work in a virtual environment, travel to visit clients and attend evening client and community events when necessary

- Ability to effectively influence and manage change and display solid leadership skills

- Sells with integrity, in alignment with compliance and internal partner business requirements

- Location: Eastern United States Candidate selected will be required to successfully complete role certification training specific to this position

- Bachelor's degree required

Dell

(http://jobs.dell.com/us/north-america/sales/jobid9053294-healthcare-provider-back-office-(bpo)-solution-sales-specialist)

Healthcare Provider Back Office (BPO) Solution Sales Specialist

JOB DESCRIPTION
Location: Remote\Field\Satellite Office

Dell, Inc. is a worldwide provider of information technology services and business solutions to a broad range of clients. We are currently looking for a BPO Healthcare Provider Business Developer to join our team.

With more than 15,000 employees worldwide (300+ MDs, RNs, PhDs), Dell is leading the way in Healthcare & Life Sciences. We support more than 2,000 healthcare providers, 100+ life sciences organizations, and over 100 health plans worldwide. We were designated by Everest Group in 2013 as a Leader in Healthcare Provider Application Outsourcing (AO) Service Providers. Dell is ranked #1 for IT Services in the Worldwide Healthcare Provider Market for 4 years in a row by Gartner. We serve more than 50% of US hospitals providing care to 90 million Americans and managing over 7 Billion Medical Images across Cloud based Enterprise Archive and 400+ revenue cycle engagements, recovering $15 billion for clients over 7 years. We also serve 7 of the top 10 pharmaceutical companies. We address almost every player in the healthcare world: Hospitals, Health Systems, Physicians, Payers, Pharma & Medical Devices Manufacturing & Retail pharmacies. Our goal is to provide better information for these clients that will lead to better health!

Location: Anywhere in the US

ROLE RESPONSIBILITIES:
Drive business growth (pipeline creation and demand management) for the Healthcare Provider BPO Practice and perform pre-sales solution function
Lead and own end-to-end RFI/RFP proposal, scope document, risk profile, legal and corresponding financials
Provide domain BPO support for due diligence and workshops for prospective customers.
Collaborate with vertical sales teams to draw out sales strategy blueprint for new logos and existing customers
Constructs risk assessments and corresponding remediation plans relative to custom solution proposals. Timely submission of proposal, often under tight deadlines
Compose applicable services agreements (e.g. Statements of Work, SLA documentation, etc.) that specify processes, technology, staffing, deliverables, commitments, risk, and project management aspects of a solution
Support deal negotiation and closure to include transition support to service delivery
Follow all organizational standard operating procedures relative to cost modeling, approvals and reviews, and all other associated workflow, documentation and deliverables
Participate in applicable win-loss reviews and incorporates learning's into future solutions

REQUIREMENTS:
8 plus years' experience in business development and/or solution architect role with 5 plus years' experience in BPO
Past experience in selling multi-year contact center and back office contracts
Deep understanding of B2C/B2B models and how to apply to customer's business.
Prior experience with staffing services deals will be an advantage

Ability to network with CxO's
Possess an understanding of BPO delivery models and standard SLA's.
Excellent presentation, communication skills and customer engagement experience.
Experience with RFP/Tenders containing BPO requirement and specifications.
Bachelor's Degree
PREFERENCE
MBA or Healthcare Certifications a plus

COMPANY DESCRIPTION
With more than 100,000 team members globally, we promote an environment that is rooted in the entrepreneurial spirit in which the company was founded. Dell's team members are committed to serving our communities, regularly volunteering for over 1,500 non-profit organizations. The company has also received many accolades from employer of choice to energy conservation. Our team members follow an open approach to technology innovation and believe that technology is essential for human success.

Why work with us?
- Life at Dell means collaborating with dedicated professionals with a passion for technology.

- When we see something that could be improved, we get to work inventing the solution.

- Our people demonstrate our winning culture through positive and meaningful relationships.

- We invest in our people and offer a series of programs that enables them to pursue a career that fulfills their potential.

- Our team members' health and wellness is our priority as well as rewarding them for their hard work.

Dell is an Equal Opportunity Employer and Prohibits Discrimination and Harassment of Any Kind: Dell is committed to the principle of equal employment opportunity for all employees and to providing employees with a work environment free of discrimination and harassment. All employment decisions at Dell are based on business needs, job requirements and individual qualifications, without regard to race, color, religion or belief, national, social or ethnic origin, sex (including pregnancy), age, physical, mental or sensory disability, HIV Status, sexual orientation, gender identity and/or expression, marital, civil union or domestic partnership status, past or present military service, family medical history or genetic information, family or parental status, or any other status protected by the laws or regulations in the locations where we operate. Dell will not tolerate discrimination or harassment based on any of these characteristics.

Come join us. For more information, visit us on the web at www.dell.com/careers.

iTelesource (http://www.telesource.com/)
Lead generation
Lead qualification
Sales outsourcing

iTelesource is looking for experienced professionals.

iTelesource is growing fast, and with this success comes the challenge of finding exceptional people with a passion for sales lead generation. iTelesource offers great perks such as the ability to work from home, flexible schedules, and excellent pay. If you are an outgoing professional with a take charge attitude please review the following positions.

Business Development Representative: Are you a sales professional with a passion for cold calling? Do you wish to spend more time at home and less on the road? iTelesource offers a great alternative to the road weary sales professional.

As a Business Development Representative for iTelesource you will make outbound calls from your home office pitching our client's solutions to their targeted accounts. You must be able to craft a solution from research and dialogue that generates interest in our clients. You will log all time and activities via CRM as well as participate in weekly client calls. You must display the utmost of professionalism in all activities representing iTelesource and our clients. Training will be provided on all client engagements.

REQUIREMENTS: (Must Meet ALL)

- Home office with unlimited long distance plan
- Ability to work 20+ hours per week during business hours
- 5-10 years sales experience in a Complex Sales environment
- Experience calling on VP and C level
- Knowledge of various technologies and business industries a plus
- Experience in multiple CRMs

Field Technician

Position will be responsible for installing and maintaining optical fiber switches, electronics, and MAN access equipment in the POP. Will perform routine maintenance & fault isolation of transmission & Sonet equipment. Duties will also include test, turn-up and troubleshooting of DS1 through OC 192 circuits at the central office. Requirements:

Must have experienced-based knowledge of central office switches and power plants, knowledge of NEBs requirements and TIRKS or similar systems, solid exposure to central office transmission equipment, and ILEC collocation standards. Must understand digital cross connects & how to read CLR's. Ideal candidates will have a strong installation background and hands-on experience with T-BERD test equipment, DMS250 or 5ESS-class switches and Gigabit Ethernet systems. Solid computer skills and a general background in networking and Windows NT is a bonus.

Candidate should understand installation of equipment (Fiber, Sonet, cabling, wire wrapping, run jumpers, cross connects. They will take a customer order (form from provisioning) then build, turn-up, and test the circuit to be sure the customer is connected and working properly. Also they will troubleshoot existing customer problems.

Email your resume to: techopps@telesource.com

Sales Agents

TeleSource is seeking energetic sales agents who desire to work as entrepreneurs in an independent agent capacity. Set your own hours and work from home as you step onto the financial FastTrack in the two hottest growth markets of the 20th century: Telecommunications and the Internet. TeleSource pays *residual income* and rewards success.

O'Currance (http://www.istayhome.com/openings.php)

Coach

PRIMARY DUTIES AND RESPONSIBILITIES

- Evaluate current sales environment, accountability systems, and agent sales skills
- Develop and implement sales strategies including scripting, ongoing training and advanced sales skills
- Increase sales metrics
- Must be able to identify trends and provide analysis
- Aid management in coaching sales skills to agents
- Possess strong motivational skills; able to drive performance in all types of people and personalities
- Monitor and track current sales and quality trends
- Monitor and evaluate agent sales skills
- Proactively develop solutions and recommendations to improve performance and/or effectiveness of client's programs
- Thrives as team player in a fast paced, high-energy, change-orientated environment
- Strong understanding of rankings, conversion, attendance, etc.
- Meet and/or exceed all client objectives
- Performs other related duties and assignments as required and as assigned by supervisor or manager
- Responsible for maintaining and tracking all key performance indicators
- Manage daily functions of the team and work closely with project manager on guidelines and next steps to success
- Be aware of what is going on within the team
- Establish high morale and motivation with the team

- Understand goals and objectives, either personal or professional, with the team
- Identify and work with all agents to create and build a career
- Ability to work with Operations staff and Client Services in a professional and productive manner
- Regularly 6 hours of phone time per month
- Acknowledge success no matter how big or small it is!

POSITION REQUIREMENTS/EXPERIENCE

- 1-2 year's previous call center experience in a supervisor capacity
- Sales/performance driven personality
- Proven track record in meeting and exceeding sales goal
- Must be analytical and understand statistics / metrics

Education

- College experience preferred

Work Environment

General office environment

Extended time typing and staring at computer monitor

May require extended periods of sitting or standing

This job description reflects management's assignment of essential functions and position responsibilities. Nothing in this job description restricts management's rights to assign or reassign duties and responsibilities to this job at any time

UTAH APPLICANTS ONLY- Two week training required on site at our Utah location.

Sales Agent

Benefits? Yes! Commissions and incentives? Yes! Flexible schedules? Yes! Casual dress? Why not?! Want to avoid the high cost of gas? Over half of our Sales Agents choose to work in the privacy of their own home.

At O'Currance Inc. you will have opportunities to work with people who are as passionate as they are talented, develop yourself and your skills enabling you to advance within the company.

Work 30-40 hours per week on site or at home answering inbound sales calls for large consumer brands.

Additionally, we like to reward our employees for the work they do with:

Medical, Dental, and Vision coverage

401(k) participation

Company paid life insurance plan

Flexible Spending Accounts

Team Contests and incentives

REQUIREMENTS:

- Prior Sales Experience
- Competent Computer Literacy
- Competitive Drive
- Excellent phone and communication skills
- Adaptable to coaching and mentoring
- Excellent active listening skills
- Adaptable to change
- Strong attention to detail
- Desire to be a team player
- Ability to follow script
- Reliable
- Flexible schedule
- Able to attend team meetings outside of your scheduled shift

UTAH APPLICANTS ONLY- Two week training required on site at our Utah location.

Sales and Customer Service Position for AT&T

PURPOSE OF POSITION

To assist AT&T customers with current products and services.

PRIMARY DUTIES AND RESPONSIBILITIES:

- Provide excellent customer service at all times
- Receive call from potential customers with questions about their AT&T service
- Offer up-sells and new products
- Answering client questions regarding programs
- Attends all training as required
- Performs other related duties and assignments as required and as assigned

POSITION REQUIREMENTS/SKILLS

- At least 6 months sales experience-Telecom experience Preferred
- Inbound phone sales experience preferred
- Technologically sound- understands cell phone and technology lingo
- Excellent phone and communication skills
- Proficient computer skills
- Ability to navigate through multiple programs
- Adaptable to coaching and mentoring
- Excellent follow-up skills
- Excellent active listening skills
- Adaptable to change
- Strong attention to detail
- Strong desire to help others succeed
- Strong desire to be the best
- Highly motivated

Education

- High School Diploma

Work Environment

General office environment

Extended time typing and staring at computer monitor

May require extended periods of sitting or standing

UTAH APPLICANTS ONLY- Two week training required on site at our Utah location.

Outbound.com http://www.outbounders.com/findwork/jobs)

Work as a freelancer sales agent for a client. On this website, you browse the sales jobs, select one, get hired and get paid.

Plus One Company (https://plusonecompany.com/)

Our teams will outperform any other call center. Our performance is documented, our agents are well compensated, and our business is thriving because we sell more. PlusOne agents aren't trained to take phone calls, they are trained to sell. Every PlusOne agent is trained by one of the industry's best; they are mentored by top producing agents, and are measured against the very best in the industry. The PlusOne system is designed to perform at levels not yet seen in our industry.

Inbound Sales Agent
Inbound Sales Agents at PlusOne aren't thrown into a typical call center sales environment. We train, empower, and mentor Inbound Sales Agents to excel at answering inbound sales calls from direct response television and radio commercials. Inbound Sales Agents must master the PlusOne Sales Method and talk passionately about the products we sell. This position is available on a part-time or full-time basis, providing a unique work-at-home opportunity.

COMPENSATION AND BENEFITS:

- Hourly + Commission.

- Many experienced agents earn $30-$40/hour. Our average agents earn approximately $20/hour.

- Unparalleled opportunity to Work From Home with proven performance.

- Healthcare benefits and Paid Time Off available.

REQUIREMENTS:

- Basic computer skills, including: experience navigating the internet, sending and receiving professional emails, communicating via instant messaging and chat tools, and moderate to advanced typing capabilities.

- Must speak English, and remain confident while communicating over the phone.

- Must be able to work early mornings, Saturdays, and Sundays.

- A professional and success-oriented attitude is crucial.

- Should be comfortable in a sales environment, and be able to overcome objections by delivering rebuttals.

Reed Tech (https://reedelsevier.taleo.net/careersection/50/jobdetail.ftl)

DESCRIPTION

The *IP Account Executive* sells leading Intellectual Property (IP) products and services to the defined market. The IP Account Executive is the Company expert in Intellectual Property (IP) research tools, workflow products and related services. The IP Account Executive leverages this expertise to skillfully assess customer needs and promote the portfolio of uniquely differentiated solutions in a targeted and highly professional manner.

The ideal candidate will be knowledgeable of IP products and search tools and be an accomplished, sales professional who can effectively and assertively support and drive new business of assigned products and services within their territory. The IP Account Executive will network and build key contacts and business relationships to initiate lead generation and drive preference for Reed Tech products and services and will work collaboratively across functions to best position and sell our products and achieve sales revenue objectives. This is a field based sales position with national territory.

KEY QUALIFICATIONS:

Bachelor's degree or equivalent combination of education and experience.

- 7-10 years of B2B sales experience preferably in the intellectual property industry. Ideal candidates will have knowledge of the Intellectual Property (IP) market and the patent process. Previous experience and knowledge of IP workflow is highly desired.
- At least 5-10 years of successful hunting and cold calling sales experience.
- Proven ability to sell complex products to new customer prospects
- Excellent oral and written communications and presentation skills
- Experience in the United States Patent and Trademark Office (USPTO) is a plus.
- Experience working as a patent attorney / patent agent, within a patent law firm, or within a corporate legal department dealing with patents is a plus
- Understanding and expertise in computer hardware and software including but not limited to: Windows , Excel, Outlook, Power-Point, Word, contact management, Sales force automation tools / CRMs,, the Internet other sales metrics and reporting tools.
- Up to 50% travel required.

Reed Tech is a provider of best-in-class information-based solutions and services to meet the broad needs of the global IP market as well as key regulatory needs of the Life Sciences industry. Our customers include the U.S. Patent and Trademark Office, IP driven companies, law firms, and a wide range of pharmaceutical and medical device manufacturers. The corporate culture is driven by a commitment to excellence, innovation and a strong dedication to its customers, employees and community. Reed Tech is a LexisNexis company.

LexisNexis & Professional is a leading global provider of content and technology solutions that enable professionals in legal, corporate, tax, government, academic and non-profit organizations to make informed decisions and achieve better business outcomes. Part of Reed Elsevier, LexisNexis Legal & Professional serves customers in more than 100 countries with 10,000 employees worldwide.

LexisNexis, a division of RELX (formerly Reed Elsevier), is an equal opportunity employer: qualified applicants are considered for and treated during employment without regard to race, color, religion, sex, national origin, disability status, protected veteran status or any other characteristic protected by law. If a qualified individual with a disability or disabled veteran needs a reasonable accommodation to use or access our online system, that individual should please contact HR-Careers@ lexisnexis.com.

Team Support (https://teamsupport-llc.workable.com/jobs/94215)

DESCRIPTION

TeamSupport is a rapidly growing provider of customer support (or "helpdesk") applications and we need to expand our sales team! We are looking for a dynamic and hard working full time sales executive to join our growing team.

Based in Dallas, TX, TeamSupport is primarily a virtual company and most employees work from their home offices. The successful candidate for this position will be able to work in this type of environment and thrive in the fast paced culture of a small and growing technology company.

The person we're looking for will be technically savvy and a self-starter, someone who has an enthusiastic, positive attitude, excellent written and verbal communications skills, and strong attention to detail and above all, a dedicated work ethic. This individual will work closely with the marketing and sales team.

The Account Executive will be responsible for establishing and maintaining profitable relationships with prospects and new customers on behalf of TeamSupport, LLC. This role will be primarily responsible for actively engaging with prospects generated as leads, prospecting for new accounts and maximizing new sales within existing assigned customers.

The Account Executive must convey a sense of expertise in our services and capabilities in our software and the SaaS model, serving as a key communicator to our prospects and customers. The Account Executive will be accountable for meeting 100% of the monthly, quarterly and annual revenue and sales goals as assigned to you individually. Because you will be in contact with current and prospective customers and you are in a key position to influence their satisfaction and our company prosperity, this position requires tact, sensitivity, and professionalism.

Our hiring process incorporates video interviews. Candidates that are selected for further review will be required to submit video interview responses.

Responsibilities will include but are not limited to:

General and Administrative

Communicate effectively with senior management, the VP of Sales, the other members of the SalesTeam, and Operations, informing and updating them regularly to guarantee that sales and client objectives are met.

File all reports and other documentation on a timely basis.

Provide timely feedback on all marketing activities.

Follow systems and procedures outlined in the company manuals.

Participate as a key team player by supporting operations as needed.

Maintain all leads, communications and tasks within the company approved CRM.

Sales

Quickly respond to all leads to determine level of interest and qualify for either further action on the part of the Account Executive or Marketing, whichever is most appropriate.

Once qualified, actively manage sales leads from sources to qualify prospects and advance them through the sales process.

Identify prospects, customers, and referral sources and develop/maintain relationships to ensure attainment of personal and company business goals and revenue targets.

Support efforts to consistently grow the base of referral sources.

Effectively demonstrate the software functions and features of Team-Support, LLC, using the company approved sales processes on current and prospective customers in a way that conveys an image of quality, integrity and superior understanding and delivery of customer needs.

Implement a strategic sales plan that identifies prospects and customers, prioritizes them according to importance and ability to provide results.

Implement a call schedule to adequately cover either assigned territory or assigned leads and provide reports and data on results.

Investigate and resolve customer problems.

Keep current on all new technology and competitive landscape.

Understand and comply with the sales methodology and processes.

QUALIFICATIONS:

Ability to work independently with minimal supervision.

Ability to adapt quickly to change within the industry and TeamSupport as directed by management.

Education at the college level and/or 5 years combined related sales experience.

Strong verbal and written communication skills.

Strong persuasive and interpersonal skills and a sales aptitude.

Ability to identify and meet customers' needs and requirements.

Must be a self-starter and a problem solver.

ADDITIONAL DUTIES:

This job description in no way states or implies that these are the only duties to be performed. You will be expected to follow any other job-related instructions and to perform other job-related duties as requested by your supervisor.

Location:

- The ideal candidate will be in Dallas, TX, but preference will also be given to candidates in Texas. We will evaluate candidates outside of Texas on a case by case basis.
- This is currently a virtual/telecommuting position, but it will require frequent visits to the Dallas office and may eventually turn into a full-time office position.

Compensation:

Base salary plus variable compensation; $65K - $75K based on experience with OTE at $110K.

Televate (www.televate.com/our-company/careers)

Is currently hiring work from home outbound telemarketing agents. I received an email from this company yesterday with a bunch of details on this particular job. I had originally emailed them last year asking if they required a land line to get info about another post I was writing, and they responded yesterday with details about the positions they are hiring for now. If you've ever sent this company your resume, you may have also gotten this same email.

Televated has different jobs available on occasion, and what you will do depends on their clients. However, today I am just going to relay the information I received in an email from Televated about the position they need callers for right now.

The Job

You are calling businesses that are launching a new cell phone product. Televated's clients sent them new phones to launch in their stores, and you are just verifying that the businesses received the phones and other items required to launch the product.

Pay

You will receive an hourly base pay of $9/hour (not commission), plus another $0.50/hour if you work your entire assigned schedule. You are paid twice per month on the 5th and 20th. Televated offers direct deposit or payment by check.

Shifts

For these calls, they have two shifts available. The first shift is Monday through Friday from 8 a.m. to 2 p.m. Mountain time (7 a.m. to 1 p.m. Pacific; 9 a.m. to 3 p.m. Central; 10 a.m. to 4 p.m. Eastern), and the second shift is Monday through Friday from 2 p.m. to 8 p.m. Mountain time (1 p.m. to 7 p.m. Pacific; 3 p.m. to 9 p.m. Central; 4 p.m. to 10 p.m. Eastern).

While this is a Monday through Friday job, they are wanting people to work the first two Saturdays and Sundays (June 1st, 2nd, 8th, and 9th) since the product is launching this first week.

Tech Requirements

No land line is needed, and of course you need computer and high speed internet. Wireless connections not allowed.

Training

The training will vary depending on the position/campaign you're working on. It may last a few days or longer.

Feedback

Televated is a legitimate company offering real work from home jobs.

Pharmaceutical Sales work at home jobs:

LABSCO

(https://www.appone.com/maininforeq.asp?Ad=430185&R_ID=1102658 &Refer=&B_ID=91)

LABSCO's Diagnostic Sales Consultant (DSC) is the frontline account manager for all diagnostic sales in the laboratory environment. As a DSC, you would be responsible for all sales in small hospitals, physician office laboratories, and medical reference laboratories, within your given geography. All DSCs are responsible for supporting LABSCO's sales revenue, profitability objectives and branding efforts through performance of the following duties:

- Achieves budgeted sales goals for supplies, reagents and capital sales

- Develops business plans for accounts in their territory covering mix, capital opportunities, new product sales tactics and submits to manager as required

- Profiles all accounts in assigned territory, identifying lab managers, micro supervisors, infection control nurses, pharmacists, and other key decision makers by contacting them in person or via phone

- Compiles data on equipment and supplies preferred by customers, instrumentation currently in use by customer and identifies potential needs based on replacement schedules or business challenges. Enters information gathered into customer relationship management (CRM) software.

- Advises customers of equipment and instrumentation for given need based on technical knowledge of products

- Provides customers with information on such areas as office layout, legal and insurance regulations, cost analysis, and collection methods to develop goodwill and promote sales

- Makes weekly routes that prioritize calling on primary accounts within assigned territory and completes pre-call planning to set agendas for each account visit

- Generates quality capital leads and works jointly with Sales Specialists and manufacturer specialist to fully develop capital opportunities and close capital sales

- Displays or demonstrates product, using samples or catalog, and emphasizes clinical, operational or financial value the product brings to the customer.

- Quotes prices and credit terms and prepares sales contracts for orders obtained

- Estimates date of delivery to customer, based on knowledge of own firm's order and delivery schedules

- Schedules joint travel with territory Diagnostic and Instrumentation Sales Specialists to build relationships with those specialists and discuss opportunities with customers

- Schedules joint travel with vendors monthly, based on guidance from supervisor, to discuss opportunities, develop vendor relationships, and show value to LABSCO's supplier partners

- Manages product mix in accordance with agreed upon goal margin for book of business

- Reports expenses as required by company policy

- Attends company sales meetings and related conventions or meetings, as required

- Represents the company at various trade shows and professional meetings

- Assists with related special projects, as required

- Completes training certification as required to maintain and increase laboratory knowledge

- Must hold current driver's license and must be able to travel 40% of the time.

Medivation (http://www.medivation.com/careers)

Area Business Manager - Mid-Atlantic

Field Based

Medivation, Inc. (NASDAQ: MDVN – www.medivation.com) is a publicly traded biopharmaceutical company located in San Francisco. We are currently seeking a qualified, highly motivated, experienced individual for the position of Area Business Manager.

- The Area Business Manager (ABM) is responsible for the development of sales strategies and achievement of sales objectives within a determined geography. This position is also responsible for the management and development of 7 - 9 Sales Specialists, market activities, and company resources within a given geographic area that are directed specifically at maximizing territory, area and national sales goals and market share objectives.

ESSENTIAL DUTIES AND RESPONSIBILITIES (Primary):

- The ABM will effectively manage 7 - 9 Sales Specialists toward achievement of sales and market share goals through coaching, training, motivation, skill development and teamwork.

- Interact with Sales Leadership and Product Management to establish field sales implementation strategies that ensure proper product positioning within the marketplace.

- Successfully interact with all Medivation departments to ensure field implementation of strategies to meet the common goals of the Sales and Marketing organizations.

- Provide consistent and accurate expectations and feedback to Sales Specialists as part of an ongoing performance management process through timely assessment of performance using measurable outcomes.

- Design and maintain personal growth programs for Sales Specialists that are focused on corporate, territory, and individual development goals.

- Initiate developmental and training programs for Sales Specialists (in conjunction with Director, Training)

- In some areas, significant overnight travel is required.

- Applying for or accepting an ABM position assumes that appropriate travel is not an obstacle.

- Must possess the ability to observe and assess job knowledge and skill requirements and develop first-hand knowledge of sales dynamics with key customers.

CORE COMPETENCIES, KNOWLEDGE and SKILL REQUIREMENTS:

- Demonstrated sales leadership ability with a proven track record as a manager.

- Strong Clinical selling skills knowledge with a strong level of business acumen.

- Excellent verbal/presentation communication skills.

- Strong interpersonal, influencing skills.

- Strong in-depth knowledge of Specialty Biotech/Pharma working in managed care environment.
- Strong analytical skills with attention to fiscal management.
- Mastery in CRM/SFA technologies.

REQUIREMENTS:

- Minimum of 8-10 years' experience in pharmaceutical sales and/or a related field required Oncology or Specialty Biotechnology/Pharmaceuticals preferred or equivalent management work experience.
- A minimum of 3-5 years of sales management experience in Oncology or Specialty Biotechnology/Pharmaceuticals.
- Proven and consistent past sales record as a high to exceptional performer.
- Must provide evidence of leadership skills and successful contributions outside immediate team (i.e., training, mentoring, process development, etc.)
- A demonstrated high degree of proficiency in managing and leading multiple projects.
- Proven presentation, coaching, and teaching skills.
- Demonstrated ability to consistently meet and exceed sales quota goals as a manager.
- Proficient computer skills.
- A valid and current driver's license with current auto insurance which meets MDVN policy requirements.
- PC literacy MSOffice skills (Outlook, Word, Excel, and PowerPoint) as well as a demonstrated proficiency in mobile devices required.

Travel, Physical Demands and Work Environment:

- The physical demands for this position must be met by an employee to successfully perform the essential functions of this job.
- The ABM may be required to travel extensively; the average travel for this position is 40-50% with some variation based upon geography and the demands of the business imperatives. This individual

must be able to sit for long periods of time while traveling to and from appointments, and/or on field days riding with Sales Specialist and waiting to see physicians. Occasional travel to sales meetings and corporate headquarters in San Francisco is required.

EDUCATION:

- Bachelor's degree or equivalent required.

Disclaimer: The above statements are intended to describe the general nature and level of work being performed by people assigned to this classification. They are not to be construed as an exhaustive list of all responsibilities, duties, and skills required of personnel so classified. All personnel may be required to perform duties outside of their normal responsibilities from time to time, as needed.

MERK (http://www.merck.com/careers/us_home.html)

Join a team that's committed to saving and improving lives around the world. Become inspired by that mission and feel empowered to advance it in the work you do every day.

We offer a wide range of pharmaceutical career opportunities from research and development and business technology to marketing and pharmaceutical sales.

Responsive Translation
(http://www.responsivetranslation.com/company/jobs/)

Sales Manager

Seeking accomplished sales leader trained in consultative sales process with demonstrated experience in winning six-figure plus engagements with Fortune 500 firms to increase revenue and grow a sales organization for salary, commission and ownership shares of a privately-held company.

Sales Lead Commissions

If you're a translator with a job that's too big for you to handle, send it to us. We'll work out a compensation plan for you before we engage with your client. You can be confident that the great service we provide will do you proud. Hundreds of our affiliates have taken advantage of this offer over the years to make extra money without extra work.

Site Staff (http://sitestaff.com/careers/)

Sales Associate: Recruiting high-energy, direct sales professionals who wish to determine their own income by introducing our live chat services to qualifying companies. If you have a successful history of researching, prospecting, presenting and closing, chat with us to learn more!

Valeant Pharmaceuticals International, Inc.
(http://www.valeant.com/)

COMPANY OVERVIEW:

Valeant Pharmaceuticals International, Inc. is a diverse and decentralized pharmaceutical company that is committed to focusing on our key stakeholders while delivering consistently high performance. Our values provide the overall direction for our company, and provide us with the tools necessary to rise to any challenge by leveraging our collective hard work and effort along with our unwavering competitive spirit. These values help us set goals based on our organization's potential and what we hope it will become.

The Area Sales Director will be responsible for managing a geographical area that includes multiple regions and will provide supervision and coaching for Regional Sales Managers (RSMs). This position will be responsible for increasing sales and meeting objectives and is accountable for the overall success of the geographical area.
Responsibilities:

PRINCIPAL RESPONSIBLITIES AND ACCOUNTABILITIES:

- Increase sales in the geographical area by coaching, mentoring, supporting and managing the group of RSMs in the area.
- Implement new programs, compensation packages, marketing pieces, etc., as provided by the Home office.

- Provide direction and training/development opportunities to direct reports.
- Routinely communicate with RSMs to share success stories, best practices, etc.
- Work in the field with sales managers and territory managers to keep abreast of current field challenges.
- Ensure that RSMs provide direction and coaching that fosters promotions efforts by Territory Managers that are compliant.
- Design and provide possible solutions to field issues and challenges.

DIMENSIONS:

- Company-wide liaison for Sales and Home office.
- Responsible for professional, first line impression of the company through interaction with physicians and staff via face-to-face presentations, telephone, written correspondence.
- Internal Contacts: Daily contact with Sales Managers, Territory Managers, Sales Administration and other employees.
- External Contacts: Daily contact with Physicians, their staff and other medical professionals.

LATITUDE:

- This position requires the ability to act independently and to take initiative with minimal supervision from the Vice President, Sales.
- Advise Vice President, Sales of work schedule, priorities, problems and of planned and unplanned absences.

MINIMUM QUALIFICATIONS:

- Education: A Bachelor's Degree in related discipline is required. MBA preferred.
- Experience: The Area Sales Director requires a minimum of four years of successful pharmaceutical sales management experience and a minimum of 10 years of related pharmaceutical sales, marketing and/or training experience.

- Skills and Abilities: Strong interpersonal, teamwork, organizational and workload planning skills are required. The Area Sales Director must be able to deliver presentations verbally. The Area Sales Director should have a travel expectation of 50-75%.

Verilogue

(https://www.smartrecruiters.com/VerilogueInc/80891294-physician-recruiting-consultant-pharmaceutical-sales-representative-work-from-home)

Physician Recruiting Consultant (Pharmaceutical Sales Representative)

WORK FROM HOME

COMPANY DESCRIPTION

Verilogue brings patients, physicians and the healthcare industry together to share information, enhance disease understanding and participate in medical marketing research. In order to develop more effective medicines and communication materials for patients and physicians, the healthcare industry requires more insightful customer data.

Verilogue's patent-pending technology system captures information at the*point-of-practice*™ and enables physicians to digitally record conversations with select patients each month. Verilogue provides a secure and confidential way for patients and physicians to share opinions during office interactions. To learn more, visit http://www.verilogue.com.

JOB DESCRIPTION

Work from Home

- Identify potential panel members given specific specially needs;
- Proactively reach out to physicians to gage their interest in participating in Verilogue's research;
- Assist Verilogue's Field service team in the coordination of physician onboarding calls;
- Follow up with interested physicians that have not yet participated and encourage them to do so;

- Building and maintaining excellent physician relationships through frequent and timely communications via phone, email, and fax;
- Responding to any questions or problems from recruited physicians;

Key Competencies:

- Strong oral and written communication skills are required
- Former experience working the physicians directly (pharmaceutical sales representative);
- High attention to detail and accuracy with the ability to prioritize and oversee complex processes is essential.

FEE = $600/physician recruited

QUALIFICATIONS:

- Minimum four (4) year degree required, with 2+ years of experience in a pharmaceutical sales;
- History of interacting with medical professionals required;
- Knowledge of the pharmaceutical and healthcare industry or specific health-related conditions a required.

Additional Information

Verilogue rewards personal excellence in the pursuit of our common goals and is extraordinarily respectful of the individual and of the creative, intellectual and cultural diversity of our team. Our culture has allowed us to attract and retain talented individuals who are driven by a vision of the way we will transform the practice of health care communication.

If you are interested in joining Verilogue, please apply online at www. verilogue.com .

In addition to applying online below please follow the link below to take a short survey outlining your skill set:

http://www.surveygizmo.com/s3/1969665/Physician-Recruiting-Consultant-Pharmaceutical-Sales-Representative

SEARCH EVALUATION

Appen Butler Hill

(https://erec.appen.com/sap/bc/webdynpro/sap/hrrcf_a_unreg_job_
search?sap-client=300#)

Termed "search engine evaluators" at this company, these freelance positions require workers to give feedback to ensure that Internet search results are "accurate, timely, comprehensive, free of spam and relevant to the search query's intent." The evaluators must be native speakers of the language in which they are working and be knowledgeable about the Internet and familiar with a wide variety of online news sources.
Contractors in these temporary positions work four hours per day (Monday-Friday).
Jobs require residency in a specific country.

*Web Search Evaluator (*https://tbe.taleo.net/CH05/ats/careers/requisition.jsp
?org=BUTLERHILL&cws=4&rid=213)

As a Web Search Evaluator at Appen, you will be rewarded for your ability to improve the Internet search relevance results for everyone. Be part of a rapidly growing global team for the world's top Internet search engine companies! We offer flexible work schedules, competitive pay and excellent training.

If you are a fast-thinking, flexible person who embraces new challenges and would enjoy evaluating the quality and relevance of the Internet for our top clients, we want to hear from you. We will provide you with standards and scoring guidelines, personal support and training so you can be successful.

Depending upon your commitment and skill level, opportunities for new projects and responsibilities that can increase your ability to earn are always there for you. We are moving fast … and so can your career. It's all up to you.

Google (Workforce Logic)

(http://workathomemoms.about.com/od/webdesignmarketing/p/Google-
Ads-Quality-Rater.htm)

Google calls this same position an ads quality rater. It is one of the only work-at-home positions the Internet giant offers, and it doesn't even hire for it directly. It advertises for the positions on its employment page but the hiring is done through WorkForce Logic.

These positions require U.S. residency.

Lionbridge

(http://workathomemoms.about.com/od/translatorsandinterpretor/p/Lionbridge.htm)

Global Localization Company has what it terms Internet assessor as well as several other similar jobs in its "crowd sourcing" division. These jobs include:

*Internet assessors who evaluate results of a web search

*Social media search consultants who express opinions on the quality of content

*Internet judges, which are similar to Internet assessor

*In-country financial consultants who monitor and document changes in regulatory requirements and national standards in a given country/market

Online maps specialist who evaluate and improve online mapping software.

Leapforce

(https://www.leapforceathome.com/qrp/public/requirements;jsessionid=269388D3780A311AD661B2EA9E1FB27A)

As a Leapforce At Home independent agent, you will enjoy the freedom and flexibility to choose when and the amount of time you work, allowing you to balance your career, family and friends.

Leapforce At Home provides an exciting home-based career opportunity where you can put your acute analytical skills to work, providing valuable feedback and critical insight for some of today's leading companies.

With no set schedules of any kind, Leapforce At Home independent agents enjoy the flexibility to choose how much and when to work.

Successful Leapforce At Home independent agents are smart, inquisitive and dig online research.

Leapforce has made a core promise to our customers to work with only the very best home-based independent agents. Each Leapforce At Home independent agent is an integral part of our shared success and we are very serious about keeping our promise. Leapforce At Home agents conduct in depth internet-based research and provide information evaluation for leading companies from around the globe.

Check out the basic equipment and skills required to become a Leapforce At Home Agent:

Equipment Requirements
High speed internet access (Cable Modem, DSL, etc.)
A personal computer running Mozilla's free Firefox web browser, version 20.x - 26.x.
Up to date anti-virus and anti-spyware software

Basic Skill Requirements: Excellent web research skills and analytical abilities Excellent comprehension and written communication skills

Many Leapforce agents must pass an assessment test before being hired.

SOCIAL MEDIA

Mylikes (http://mylikes.com/publishers/overview)

Earn money by creating a social website OR embed our sponsored widget on your site to increase revenue and engagement

Pin Booster (https://pinbooster.com/site/page/view/pinners)

1. Sign up and set your price per pin
We'll give you an idea of a reasonable amount to charge, based on other pinners, but we leave the final price up to you. At Pin booster, you might notice a trend that you're always in the driver's seat.

2. Select the boards you pin in more often
Always pinning home décor? Tell us! This kind of information helps us find the right advertising fit for you. We want your Pin booster pins to be at home with all of your other favorite things.

3. When you receive an offer, decide to accept it or reject it
You'll receive a notification that someone thinks you're awesome and wants to pay you to pin, but then it's up to you whether you want to pin the image or not. Again, you're the boss!

4. If you accept it, pin away!
Love the pin? Accept the offer and get started. We'll walk you through the specifics to make sure that everything goes well, but it's pretty straightforward.

5. Get paid (the good part) within 24 hours of the pin going live
You did your part, now it's time for us to do ours. You should see funds show up in your Pin booster account within 24 hours. Feel free to spend that time scouring Pinterest for ways to spend it.

Shutter Stock (http://submit.shutterstock.com/?language=en)
Submit photos and sell them

SociBuzz (http://www.socibuzz.com/)
Get started today by promoting the products, services, and causes that match the "voice" of your social media accounts. SociBuzz advertisers will pay you for each visitor you send to their websites.

TRANSCRIPTION (not medical)

Aberdeen (https://www.abercap.com/careers/)

Company provides captioning, transcription and translation services and hires transcribers, real time captioners, editors and translators to work at home and in its office in Orange County, CA.
Transcription jobs pay $1-$1.50 per audio minutes; real time captioners are paid $75/hour.

AccuTran Global (http://www.accutranglobal.com/)

Transcribe conference calls, meetings and interviews for the financial sector in this Canadian company's home transcription jobs. It hires transcribers as independent contractor on a part-time basis.
Pay ranges from $0.005 to $0.0066 per word. 70 WPM preferred for most jobs. Other jobs available include transcription reviewer, editor, real-time writer or captioner, formatter and supervisor. Hires in U.S., U.K. and Canada.

Alice Darling Audio Transcription Services

(http://www.alicedarling.com/about/employment.html)

Boston-area company hires experienced transcriptionists to work from home or from its offices. Company's clients are in the fields of science, biotechnology, academia, business, technology, finance, Medicine, film, advertising and the law.
70 WPM required for transcription jobs.

American High-Tech Transcription and Reporting
(http://www.htsteno.com/jobs.html)
Firm offering transcription and translation services to government, law enforcement, corporations and other organizations hires both on-site and work-at-home transcriptionists.
Applicants must pass and pay for FBI and state criminal background checks with fingerprints.

Birch Creek Communications

(http://birchcreekcommunications.com/3894/index.html)

Transcription Positions
We have openings in our transcription department for high quality corporate and legal transcriptionists, doing audio files for Social Security, Veterans Affairs, Immigration, as well as legal and corporate clients. We do not do any medical transcription.

These positions are Independent Contractor (IC) positions. You are not an employee for our company, but rather, work for yourself, providing us with your services.

We do not withhold taxes for independent contractors. Similarly, as an IC, you are not eligible for unemployment benefits or Workmen's Compensation Insurance.

We cannot provide any technical assistance, training, software, or other support.
Compensation

For corporate and financial, we pay by the audio minute, ranging from .40/audio min to 1.25/audio min.

For general legal, we pay by the page, ranging from .75/page to 1.75/page.

Rates of pay depend on the job, turnaround time, and the quality of your work. The upper range of the scale will be given to those with 99% accuracy consistently.

Must be a U.S. citizen. Background check may be required.

Capital Typing
(http://www.capitaltyping.com/employment-application)

Outsourcing company based in South Carolina provides virtual office services.
In addition to its data entry and transcription jobs from home, it offers online customer support, translation and secretarial services.

Cyber Dictate (http://www.cyberdictate.com/company/employment/)

Recruits U.S. citizens as independent contractors for transcription jobs.
Minimum of 70 WPM and 2 years of experience required.
Hires both legal and general transcriptionists.

DionData Solutions
(http://www.diondatasolutions.net/opportunities.htm)

Hires typists with a minimum of 60 wpm and basic computer skills for home transcription jobs. No fees.

e-Typist.com
(http://www.e-typist.com/Employment_work_at_home-dictation-service.htm)

Company hires work at home transcriptionists for legal and insurance-rated transcription jobs. Submit resume and company will contact applicants when it has openings. 60 WPM and knowledge of legal terms required.

Fantastic Transcripts

(http://www.fantastictranscripts.com/employment.html)

Fantastic Transcripts is a fantastic place to work. We offer a casual work environment in our downtown Boston offices.

We also offer great flexibility in scheduling - work when you want to - and the Pepsi is free.

With Suffolk University and Emerson College only a block away, our part-time jobs are perfect for mature students with typing and transcription skills.

Our central location at the intersection of five transit lines also makes us easy to get to from just about anywhere in the metropolitan area.

You must type a minimum of 60 words per minute, transcribe a minimum of 35 words per minute, be comfortable using a computer, and you must pass a transcription aptitude test taken in our offices. We pay $10 to $12 to start, and overtime after 40 hours if we really get busy.

Our office is standardized on Windows XP and Microsoft Word 2000 with documents saved in the Word 95 format standard.

To apply, please e-mail your resume to us at jobs@fantastictranscripts.com and include your typing speed. If your background meets with what we are looking for, we will contact you to set up a time for an interview and a transcription test.

Freelance Transcriptionists
We are always interested in hearing from experienced transcriptionists to work on a sub-contract, freelance basis from your home or office.

When contacting us, please let us know what you charge to transcribe an hour's worth of audio because this is how we charge our clients.

To figure out your per hour of audio charge, estimate how long it usually takes you to transcribe an hour of audio and then multiply that number by what an hour of your time is worth.

E-mail your resume and background information to us at jobs@fantastic-transcripts.com and we will consider you for future work.

Fantastic Transcripts is a fantastic place to work. We offer a casual work environment in our downtown Boston offices.

We also offer great flexibility in scheduling - work when you want to - and the Pepsi is free.

With Suffolk University and Emerson College only a block away, our part-time jobs are perfect for mature students with typing and transcription skills.

Our central location at the intersection of five transit lines also makes us easy to get to from just about anywhere in the metropolitan area.

You must type a minimum of 60 words per minute, transcribe a minimum of 35 words per minute, be comfortable using a computer, and you must pass a transcription aptitude test taken in our offices. We pay $10 to $12 to start, and overtime after 40 hours if we really get busy.

Our office is standardized on Windows XP and Microsoft Word 2000 with documents saved in the Word 95 format standard.

To apply, please e-mail your resume to us at jobs@fantastictranscripts.com and include your typing speed. If your background meets with what we are looking for, we will contact you to set up a time for an interview and a transcription test.

Freelance Transcriptionists
We are always interested in hearing from experienced transcriptionists to work on a sub-contract, freelance basis from your home or office.

When contacting us, please let us know what you charge to transcribe an hour's worth of audio because this is how we charge our clients.

To figure out your per hour of audio charge, estimate how long it usually takes you to transcribe an hour of audio and then multiply that number by what an hour of your time is worth.

E-mail your resume and background information to us at jobs@fantastic-transcripts.com and we will consider you for future work.

Morningside Partners (http://www.fdch.com/careers.html)

Morningside is seeking to hire qualified applicants in a wide range of fields related to transcription, editorial and content verification, video technical services and data management. Most of these positions are resident at the company's offices in suburban Washington, D.C. (Lanham, Maryland).

In-House News Transcribers
Fast-paced, deadline-driven political news transcript service seeks transcribers for media briefings, newsmaker interviews, congressional hearings and other news events. Must have excellent grammar and knowledge of current events. Min. 70 wpm. Part time or full time; hours available from 10 a.m. to 9 p.m. Lanham, Md., location; own transportation required. Please send cover letter and resume in the body of an e-mail to Careers @ ascllc.net.
Attachments will not be opened and please include "In-House Transcriber" in the subject line.

News Transcribers
At-home transcribers needed to produce verbatim transcripts for media clients such as CNN, FOX and MSNBC. Ability to work independently and meet deadlines a must. Familiarity with current events and AP style a plus. Requirements include: high-speed Internet connection; digital foot pedal system; bachelor's degree in English or journalism; at least three years of work experience. Please send cover letter and resume pasted into the body of an email to Careers @ ascllc.net.
Attachments will not be opened. Please include "News Transcriber" in the subject line and WPM typing speed in your cover letter.

Financial At-Home Transcriber
Experienced transcribers sought for at-home financial transcription. Must be accurate, deadline-oriented, and reliable. Hrs. flexible. Deadlines firm. PC requirements: Internet connection (dial-up or high speed), RealPlayer, Transcription software/foot pedal for digital .ra sound files. QUALIFIED applicants, send résumé to Careers @ ascllc.net.

Mountain West Processing

(http://someplacespecialpizza.net/transcription/mountain-west- entry-level-transcription/)

Company hires independent contractors to work as legal, corporate, general and Medical transcriptionists. Rates for these transcription jobs may be per page, per audio minute or per word.

Mulberry Studio

(http://www.mulberrystudio.com/mainsite/jobs.html)

Company offers full- and part-time transcription and proofreading positions either on-site in Cambridge, MA, or on a freelance basis from home. Typing speed of 75 wpm, excellent grammar and language skills, and two years of experience in transcription and word processing are required.

Neal R. Cross & Company

(http://www.nealrgross.com/transcriber-employment-details)

Neal R. Gross & Co. is a Washington, DC based court reporting and transcription company. We have been in business over 35 years and provide verbatim court reporting and transcription services to a broad range of government and private clients.

REQUIREMENTS:

Must type at least 60 WPM
Excellent command of the English language

MUST BE ABLE TO WORK A MINIMUM OF 30 HOURS PER WEEK
If you type over 60 words per minute and need to work from home, you may be what we're looking for in a legal transcriber. No transcription experience necessary, but you must be willing and able to work on overnight delivery. Timeliness is a must, as are excellent English language skills. Please apply only if you can transcribe at least 5 hours of audio per week.

Most of our recordings are digital, so please indicate in your resume or cover letter if you are familiar with digital audio and with using an FTP program.

To inquire about taking a transcription test for this position, please send a cover letter and resume to: transcribe@nealrgross.com.

All NRGCO transcribers are independent (1099) Subcontractors.

Net Transcripts

(http://www.nettranscripts.com/careers.htm)

Law Enforcement Transcriber

Individuals who can transcribe audio content of criminal investigations, internal affairs, and patrol reports. You must have prior experience transcribing for a law enforcement agency (police department, sheriff's department, etc.), type 80+ WPM, have excellent grammar, outstanding accuracy and proofreading skills, have experience with MS Word, and must demonstrate strong computer literacy.

A full criminal background check is required for individuals completing this work.

There is an initial assessment period before any individual is able to complete client work. Therefore, it is essential that you have prior Law Enforcement transcription experience and be able to proof your work to be at least 99% accurate.

General Transcriber

Individuals who can transcribe audio content of financial results conferences, medical training seminars, group project meetings and other general business meetings. Must type 80+ WPM, have excellent grammar and proofreading skills, have experience with MS Word and Excel, and must demonstrate strong computer literacy.

There is an initial assessment period before any individual is able to complete client work. Therefore, you should have prior experience in transcription. Those most successful candidates will have had work experience creating, reviewing or interpreting corporate financial information (e.g. 10Q, 10K, Annual Reports).

QuickTate or iDictate
(http://typists.quicktate.com/transcribers/signup)

Company provides transcription of short audio files such as voicemails and dictated notes by hiring Work-at-home transcribers. Quicktate pays $.0025 per word (this pay may vary—see their website).
Successful Quicktate transcriptionists may receive work from iDictate which transcribes a wider range of documents. Bilingual, particularly Spanish-language transcribers are needed.

Scribie
(https://scribie.com/freelance-transcription#intro)

Freelance transcriptionists choose audio files to transcribe at $10 per audio hour.
Files are 6 minutes or less. Opportunity for advancement to reviewer.

SpeakWrite
(http://www.speakwrite.com/WEB/sw/employment/typist/typist-home.aspx)

Hiring home-based typists throughout the United States and Canada to work as independent contractors.
SpeakWrite requires a typing speed of 65 WPM for its transcription jobs.

Talk2Type Transcriptions
(http://www.talk2type.net/transcriber.html)

Independent contractors must type at least 75 wpm and have their own Equipment to qualify for this telecommuting position

Terescription
(http://www.terescription.com/site/terescriber/terescriberSignUp.aspx)

Independent contractors transcribe for the entertainment industry. A foot Pedal is required. Work pays $.07/line for a one-person interview and potentially more for multiple-speaker interviews.
A transcriber typing at 70wpm can earn between $12 and $15 per hour.

Terescription provides affordable and professional transcription services for the entertainment, business, legal and educational markets.

(At the time of this printing, this company said they have all the transcribers they need but did say they would accept applications and contact you when there is an opening).

TRAVEL AGENTS

Jet Blue Reservations
(http://work-here.jetblue.com/category/careers/customer-support/)

Most Customer Support crewmembers are based out of our Salt Lake City Support Center (SSC). Upon hire, new Reservations Crewmembers attend orientation and training at SSC before starting work from home.

Travel Outlook (http://traveloutlook.com/jobs/)

Travel Outlook is a virtual hotel reservations company. We answer reservations calls for our hotel clients in North America and the Caribbean. We're a stable, growing company, and we are looking for mature, professional people who enjoy working from home. When you're working with us, you will receive reservation requests and inquiries from multiple hotels from around the country.

We all love working from home. It provides more free time, and because we can avoid the hour long drive to the office with gas at $4 a gallon or the packed subway. We can also avoid the loud mouth in the next cubicle, or having to worry about a work wardrobe.
We're looking for full time and part time reservation agents. Prior hotel and/or work-from-home experience is preferred. You will be an employee. So, if you are looking for a professional work-from-home opportunity, consider working with us. You'll be required to have some basic equipment and Internet service available at your home office:

- A Windows XP or later computer system.
- A valid company-approved DSL/broadband internet service with minimum broadband capacity of 2Mb up/7 Mb down service speed.

- A dedicated landline or company-approved VOIP telephone.
- Other essential items:
- Knowledge of basic hotel operation and services (not required, but important)
- A quiet home work environment
- Strong customer service skills
- Strong data entry and good overall writing skills
- Positive, sales-oriented phone personality
- Personal transportation to perform onsite tours of local clients
- Moderate to high general computer knowledge, including experience with specific hotel management systems, Microsoft Office products, 3rd party email applications (Outlook, Thunderbird, etc.), virtual private networks, etc.
- Flexible availability for scheduled work hours.

Travel with the Magic
(http://travelwiththemagic.com/about-us/apply/)

Are you ready to join our team? Do you love to travel? Do your friends and family always ask you for help when they are planning to go to Disney?

Travel with the Magic is CLIA and IATA accredited and all our Consultants are graduates of the College of Disney Knowledge. We are looking for passionate, hard-working planners who are self-starters and want to grow and maintain a successful and profitable business selling Travel. This is a sales job, not just for the average Disney fan. You must be motivated to increase your sales.

As an Independent Contractor/outside sales consultant you have access to:

- Monthly conference calls
- Access and training on DisneyTravelAgents.com
- Online training and webinars from various suppliers such as VAX, Royal Caribbean, Celebrity, Carnival Cruise Line, Universal Orlando, Go-Go, and more!

- Support via email, phone and instant messaging
- Opportunity to obtain discounts on your personal travel (after goals have been met)
- Invitations to attend FAM and Agent Education programs
- Internet leads if available and after you complete training and meet sales goals
- Candidates must have:
- Personally experienced the Walt Disney World Resort in Florida in the last two years
- Excellent computer skills
- Excel in a team environment
- Be a self-starter and take ownership of growing and maintaining a profitable business
- Be professional, honest, and hard working
- Attention to detail
- Sailed on at least one cruise
- Thought about HOW you will grow a profitable business
- Have a passion for helping people with their vacations
- Open to selling all types of Travel
- Must reside in the United States

World Travel Holdings

(http://www.worldtravelholdings.com/careers,work-home#.VmNMrnarTIU)

Interested in our Travel Professional, Customer Care Representative or Luxury Travel Sales work at home positions? *Connect now* to receive information on when these positions become available and other World Travel Holdings news!

Embark on a fun, exciting, and dynamic career with World Travel Holdings. As an At-Home Agent, the leads will come to you (no cold calling). You will sell and service fabulous resort and cruise vacations for more than 40 top travel brands while building customer loyalty. Your extensive onboarding and training builds a solid foundation for your success here. Check out a day in the life of a Travel Pro.

NO SHOES, NO PROBLEM

Get all the advantages of working with a travel industry powerhouse from the comfort of your home.

- Create your own dress code ... pajamas and bare feet are always okay
- Become an employee and member of the World Travel Holdings team
- Receive paid training as well as ongoing training and support
- Get a computer and access to our at-home agent support team
- Enjoy great benefits and paid time off
- Get access to great travel discounts and perks

WHAT YOU NEED TO WORK FROM HOME*

A private area to work in free of distractions. Sorry, Fido, your cute little bark still counts as a distraction.

Internet service (DSL or cable modem required). We DO NOT support dial-up, satellite connections or wireless networks. Trying to connect to the Internet with aluminum foil on your antenna doesn't work so well either.

A regular phone line with no features such as call waiting or long distance. When we say "regular" phone, yes we mean the one that plugs into the wall, not over the Internet.

Internet with 1.5 Mbps upload speed and 5 Mbps download speed. (To check your Internet speed go to http://www.speedtest.net/)

World Travel Holdings provides you a computer, monitor, keyboard, mouse, phone and headset. You just need to supply the voice and a passion for travel.

YOUR INVESTMENT

- Refundable $500 deposit for a company computer and phone (deposit will be spread out over 5 payroll deductions)
- Initial setup fees (cable/DSL) - $0–$200

- Start-up office supplies - $30
- Printer/Fax $150–$175 (optional)
- UPS/Surge Protector $50-$100

Working Solutions

(http://www.workingsolutionsjobs.com/Program-Areas/Corporate-Travel)

We're looking for skilled professionals who can understand the business, can master the technology, and deliver great service—call after call, customer after customer. We'll pay you well to do it, working at home or any safe, secure and quiet location with landline access.

What it takes—program details: Working Solutions is seeking on-demand travel agents to support corporate clients. Agents will make air, hotel and car reservations for corporate clients, using a web-based Sabre application.

They will provide routing and pricing—plus rerouting and re-pricing—information to facilitate customer decisions on itinerary selection and ticketing options for new air, car and hotel reservations. Agents also make changes to existing reservations. Calls will be routed to the agent's workspace, with reservations being made through the client's reservation system.

Agents on this program will need a background in travel and recent global distribution system (GDS) experience. If your GDS experience is rusty, we offer refresher courses in Sabre.

We ensure quality service through the best agents, which could be you.

Program hours: This client's operating hours are 24/7. Agents need to commit to a minimum of 25 hours a week.

Program requirements:

- Recent GDS experience (Apollo, Amadeus, Galileo, Sabre and WorldSpan)
- Knowledgeable of corporate bookings and business demands
- Experience in travel industry and delivering world-class customer service—the same you would expect

Rewards: Agents on this program will earn $12 - $17 an hour, based on productivity and certifications.

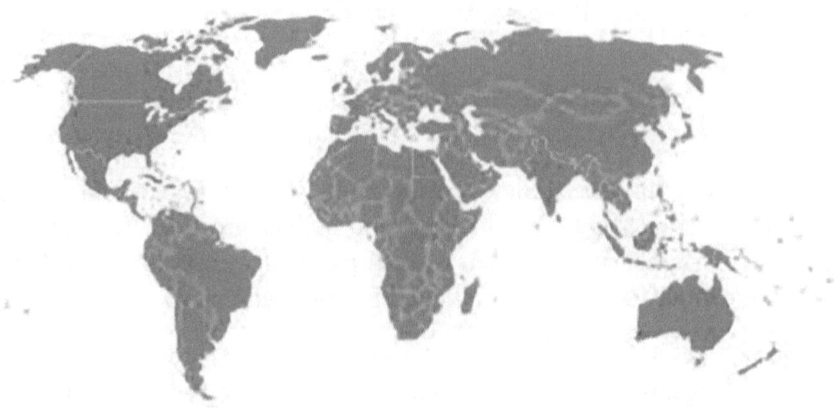

VIRTUAL ASSISTANT

BCD Travel

(http://www.bcdtravel.com/get-to-know-us/careers/search-global-jobs/)

Client Data Solutions Analyst

Job Description: The department Global Client Data Solutions delivers Business Intelligence through the collection of our customers travel data globally and provides this to our consolidated & local customers in a meaningful end product. The information we provide supports our customer in general making decisions in their travel policies as it relates to compliance, spend management and negotiation of global contracts.

In this role you will be responsible for reviewing client data for trends and areas that are important to client or industry changes. You proactively communicate your findings with the account management team. You assist account manager to develop, implement and deliver KPI's and SLA's. You are an accurate person that makes sure data reports are complete and ensure proper framework is in place to deliver future consistent data. Working together with global implementation and account management teams you ensure accurate, timely set up and implementation of global MI.

RESPONSIBILITIES:

Client Trending: Benchmarking, trending, data mining and data analytics

Process Improvement: Construct data analysis to support process reengineering efforts

Strategic: Gain understanding of the strategic vision, business and tactical plan and culture

Analytics: Analyze customer travel patterns and make recommendations to account management for cost savings and productivity enhancements

Consultative: Provide consultative input and delivery of strategic business reviews which may include presentation and delivery

KPI / SLA Development: Assists account manager to develop, implement and deliver of KPI's and SLA's

MI Management : work with global implementation and account management teams to ensure accurate and timely set-up and implementation of global MI

Training: Organizes, provides or participates in global account management training

Communication: Gather and distribute GAM relevant market/country specific intelligence. Make sure the best service is delivery to BCD Travel clients

REQUIREMENTS:

Under graduate degree in a related field with 3 years of relevant experience

Flexible, able to multi-task and manage workflow across different time zones

Minimum 3 years of travel industry experience

Proven flexibility and adaptability in effectively driving results and developing/implementing process strategies in an environment of changing priorities

Experience with account planning, execution and strong decision making and problem solving skills

Strong collaborating and influencing skills

Ability to work with complex global initiatives

Data Visualization experience (Tableau, Microstrategy, etc..) and Process mapping program experience(Visio, SmartDraw) is preferred

Apply

Please apply by creating a profile and upload resume and cover letter.

Global CDS Project Specialist

JOB SUMMARY:

Responsible for project and implementation management of Global, Regional and Country specific CDS technology projects. Works as a functional coordinator on larger scale projects as dictated by the matrix of the individual projects and Scope and leads mid-range complexity projects
- Responsibility for project planning and execution
- Responsibility for communication needs identification, delivery to Project Manager and execution of reconciled communication measures
- Responsibility for project status reporting
- Responsibility for assigned project tasks

ESSENTIAL DUTIES AND RESPONSIBILITIES:

- Capable of Leading mid-range complex projects
- Executes Implementation tasks
- Facilitate Customer requirements sessions and documentation sign off with Account Management and BCD resources
- Capable of coordination as sub project leader on high complexity projects
- Execution of project tasks in time and quality based on project scope provided by Project Manager
- Structured preparation of decisions
- Presentation of alternative solutions for project
- Manage and tracking of day-to-day project tasks

- Risk Management
- Adherence of technical and economical parameters
- Knowledge management
- Project documentation
- Abide by CDS Project Management Organization processes and procedures
- Expert in Client Data Consolidation Requirements for customer reporting
- Expert in CDS products for crisis and management information reporting
- Accountable for project deadlines and deliverable for CDS projects
- Facilitate and attend meetings/conference calls with internal and external clients
- Coordinate collection and distribution of required implementation data
- Identify potential risks associated with projects
- Leverage Global resources as necessary
- Manage and deliver clear and concise communications related to project work
- Identify and communicate elements which are in and or out of scope for department projects
- Interact with internal technology teams on a regional and or Global level
- Monitor project cost for budget and time tracking
- Planning and executing complex multi-departmental projects with internal and external stakeholders
- Excellent communication skills utilizing various media
- Deliver training and support as required
- Travel as necessary for internal and client meetings as projects dictate

TRANSFERABLE SKILLS:

- Thorough knowledge of travel agency, operations and industry
- Capable of problem solving, anticipating, initiating and resolving customer, vendor and account issues
- Capable of working in a team environment, supporting management and staff, following policies, providing feedback, assisting in special projects and taking on additional responsibilities
- Able to respond to change; able to be flexible and work with ambiguity

- Strong analytical skills
- Ability to work independently, developing strategies an action plans and implementing goals and objectives
- Ability to work in a virtual environment
- Ability to be concise
- Ability to articulate opportunities and risks
- Excellent oral and written communication skills
- Professional manner and appearance

QUALIFICATIONS:- Demonstrated project coordination in complex multi-departmental projects

- Proficient use of project management software and processes
- 2 years minimum experience in the travel industry, including agency operations, account and or technical management
- Proficient using Microsoft Office applications including but not limited to Outlook, Word, Excel, PowerPoint and Visio
- Technical project management experience preferred
- Thorough understanding of BCD Travel front-mid and back office processes (preferred)
- Thorough understanding of BCD Travel client reporting offerings (preferred)
- Strong people management and leadership skills
- Ability to work on multiple projects concurrently
- Strong problem solving skills and process reengineering skills
- Experience working within an international environment preferred
- Ability to work weekends and nights when necessary
- Ability to travel globally if/as needed

Virtual Assistant Jobs

(http://www.virtualassistantjobs.com/virtual-interviewer-salaried-full-time/)

FEATURED PROJECT: Virtual Interviewer-Salaried

HOURS: Part time (with approval), and F/T hours

JOB DUTIES:

Duties: We are currently searching for an experienced full-time, independent contract Interviewer to work from their home office. The Interviewer will specialize in assessing and pre-qualifying candidates for active positions and ensuring they meet the requisite skill set and competencies required by our clients.

JOB REQUIREMENTS:

Your Required Skills & Experience: You have three or more years' experience as a recruiter or interview specialist in the talent identification and staffing industry or corporate recruiting environment. You have an established track record of identifying top talent through intensive interview processes and techniques. You have the ability to read scripted questions (when necessary) and are able to clearly convey the answers in writing. You have a keen sense of discernment to determine if a candidate is the best fit holistically, not just from a technical standpoint. You are an obsessive "note taker" and can produce a concise and qualitative analysis for candidate recommendation. You have the ability to conduct professional interviews by telephone, uninterrupted, to candidates in different time zones. You are an expert communicator and have the ability to command a telephone interview. You have a high sense of urgency and the ability to multi-task. You have a fully networked home office with high-speed internet access and land line phone or installed software. You possess the ability to work on a full-time, flexible, yet consistent, schedule.

How This Position Will be Paid: Direct Deposit, excellent salary.

WEBSITE DESIGN

Chalk & Chisel (https://chalkchisel.workable.com/jobs/116588)

Senior Interactive Developer

At Chalk + Chisel, a Senior Interactive Developer is a leader. You'll work with our interactive team to determine the best technical approach, then take the lead as you and other developers practice your craft. You'll be responsible for ensuring interactive team members contribute to each project's success – tracking deadlines and team progress, and communicating with the larger team.

We've built a unique development team with skills and experience ranging from Django-based websites to iOS apps to interactive physical installations. We all develop comfortably in JavaScript building Node.js backends and React-based products for web and mobile devices. We're looking to expand that team.

You'll get to choose and work with new technologies, like React Native and GraphQL, on a team that thrives on continuous evolution.

RESPONSIBILITIES

- **Develop.** Write code, build systems and devise solutions. Consider the strategic, design and technology goals of a project.
- **Lead.** Manage the development process and work with other developers to ensure their work is in support of a larger goal.
- **Collaborate.** Engage with account strategists and designers. Keep them up-to-date on progress. Communicate ideas, explain technical challenges and propose alternatives.
- **Strive.** Aim to produce high quality work and seek to improve the development process.

About You

- Solid foundation as a web and/or mobile developer.
- Experience working with a cross-functional team and managing other developers.
- Open to using new technologies and approaches – not because they're novel, but because they can make the work better.
- Familiarity with technologies like Node.js, React, ES2015 (or similar technologies, frameworks and languages).
- Comfortable working on both front-end and back-end problems, even if you prefer one more.
- You can debug a problem (even if it's not code you wrote).
- Your peers might call you a "hard worker", but you have a life outside of code.

The Location

- We'll consider all applicants, but have a strong preference for those who can join us in our office overlooking Baltimore's Inner Harbor.

- Remote employees will be asked to visit the team in Baltimore a few times a year.

Crossover

(http://www.careesma.in/jobs/angularjs-nodejs-engineer-30k/remote-work-from-home/1498239?utm_source=Indeed&utm_medium=organic&utm_campaign=Indeed)

Angular JS + Node JS Engineer

JOB DESCRIPTION

Ready to make $30,000 USD while working for a fortune 500 company from the comfort of your home? Eager to join a network of the most talented remote workers in the world? Do you have extensive experience with structural frameworks for dynamic web apps and open-source, cross-platform runtime environments for developing server-side web applications? If so, this role is for you. Work for Crossover, and you'll earn the most competitive wages on the market, collaborate with the most skilled teams in your field, and work for the most elite companies in the world. Sound too good to be true? Take a closer look...

What to Expect as an AngularJS and NodeJS Engineer at Crossover

Join Crossover and you'll be given the responsibility of engineering backend services with supporting front end UIs for enterprise consumption in a cloud stack. You will assist a global team of web designers and developers in utilizing the best-in-practice architecture, tools, and design patterns in web development. You will be expected to think in an abstract or computational way to provide solutions to help scalability and handle complex business logic. Creativity in solution implementations are welcomed!

QUALIFICATIONS FOR THIS OPPORTUNITY

If you want to work with the best, you have to be the best. A successful AngularJS + NodeJS Engineer at Crossover will demonstrate the following qualifications:

At least four years of hands-on experience with developing web applications

Bachelor's Degree in Computer Science or related field

General knowledge of both front-end and back-end web development from a consumer perspective

Excellent communication skills (in English)

Proficiency in the following skills and technologies is mandatory:

Node.JS

Angular.JS

Express

Mocha

Test Driven Development / Continuous Integration/Delivery

Service Oriented Architecture / Microservices

SQL (Any SQL)

Material Design Understanding

Docker

Vagrant

AWS Experience

JavaScript

Compensation

At Crossover, you'll earn extremely competitive wages while enjoying the flexibility of working from virtually anywhere on the face of the earth:

Salary: 15 USD/hr
Position type: Full time (40 hours per week)
Location: Global

The Type of AngularJS and NodeJS Engineer We're Looking For

Crossover values a culture of excellence. We need web developers who are not only technically proficient, but also demonstrate the following qualities:

Perfectionism when it comes to code quality
Commitment to developing a simple, clean, and attractive UI

Confidence that your talent is significantly above your peers and competitors
A willingness to embrace the concept of iterative development as the means for building excellent products
And obsessive commitment to quality

Gauge Interactive
(https://gauge-interactive.workable.com/jobs/116305)

eCommerce Project Manager

THE POSITION:

Often you'll act as a Relationship Manager or Business Analyst, in addition to managing project details with humor and professional self-confidence. This position is perfect if you are really into getting all the details right, love to learn, relish a challenge, and consider yourself a tactful mediator. This position will focus on clients who hold a long-term retainer agreement with us. You will work with them to maintain their storefront, build marketing strategy, develop new store features, and implement marketing objectives. You will work in close partnership with our two current Project Managers and our leadership team to manage overall production and capacity for new and existing clients.

In order to be successful in this position, you will need to learn about and understand the basics of many different technical systems and processes as they pertain to an eCommerce business. Being able to step back from the details of this week and plan what next month will look like is a critical discipline you will need to have mastered. To totally own this position, manage the above and show us new ways you can help us do things better. We'll love it!

Your typical day will involve a few meetings, and working closely with the rest of the team to align around the priorities you've set for us. You'll be in contact with our clients a lot, as you will be the grand arbiter of all project details. Depending on where you are in a project, you could be writing a sitemap, talking with a designer about a home page layout, discussing some pesky IE9 bugs with a developer, or organizing a final launch checklist for a client.

KEY TASKS AND RESPONSIBILITIES

- Your objective: to collaborate with, organize, and lead your team through multiple project timelines
- Our clients deserve excellence; set reasonable expectations and carry them out
- Your ability to understand and translate how eCommerce, email marketing, shipping, and accounting software integrate with one another will be crucial to our clients
- You'll own the agenda and schedule for project meetings and client communication
- Always be researching and recommending needed Magento features & extensions
- You're behind the wheel; navigating the speed bumps and roadblocks, while keeping the clients appraised
- Become a master of Magento features and functionality; share your great knowledge with clients
- Deadlines, milestones, priorities, and other big words - you'll set them up!
- We carefully craft our project estimates, and your input is highly valued and needed
- All good processes are built around great documentation. Create it, and always improve the process

REQUIREMENTS

- At least one year of successful experience as a Project Manager at a web agency
- Excellent written and verbal communication skills (of course!)
- Brilliant organizational abilities, time management, and attention to detail
- Working knowledge of CSS and HTML, plus some SEO insights
- A desire to dig under the surface to see how things work
- A strong and disciplined work ethic

Viralstyle (https://viralstyle.workable.com/jobs/111440)

Senior Front End Developer

We like to work with people who are like us: driven, career-focused over-achievers that enjoy recognition and are willing to challenge themselves in order to attain it.

You should be a confident self-starting individual with the following skills and experience:

- Expert knowledge of HTML5 and CSS3
- Strong JavaScript knowledge
- Experience with Javascript MV* frameworks such as AngularJS, Ember, Knockout, or Backbone
- Able to set up a local PHP environment, including setting up Laravel and working knowledge of Blade templating
- Familiar with Social media API's (FB, Twitter, Instagram, Pinterest) and integrating them into web projects
- Comfortable with version control systems – Git
- Extensive experience with object-oriented design and programming
- Proficient at analyzing, decomposing and solving problems
- Sound judgment and direction in work prioritization

Highly desirable additional skills:

- eCommerce development experience
- Development of Retail or CRM systems
- Experience in UX (User Experience) Design/Development

We value attitude, adaptability and aptitude over experience, if you do not have the experience outlined but think you can do this role tell us why you should be considered in your application.

WEBSITE/MOBILE INTERNET SITE TESTING

Analysia (http://www.analysia.com/user.asp)

Get paid to test out websites. Simply fill out the user registration form and wait to be contacted by email for tasks. Each task will require you to read the instructions, complete the set task on the website, and record your session. Tests usually take between 10 – 15 minutes and pay $10 per test. Payments are made via PayPal.

You will be asked to read some instructions and complete task on a website, this session will be recorded, your screen and audio will be saved. It typically takes about 15 minutes.

Anybody with an Internet connection and a microphone qualifies, we accept a good variety of users from many locations and many different profiles.

You will get paid $10 for each test. We will send you a payment via "PAYPAL"

You will get an email from us when we need you to complete a task

This opportunity is very popular! Getting paid $10 for just a few minutes, many testers want that and statistically, they are less customers than testers.

So you cannot expect to do a test per day. It will depend about your profile as some company needs specific tester profile. But being on the target profile, you can be invited to do a few test per months!

Enroll (http://www.enrollapp.com/)

See what real companies are working on right now and let them know what you think! You'll be the first to get sneak peeks behind the screen.

Take user tests on any device: phones, tablets, desktops----whatever you prefer!

Earn rewards: Collect badges and get compensated for each test conveniently via PayPal.

Change the Web: Be a part of the Internet's next revolution. Help good ideas happen, make suggestions, and stop bad ones in their tracks.

Feedback Army (http://www.feedbackarmy.com/)

Make money answering questions about various websites. Tests consist of 10 questions. If you'd like to work for Feedback Army, you'll need to sign up through Amazon Mechanical Turk. After you complete your task through Amazon Mechanical Turk, the requester will approve your work, and your money will be deposited into your Amazon Payment account.

StartUpLift (http://startuplift.com/get-paid-to-provide-feedback/)
Type of micro job: Remote website tester
Pays in USD in PayPal weekly

Testers are paid $10 to spend 10-20 minutes on a website using a screen and voice recorder and giving feedback. Mobile tests pay $15. Jobs are made available based on the demographics of the tester.

Try My Ui (http://www.trymyui.com/)

Earn $10 for 15 – 20 minutes of your time. To become part of the Try-MyUI team first sign up for an account. Next you'll need to take and pass a qualification test. The qualification test is a sample test that shows you understand the process and requirements. After you qualify you'll be sent test opportunities via email. Payments are made biweekly via PayPal.

Userfeel.com

(http://www.userfeel.com/index.php?option=com_content&view=article&id=9&Itemid=23&lang=en&hide=1&utm_expid=32266794-0.QdRzIADkRruvRlxpPKPF_w.1)

He or she conducts a usability test on a site to reveal usability problems on the client's sites.

A good Tester can provide useful information on a site's usability. In a few words:

- Speak her thoughts on the microphone.
- Tell us what confuses him, and what attracts his attention.
- Explain what and why she does what she does on the site.
- Propose something that would help him perform the required task.
- Provide useful comments.
- Perform the required tasks according to the test scenario.
- Speak loudly and clearly on the microphone.
- Thoroughly answer the questions in writing, at the end of the test.

For each test you conduct after the initial sample test, you get paid $10 at the end of each week, via PayPal. The amount of money you can earn depends on how well you speak your thoughts into the microphone, and how useful your usability remarks can be. Also, the amount of tests you get assigned depends on the amount of orders we have. For each test you perform, you get rated by the site's owner. Your overall rating determines the amount of tests you'll be assigned. Anyhow, we don't suggest quitting your regular job, but good testers can earn up to $100-$200 per month.

Userlytics (http:www.userlytics.com/tester)

Userlytics is a highly recognized and respected website usability testing company. Top businesses and well-known websites companies are clients of Userlytics. Seeking the viewpoint of the average online user,

Userlytics clients are able to gain a better knowledge of whether they have a user-friendly website. Because clients of Userlytics are interested in the perspective of everyday people, Userlytics allows anyone to become a tester for their clients!

What Do Userlytics Testers Do?
Based on the demographic information provided by Userlytics testers, a variety of assignments may be available. Using Userlytics downloadable program, testers can check the availability of open tests. When one is available, Userlytics testers can choose to start the test. The program window will open the client's website and provide a set of tasks and instructions.
For instance, if such said company, XYZ.com sells alphabet toys, they may be interested in knowing how easy it is for their visitors to find the cost of ABC building blocks. Therefore, the type of tasks may be to search the site for ABC building blocks and locate the price. The Userlytics program records the actions taking place during the test.
Testers are also recorded visually and through audio. It is important for testers to think aloud. Clients of Userlytics want to see and hear the reactions and the thinking process of the testers. Remember, the goal of Userlytics is to project the average online user's experience.

How Does Userlytics Pay?
Userlytics pays through PayPal within two weeks of completing each test. Every test that is completed within the guidelines given pays a generous $10. Each test takes no more than 10 minutes to complete, making the pay well worth the time.

What Are Userlytics Requirements?
Because Userlytics uses both Audio and Visual responses in formatting a user's experience, testers need both a microphone and a webcam. Additionally, a user will need to download Userlytics software, which is quick and easy. Testers with Windows operating system will need to have XP or higher (XP/Vista/7) or Mac users will need Leopard 10.5 or newer. Finally, at least 200 MB of free hard disk space is required. Userlytics looks for people of all demographics and computer experience.

How Can I Sign Up To Be a Tester for Userlytics?
Because Userlytics needs to provide feedback to their clients that include user experience from a range of types of people, anyone who meets the above

requirements can work for Userlytics! There is no application approval process, just sign up! Simply visit http://www.userlytics.com/tester/ and register.

User Testing (https://www.usertesting.com/be-a-user-tester)

Pay is $10 per test. You do not need a web cam with this company.

U Test (https://www.utest.com/)

Join the world's largest community for software testers. Gain access to paid testing projects from brands like Google, HBO, Amazon and more.

Uxline (https://www.uxline.com/team/join)

Make $10 for completing 5 website tasks and answering 5 written questions. Just register as a user, complete a qualification test, and once approved wait for assignments to be sent via email. Payments are made to PayPal within 15 days.

Validately (https://validately.com/panel_signup)

Validately hires testers to complete mobile and website tests for companies. Compensation varies: Complete a 5-minute test and get paid $5 bucks. Live tests where you speak via phone and share a screen with a moderator pay a minimum of $25 for 30 minutes. Payments are made via PayPal within 5 business days of the test.

What Users Do (http://whatusersdo.com/panel/)

Get paid to give feedback on our clients' websites. Use your own computer from home. Our software records your screen and spoken thoughts. Pay is up to $8 per test.

YouEye (http://join.youeye.com/participant-101/)

Online usability studies are an easy way to earn money from home. You'll be asked to perform simple tasks on a website, such as signing up for an account or adding an item to your shopping cart.

Desktop
You must be 18 years or older and speak English fluently
The current minimum system requirements are Mac with OS X 10.7 or
higher or PC with Windows Vista, Service Pack II or higher
You must have access to a webcam and microphone
You must have a fast internet connection - DSL or faster
You must be able to follow instructions

Mobile
You must be 18 years older and speak English fluently
You must have a mobile device with a front facing camera
You must have iOS 6.1 or higher
You must have Android 2.3 or higher
You must have Wifi connectivity or cellular connectivity (WiFi preferred)

WRITING/EDITING

About.com (http://experts.about.com/)

Those freelancers who are most successful writing for About.com are highly
skilled, self-motivated, and experienced web content creators with a deep
passion for their topic area and impeccable journalistic integrity. They create original and easy-to-consume articles to meet the diverse needs that arise
in readers' everyday lives; are able to produce content on a regular basis on
their own time; and have the entrepreneurial spirit and conviction necessary
to build independently upon their expertise and authority.

About.com contracts with more than 100 experts in many different fields.
They write online content from home and are paid a minimum based on the
number of articles they create. However, compensation increases with page
view growth.

allcustomcontent.com
(http://www.allcustomcontent.com/work-from-home/)
We are currently looking for serious-minded freelancers to provide assistance in our growing content providing and transcribing business.
We are currently looking for talented and detail-oriented writers with an
excellent command of the written English language.

Positions Available: Freelance positions ghostwriting articles, reports, e-books and other content. We are also looking for writers to be able to rewrite transcriptions and other documents to put them in a useable format for end-users.

Potential for Growth: There may be future opportunities to become a Senior Writer or a Team Leader. Both positions include more available work and increased rates of pay.

Writing Skills & Qualifications: Please read through these qualifications to ensure this position is right for you.

- Some experience: It is not required that you have written as a professional or freelance writer for clients before. We are more concerned with quality writing and will ask you to conduct a writing exercise during the application process.
- Research Skills: Your writing projects will, in some cases, require initial research and will be focused on topics easily searched for on the Internet. More technical writing will only be provided to you if you indicate you already have a knowledge base in that particular area.
- Ability to Adjust Writing Style: The projects you receive will range from formal to casual writing styles. You must be able to adapt to those styles where required and outlined in each project description.
- Ability to Learn Industry Jargon: Writing projects will be on a number of different topics. You don't need to understand all jargon prior to starting, but you will need to be able to research terminology or ask for help, when needed.
- Nonfiction Writing Only: We are only looking for nonfiction writers to write and rewrite informational content. We are not looking for fiction writing at this time.

General Skills and Attributes You Must Have:

- Detail Oriented: You will be responsible for editing and proofreading your work prior to submission and must pay close attention to details.
- Be Willing to Accept Constructive Feedback: To provide the best service possible to our clients and in order to keep bringing you more work, you must be able to accept and adapt to the constructive feedback provided to you.

- Excellent Communication Skills: As a freelancer, you will be in regular communication with your Team Leader who is responsible for timely and quality service delivery to our clients. Your communication must facilitate this process for your Team Leader.

- Commitment to Quality Client Service: You must respect deadlines and complete projects that you accept from us.

- Maintain Confidentiality: Client confidentiality is of utmost importance in working with All Custom Content. Any breach of confidentiality will result in the termination of your contract.

Allvoices (www.allvoices.com)

Writers are paid based on the performance of their "brand" or page views of the news content they write. Payment is based on page views and contributors are paid in minimum $100 increments.

As the world's premier platform for citizen journalism, Allvoices is committed to delivering a community-driven platform for open, global news and idea exchange. In support of this mission, Allvoices:

Empowers contributors around the world to share news and views

Fosters an engaged community of contributors and audience members who value critical thinking and intelligent discourse while remaining respectful of one another rewards contributors financially for the page views their content generates in a regular and reliable fashion delivers technology solutions that help contributors gain exposure and build a following provides contributors with resources to help their stories stand out, including licensed photos, writing tips from other members of the community and social media tools helps contributors improve their writing voice and gain valuable experience and mentoring by enabling mentoring exchanges with other contributors. Responds quickly and effectively to users' flags of inappropriate content.

Article world.net
(http://www.articleworld.net/pages/Author-Guidelines)

A website company that promotes freelance writers and publishers.

Articlesmasters.com
(http://articlesmasters.com/the-writers-at-content-writing-services)

The writers at content writing services follow certain specific formats, such as 12pt Times New Roman font, double spacing and one inch margins on all sides. These are the requirements of most academic assignments and are in accordance with APA formatting. The versatility in prices at content writing services offers clients the option to choose a payment plan that fulfills their requirements.

Writers generally post their sample writings at content writing services or when they apply for a specific job to ensure the client that they have relevant experience. The client can also ask for a sample article or a small portion of their writing project before they hire a writer so that there is better understanding of what each side needs in terms of writing, format, vocabulary and style.

ArticleZ.com (http://www.articlez.com/)

A website company that allows articles to be submitted as a means to drive traffic to website.

Blogmutt.com (https://www.blogmutt.com/pages/writer)

Blogmutt serves businesses that have websites with blogs, and the people there just don't have the time or writing talent to fill up that blog them.

Our system is more straightforward than any of the content farms:

1. You write posts for businesses.
2. If they like and use those posts then you get paid.

The customers get their pick of posts, but they have an ongoing need for original content, so even if your post doesn't get used the first week, most posts eventually get picked. Our acceptance rate right now is at about 90 percent.

We also give you tools so you will have the best opportunity to write posts that our customers will love.

Within the Blogmutt platform we have a point system. You earn points for posting, for posts that get picked and for a variety of other internal goals. As you earn points you move up in levels. At certain levels you earn status, such as an exclusive, invite-only LinkedIn honor for success as a professional writer. At higher levels you'll become part of an elite group of writers that gets access to higher-paying work.

Caption Colorado
(http://www.captioncolorado.com/captioning-careers)

Caption Colorado offers full and part-time captioning positions and a world where competitive rates, flexible hours, technical support, 401K, flex spending accounts, health/dental/vision and training are all available from the comfort and convenience of your home. And, on top of that, wouldn't it be great to know that what you do every day has tremendous value and purpose.

Our captioners deliver the missing soundtrack and provide access to what's happening in the world, and you can too! Trading in your shoes may be easier than you think…

Am I ready to be a Caption Colorado Realtime Captioner?
You're Ready if You Are…
A clean, complete, and consistent writer with 98+% accuracy.
A writer who is conflict-free and uses prefixes, suffixes, etc. in your writing style.
A team player who is able to work within Caption Colorado's policies, procedures, and guidelines.
A reliable and punctual person who is dedicated to delivering exceptional customer service.

A writer who actively seeks ways to develop and maintain superior real time captioning skills through self-correcting, continuing education, and a willingness to give, receive, and incorporate feedback…..then apply.

Your application will be screened and selected candidates will be invited to take a real time assessment, which consists of a 30 minute local news program. When an opening becomes available, candidates with the top assessment scores will be interviewed and candidate selection will be based on the assessment score and the final interview. Assessments are reviewed on the basis of keystroke accuracy, conflicts, word boundary problems, overall flow, completeness, and comprehensibility. Candidates may be asked to complete more than one assessment.

ChaCha (http://becomeaguide.chacha.com/)

Like a search engine but with live work-at-home guides answering the questions, ChaCha pays per answer, which it says averages out to $3-9 per hour.

Constant-content.com
(https://www.constant-content.com/area/registerauthor.htm)

Constant-Content attracts professional Web content writers who care about quality and uniqueness as much as you do. With strict quality controls in place, we are able to offer custom content writing services and a huge catalog of Web content and articles written by writers who thoroughly know their craft.

All content writers must pass a screening quiz before their work will be considered. From there, every article and every page of website content submitted undergoes an extensive editorial review. Content writers must consistently submit quality Internet content in order to remain a part of our article writing service. With extensive editorial guidelines and high writing standards in place, only those with exceptional article writing skills and a commitment to providing unique, original content make the cut.

The Content Authority (http://thecontentauthority.com/)

The Content Authority, commonly referred to as TCA, is very similar to Textbroker in terms of topics and pay rates. They also have four tiers of writers with rates ranging from $.007 per word to $.03 per word. The minimum amount earned for payout is higher, at $25, but the pay is still weekly. They pay each Monday via PayPal.

Contently.com (https://contently.com/journalists)

A website company that promotes freelance writers and publishers.

Copypress.com (http://community.copypress.com/work-with-us/)

CopyPress Community is place where creatives' collaborate and work together. CopyPress frequently works with certified marketers on a variety of paid assignments in the following departments:

Writing

CopyPress utilizes a team of trained writers to produce large scale, quality-content campaigns for clients in a variety of industries.

We are always accepting applications from writers interested in receiving paid assignments. All CopyPress writers must:

- Have a high-level knowledge of grammar and writing mechanics
- Have a strong command of the English language
- Be able to construct clear, well-written copy
- Be able to follow directions to accomplish defined editorial objectives
- Be reliable and dependable

Design

CopyPress utilizes a team of talented designers to produce infographics, videos, and illustrations for a variety of industries and platforms.

We are looking to add talented designers to our team. If you are a designer, artist, videographer, or illustrator interested in producing high-quality online media, we want you on our team. CopyPress Community is a learning center, training facility, multimedia educational portal, all rolled into one. This free training portal is for all online marketers (writers, designers, publishers, and everything in between) who want to join the Content Revolution.

CyberEdit, Inc. - ResumeEdge.com
(http://www.writejobs.info/2012/03/freelance-writing-cyber-edit-resume.html)

Job Description: Professional resume writers and editors wanted for all shifts, including weekend work -- Friday - Sunday

* Make $35 and upper job
* Work From Home From Anywhere in the World
* Telecommute
* Choose Your Hours (10 - 40 hours per week)
* You Can Begin Now

Creative writing talent wanted. ResumeEdge writers work from their own home or office from anywhere in the world via the Internet 7 days a week.

You would help our IT, Engineering, and tech industry clients write and edit their resumes and cover letters using their existing resumes and cover letters (if available), a phone conversation (we pay for the calls), and information submitted over online forms. This is challenging work requiring a strong knowledge of the IT & Engineering fields.

ResumeEdge provides the resume writing services to thousands of sites, including The Wall Street Journal`s Career Journal, Lycos, SallieMae, and Wet Feet. We are the net's premier resume writing service because of our talented resume writers.

Education: College Degree (or equivalent work experience) in IT (all fields) and/or Engineering (all fields), and/or tech industry (all fields).

EXPERIENCE: REQUIREMENTS

- 2 + years professional experience
- BA or higher (or equivalent professional experience)
- Ability to meet/beat deadlines
- Certified Professional Resume Writers (CPRW) and Nationally Certified Resume Writers (NCRW) are preferred
- Expert in MS Word

Please do not apply unless you have knowledge and/or experience in the IT, Engineering fields or the tech industry and are an expert in Word. Writers with weekend availability are also preferred.

Hours: 10 - 50 hours per week. Flexible Hours.

Salary: $35 and more per job

How To Apply: To apply, please submit your resume (in Word as an attachment, no pdfs, please), cover letter, and one `before` and `after` example of a resume you have edited or written (if available) using this link.

After we review your material, we will email selected applicants with one test resume that requires editing and allows us to make final decisions. Given the large number of applicants, we ask that you please not follow up regarding this job by phone or email until you are selected to take the test.

To begin application process, please submit your resume here.

Please only use the above link to submit your information.

Compensation: $35 and more per job

Ecopywriters.com
(http://www.ecopywriters.com/about/employment.html)

ECOPYWRITERS prides itself on hiring only the very best talent. Our company is made up of a vast network of freelance copywriters and our operations team located in San Diego, California.
Our standard employment package includes a base salary plus a discretionary performance bonus. Additionally, we provide health insurance and three weeks paid vacation per year for salaried employees.

Edit Fast (http://editfast.com/english/editjobs.htm)

We need you because you are a skilled proofreader, editor, or writer. Edit Fast takes pride in the quality of the work we do and in the speed of our editors. We want the best!

This is a freelance opportunity. We cannot guarantee that there will be work available, but if you have the qualifications Edit Fast's clients are looking for, and if you are patient, there may be projects for you in the future. You should be aware; however, that Edit Fast has no obligation to provide work for you now or at any time in the future. Completing the registration process and passing the Edit Fast review does not necessarily mean you will receive projects. It simply means you are eligible to receive projects and your Web page is available for Edit Fast's clients to view and perhaps choose you as their editor. If you are selected for a project by a client or by the Edit Fast administration you will be notified and that project will be directed to you.

Only those editors who's Web pages have been activated are eligible to receive New Project Notifications. For those who are not successful, all information connected to your email address will be deleted, and notification of this will be sent (This can take anywhere from one day to two weeks).

Examiner (http://www.examiner.com/About_Examiner)

Writing jobs at Examiner.com are for writers with insights and knowledge about local events and communities in topics ranging from sports and parenting to food and green living. Pay is based on the size of your readership.

Families.com
(http://www.families.com/become-a-blogger)

A Families.com Blogger is a paid professional writer who posts regularly on a given topic. A Families.com Blogger writes articles with a minimum of 300 words. Bloggers can blog for many different topics–as long as they have the expertise to write in that subject area.

A Families.com Blogger must be versatile, creative, experienced and well informed on their chosen topic. They must have a solid grasp of the English language and be able to edit their own work as well as take the direction of an editor.

Families.com is the blog network for family topics. We currently have more than 30 blogs on topics such as parenting, marriage, family fun, frugal living, and home & garden. Incomplete applications will not be considered, so please see below for exactly what should be included in your application package. Applications are accepted on an ongoing basis, however, we generally do not have immediate openings. When we have an opening, we look for the best qualified writer for the position.
What Do You Get by Writing for Families.com?

The opportunity to share your passion, to be published and to have your voice heard by large numbers of readers.

We take care of the technology, hosting, graphic design and marketing. There are no fees to you.

We will cross-promote your blog on Families.com.

We pay $4 per blog entry (There is a 90 day training period). We give annual raises, up to $5.50.

Bloggers are eligible for quarterly bonuses based on their performance.

What is Required of Families.com Bloggers?

- The Families.com blogs will only be as good as our bloggers. We are looking for amazing bloggers who can write passionate, high-quality, interesting, and thought-provoking articles.

- Some of our bloggers write 100+ posts per month while others only update their blog once or twice per week. How many posts you are able to write depends on the blog you are writing for. We do expect our bloggers to commit to their assignments and communicate with the editor should there be an issue in getting them done.

- Entries should be at least 300 words, but can be much longer. A post could include a tip or idea, a top 10 list, a story or quote, "how-tos", demos, photos, essays, or a product or entertainment review. The important thing is that whatever material you write is informative and/or entertaining for our readers.

- Review comments to your blog entries, delete inappropriate comments and respond to comments where appropriate.

- Avoid topics that are not appropriate for the Families.com family-values centric audience, such as drug and alcohol abuse, profanity, gambling, pornography, extramarital sex, and nudity, except in the context of helping families to overcome these issues. There is definitely a place in the blogs for PG-rated discussions of intimacy and sexuality in marriage; however, these blogs are not the appropriate place for sensualized sexuality. Do not use the blog to advocate for a specific political party, religion, alternative lifestyle, abortion, etc. Please see us if you feel an exception needs to be made to this rule. It is appropriate to talk about faith and spirituality without advocating for a specific religion, or to talk about advocating for families without endorsing specific political candidates and parties.

- Successfully complete Families.com Blogger Training and a 90 day probationary period. Then, continue to maintain a high quality of blog posts and work well with the Families.com team.

We are looking for bloggers who are self-motivated, who have expertise in their topic, and who can add personality to their blog.

How Do I Apply to Be a Families.com Blogger?

- Select a Topic – Select 1 to 3 topics either from our list of current topics or topics you feel would add value to our community for which you would like to write. We do consider adding new blogs occasionally. PLEASE NOTE THE TOPIC(S) IN YOUR SUBJECT LINE.

- Samples – Please send two sample blogs. They should be related to your topics. If you have noted 3 topics, we still only need two samples. Samples should be at least 300 words long and give us a feel for your writing voice. Note: Please write an original sample related to your topic choice. We do not look at links in lieu of samples. (Additional information about the hiring process is on the website)

Funds for Writers (http://fundsforwriters.com/submissions/)

Freelance Submission Process for FundsforWriters
Articles should fall between 500 and 600 words. Why so short? Writers look to FFW for sources. So each FundsforWriters newsletter lists only one article – short and sweet and to the point. That leaves more space for awards, contests, grants and markets. So make each word count. MAKE YOUR WRITING TIGHT. Watch the passive voice.

NOTE: The newsletter is booked through January 2016. We never close the door to submissions, but we are very particular now, and just know that any pieces we purchase will appear in a 2016 edition of FundsforWriters.

If you are up to it, we'd like to hear about your success, thought and/or advice about some aspect of earning funds through writing. Resources with links are much desired.

We do NOT want stories about…

- how to write
- how to develop plot, characters or settings
- topics that cannot relate in some manner to making more money as a writer

We DO want…

- ideas on breaking into a particular market
- pointers on winning contests
- unique ways to develop an income with words
- success stories with ideas for others
- profitable business practices related to writing
- seasonal material affiliated with particular markets
- grant success stories
- nonprofit partnerships
- unique markets
- unusual writing income ideas
- anything to help a writer make a dollar penning words
- a dash of humor, if possible; a positive note and a happy ending

Hint: List markets with links, and we'll look even harder at your submission! Our readers like to walk away with tools to use. DO NOT USE WORDS IN ALL CAPS. Do not query in smartphone text-ese. Your introduction is as important as your submission.

Query or Manuscript:
We accept either one, but to save you time and trouble, you might want to query unless you are pretty sure about the topic after reading Funds-forWriters for a while!

Payment:
Via PayPal – $50 for unpublished original articles; $15 for reprints.
Via check – $45 for unpublished articles; $10 for reprints.

Please indicate which you are submitting. If a reprint, list where and when the piece was published. Payment made when article is accepted, usually within a week of submission. Please do not email and ask when we will get to your piece.

FFW purchases one time electronic rights and archival rights in the newsletters' archives. Occasionally an exceptional piece may be listed on the website under Latest FFW Tips. After publication in the newsletter, you may resell your article after 30 days. FFW purchases articles for use often three to six months downstream. Please do not ask when it will be published as the editor retains the right to move articles around due to unforeseen circumstances.

Final Manuscript:
When you submit the manuscript, include:

- word count
- title
- piece
- a brief bio at the end to include your website/blog
- how you'd like to be paid – PayPal or check. Tell FFW either the email address for PayPal or the postal address for the check omitting any of the above can result in rejection.

Email:
We prefer all submission by email and WITHOUT attachments unless you are given the nod to send an attachment. Submit your manuscript to hope@fundsforwriters.com

Helium Network (https://www.heliumnetwork.com)

We match you to freelance assignments that are right for you. Qualified writers, editors and fact-checkers work on a wide range of projects through RRD Content Source. Freelance professionals like you provide content for newsletters, articles, blogs, retail product descriptions, customer websites and more. Our clients range from major newspapers and national department store chains to small businesses and local or niche publications.

Hirewriters.com (http://www.hirewriters.com/signup/writer)

If English is your first language, join HireWriters.com today for FREE and you will have access to HUNDREDS of paid writing jobs. Clients post writing assignments and you can then accept the job and get paid when you complete it!

Hub Pages (http://hubpages.com/)

HubPages bills itself as the "leading online publishing ecosystem." Writers sign up and publish their work. Revenue from Adsense and affiliates is split with HubPages, which receives a 40 percent share.

Interact Media (http://www.interactmedia.com)

Interact Media has several more levels, each with higher pay rates. They range from $.007 cent to $.16 per word. They pay via PayPal twice per month on the 1st and 15th. The most glaring difference between Interact Media and Textbroker is that the editors only review your first article, after that all reviews and even ratings come from the clients. The rating system is similar, from 1 to 5 stars. Also, clients have the option of offering "tips" for material they consider to be worthy of more than the price originally charged.

International Living
(http://internationalliving.com/about-il/write-for-il/)

> We know from experience that there are a host of places around the world that are cheaper, healthier, safer and freer than you ever thought possible.
>
> **Can you write about them for us?** You read about one side of the world in your daily paper, you see it on TV newscasts. Murders. Wars. Airplane crashes. Politics. But there is another side of the world…one you can't find out about by reading the paper, certainly not by watching TV. It is a world of delightful opportunities for fun…pleasure… financial security and profits…romantic discoveries…adventure… It is

a world full of things you can do to make your life more fun—and more profitable.

Write for *International Living*'s Daily Postcards

Every day, *International Living*'s Daily Postcards bring stories from expats around the world to readers. If we use your postcard, we will pay you a one-time rate of $75, including any photos you may wish to include. (Please note: photos are not a requirement.) But before you submit an idea to us, familiarize yourself with the style and subject matter of the postcards by signing up at the website.

Who can write for us?

If you're an expat living overseas, we want to hear from you. Don't worry if you're not the new Hemingway—we're not just looking for professional writers (though professional writers are encouraged to get in touch, too). We're more interested in *what* you have to say than how you say it.

What are we looking for?

We want to hear *your* story—whatever that may be.

Imagine you're talking to your friends back home. What do you want to tell them about your experience overseas? What are the most important things you can tell someone about your life in another country?

Some writers have told our readers about how and why they chose their new overseas destination. Many tell us about the magnificent homes they have bought or built, about the cost of living, the rich culture of their new hometowns, and the warm and friendly communities. Some have told us about how they availed of low-cost health care, or discovered secret slices of paradise...

Some tell our readers quirkier stories. Like the one about how experts in Cuenca, Ecuador are effortlessly shrinking their waistlines and dropping to a healthier weight. Or like the one from Lynne Martin who, along with her husband Tim, sold everything she owned to roam the world.

Whatever it is that makes you happy in your new life, sum it up—in 500-600 words.

To submit your ideas email: *postcards@internationalliving.com*

Internet Brands (http://www.internetbrands.com/ib/careersdivision/)

Internet media company that operates community and e-commerce web sites in the automotive, careers, home, shopping, and travel and leisure categories hires telecommuting writers and editors.

Iwriter.com (http://www.iwriter.com/signup.php)

iWriter pays up to $15 for each accepted post. That may seem small, but they aren't as strict as many of the others above and they also allow you to pick exactly what you write. You can write as many or as few articles as you want.

A List Apart (http://alistapart.com/about/contribute)

A List Apart pays $200 for each accepted post. They're not first on the list, because they tend to publish less articles, which means you have a smaller chance of getting accepted. Same guidelines as above, 1,500 word minimum.

We're always looking for new authors. If you've got an idea that will challenge our readers and move our industry forward, we want to hear about it. But you don't need to wait for an idea that will *redefine web design*. Just aim to bring readers a fresh perspective on a topic that's keeping you up at night.

We'll be honest, though: writing for *ALA* takes work. We want your article to be at its best, and we'll push you to get there. You'll get extensive feedback from our team, and you'll work closely with an editor on revisions.

It's also rewarding. Thousands of your peers (and potential employers, clients, or publishers) will read your work, and you'll also learn a lot in the process—about communicating your ideas, about writing, and even about the topic you thought you already knew when you started.

We pay $200 per article, typically within a month of publication.

What we publish

We accept submissions for original, feature-length articles only (not blog posts or columns). These typically run between 1,500 and 2,000 words. We do not publish anything that's been published elsewhere (including on your blog).

You may submit a rough draft, a partial draft, or a short pitch (a paragraph or two summarizing your argument and why it's important to our readers) paired with an outline. The more complete your submission is, the better feedback we can give you.

Before you submit, look at our style guide and recent articles for insight into structuring and formatting your piece, and make sure your submission:

- Offers a clear argument, not just a list of tips and tricks.
- Has a voice. Be bold, interesting, and human.
- Is written for an audience of designers, developers, content strategists, information architects, or similar.
- Is supported with convincing arguments, not just opinions. Fact-check, and cite sources where appropriate.
- Follows our style guide.

See our article, "Writing is Thinking," for help in the writing process.

How to submit (and what happens next)

Email us your submission. We *prefer submissions as Google documents*, so that editors can easily provide feedback and guidance within your draft. You may also send us a link to an HTML file (please do not send a .zip of assets unless requested by an editor), a plain text file, or a markdown file.

Here's what happens after you hit send:

- An editor will review your submission and determine whether it's a potential fit. If so, the whole team will review and discuss it. This typically happens once a week.
- The editor will collect the team's feedback and get back to you with notes. (We rarely accept an article on the first draft, but we'll tell you if we're interested.)

- Once you've addressed our comments, you'll send your revised draft back. We'll discuss it again and let you know if it's accepted.

- If we accept your article, an editor will work closely with you on issues like organization, argumentation, and style.

- We'll schedule you for an upcoming issue as soon as revisions are complete. We can't promise inclusion in a specific issue until we have a nearly publication-ready article.

List Verse (http://listverse.com/write-get-paid/)

We will pay you $100 for your efforts. You don't need to be an expert—you just need to have great English, a sense of humor, and a love for things unusual or interesting.

It works like this: You write your list (1,500 words/10 items minimum), you send it in, we reply and say "Great—we'll publish it" and send you $100 by PayPal (don't have an account? just make one—it's easy and free) or Bitcoin; or we reply and say "Sorry—it isn't the sort of thing our readers will love—give it another shot."

Either way you win—your list will be read by us and reviewed, and if it's amazing it will appear on the front page of Listverse to be read by over 15 million people a month!

The rules are really pretty simple. As long as your list (and we do mean yours—don't steal other people's stuff) is over 1,500 words you can choose any topic you like. We also need you to link to reputable sources (see Section 7 for more details) so we can verify what you're saying. Just remember—if it's good enough to publish (by our standards) you get 100 bucks—simple as that.

To help you out with some ideas, the lists that our readers love the most (and the ones we will most likely pay for) are usually offbeat, looking at something normal in an unexpected way (ways college makes you dumb, for example), hidden knowledge (things most people don't know), misconceptions, facts, and just really good general knowledge about anything—science, for example.

Oh—and there's one more thing: If you have a blog, a Twitter account, or a book you want to promote, mention it in the submissions form and we will stick it at the bottom of your list.

Mahalo (http://blog.mahalo.com/careers/)

Mahalo calls itself "a human-powered search engine dedicated to delivering carefully curated search results featuring the highest quality, spam-free links available." It hires freelance writers for $10-12 an hour for a minimum of 20 hours a week to fulfill this mission.

Matador Network
(http://matadornetwork.com/content/about/jobs/)

Matador seeks original writing, photography, and video that speaks to the adventures, cultures, and identities of people around the world.

1. Familiarize yourself with what we like to publish by spending time on the site before submitting.

2. Avoid submitting on specific topics or story angles we've already published. Use the search function in the navbar above to review existing content.

3. Publishing rights – read our full Author's Rights.

4. Payment – standard payment is $40, depending on article type and length. (Higher rates may be offered in special circumstances; please note this is determined on a case-by-case basis.) Payments are made via Paypal[1] the first week of each month for all content published by the 21st of the previous month.

Sending in your draft

1. Send an original draft (max 1500 words). Check spelling, punctuation, grammar, and facts. Submissions sent with numerous errors are unprofessional and will not be considered for publication.

2. Please do NOT embed photos in your submission document; simply indicate that photos are available upon request. If submitting a photo essay or other image-based piece, provide a link to a Flickr gallery or other URL where the images are viewable.

3. Submissions received without all accompanying info requested on the submission form will not be considered.

4. Because of the high volume of submissions we receive, we can't guarantee a response if we've decided your piece isn't a good fit. Please don't take it personally — and after a month or two, feel free to submit something else.

Matador Network

(http://matadornetwork.com/content/about/jobs/visual-content-editor-producer/)

Visual Content Editor / Producer (http://matadornetwork.com/content/about/jobs/visual-content-editor-producer/)

Matador is bringing on a new visual content editor / producer. This is a highly creative position with the following KPIs:

1. How many stories you produce (individually and via soliciting other media creators)–and how efficiently,
2. The social engagement your stories generate,
3. The number of new media producers you bring on / work with as regular contributors.

An ideal candidate will be an action-taker, an excellent communicator, and someone with a demonstrated track record of hustling in the media industry to produce stories and network with relevant media outlets and other producers.

All candidates must:

-   Be a self-starter animal — a doer, no hand-holding required
-   Be in a US (Eastern through Pacific) Time Zone at least 3 weeks / month (i.e. extended travels disqualify you from this position)
-   Be working or have worked as a professional shooter and/or editor professionally
-   Have a strong vision for visual storytelling as demonstrated by their work in travel / culture / lifestyle
-   Have an active social media presence and incorporate this work into your channels

- Be excited about working with and helping mentor young, up-and-coming media producers

Commitment & Compensation: ~20 hrs./week, hourly depending on candidate. This is a remote-based, independent-contractor position. The chosen candidate will have a one-month trial period.

Video Producer (http://matadornetwork.com/content/about/jobs/video-producer/)

Matador Network is hiring for a part-time video producer to work primarily on our branded-content team.

This person must have experience in:

- Scouting shooting locations via phone and internet research
- Applying for filming permits
- Researching locals to use as on-camera talent
- Booking flights, hotels, rental cars, etc.

This person is:

- A self-starter animal — a doer, no hand-holding required
- A critical thinker and problem solver who always finds a way
- A 3rd-degree black belt at using Google to find very specific things, places, people
- Based in the US with a US cell phone in a US time zone
- Someone with sales experience ++
- Someone with event-planning experience ++
- Someone who will not lose their cool when dealing with difficult clients, talent, and subcontractors

Video Editor (http://matadornetwork.com/content/about/jobs/video-editor/)

Matador Network seeks a skilled, versatile video editor to assist our creative director with video projects. A successful candidate will be able to work under the creative director's lead to turn raw video into finished, story-driven videos of varying length and style. From epic drone footage of exotic destinations to short, snappy Facebook videos, we want a video editor who is capable of editing in a variety of styles.

A huge bonus if you're good with AfterEffects.

In addition to editing, this position will be expected to communicate with subcontractors, collect signed agreements and work on special projects as needed.

This is a remote-based (in the US strongly preferred), independent-contractor position estimated at 40 hours/month. Pay is per video or hourly, depending on the candidate. We're a travel and adventure website, so interest in travel sure helps around here.

Is this you? Please email your resume, at least three examples of your work and salary requirements.

Morningside Partners (http://www.fdch.com/careers.html)

News Transcript Copy Editor
Full-time editorial positions are currently available with the Network News department at Morningside Partners. Copy edit verbatim transcripts for media clients such as CNN, FOX and MSNBC. Ability to work independently and meet deadlines a must. Strong problem-solving skills and ability to professionally work with clients in a fast-paced environment required. Evening hours. Bachelor's degree in English or journalism and at least one year of experience required. News sense and knowledge of AP style a plus. Lanham, Maryland, location; own transportation required. Please send cover letter and resume pasted into the body of an email to Careers @ ascllc.net.
Attachments will not be opened. Please include "News Copy Editor" in the subject line and WPM typing speed in your cover letter.

Editor/Proofreader
Part-time, entry-level positions for copy editors/proofreaders are currently available with the WordXpress Department with Morningside Partners, LLC. Bachelor's degree in English or journalism and/or at least one year of experience preferred, but qualified college students are encouraged to apply. Day, evening and weekend scheduling

available. Knowledge of AP style a plus. Please send résumé to Careers @ ascllc.net.

Financial Editor

Experienced editor with strong online research skills. Related coursework or experience required. English/Journalism degree preferred. Flexible hrs. QUALIFIED applicants should send résumé and cover letter to Careers @ ascllc.net.

Penny Hoarder

(http://www.thepennyhoarder.com/contributor-guidelines/)

We're looking for freelance writers that have fun, unique ideas for earning, saving or investing money. We'd love to hear your personal experience, especially if you can share detailed numbers, strategies and advice.

Do you have a story to share or an idea we haven't covered? Get in touch with TPH Editor Heather at editor@thepennyhoarder.com.We're also hiring full-time writers and editors; see the job descriptions for more information.Want to give your post its best shot at being published?

Here's what to do:Read other Penny Hoarder posts. Get a feel for the tone of the site. We're informative, relaxed and excited about earning — and saving — money. Make sure we haven't already covered the topic you're pitching!Aim for 700 to 900 words. Write in a bloggy, friendly style that's fun to read.Focus on being useful. How will your post help readers save, earn or grow their money? We like practical, actionable advice that our readers can put to use in their own lives. Share detailed instructions to help someone else follow in your footsteps.

Include real-life examples. If you haven't personally experienced what you're writing about, be sure to refer and link to stories or examples of people who have managed to earn, save or invest money in the way you describe.

Add relevant links to other Penny Hoarder posts. We always appreciate it when you link to other articles we've published.

Include a two-sentence bio at the bottom of your post. Share a bit about yourself and your experience. What makes you an expert on your topic?

Feel free to add a link to your website, blog or social media profile so readers can find you.

Submit your post as an editable Google Doc to editor@thepennyhoarder. com. Follow **these easy instructions** to share your doc with us, and remember to select "Can Edit." Google can be finicky, so it's best to create your post as a Google Doc by copying and pasting from Word, rather than uploading a Word doc. If you'd like to include a note with your submission, check "Add Message" before you hit "Send."

What should I write about? The best way to get a feel for the types of posts we publish is to read them! We like fun, interesting, actionable advice that helps readers earn, save and grow their money

Do you pay? Only when pre-arranged with our editor. We do, however, offer a link to your website in your bio, and since our site sees about 2 million unique visitors monthly, that means you'll likely see traffic back to your site. (Paid writers do not get a link in their bio.)

We also offer a bonus system for all posts. Effective September 1, 2014, contributors whose posts hit certain traffic milestones receive bonus payments. Here's the breakdown:

When your post hits 50,000 page views, you earn $100.

When your post hits 100,000 page views, you earn another $200.

When your post hits 250,000 page views, you earn an additional $500.

The total possible bonus on each post is $800. All posts over 700 words are eligible, and traffic received on or after September 1, 2014 counts toward the bonus. We pay via PayPal at the end of each quarter, and reserve the right to adjust the bonus payments at the start of each quarter (if there's a change to the bonus thresholds or amounts, we'll update this page).

Should I pitch you my idea before writing the post? If you'd like to, go ahead — it might save you time in case we've already covered your idea. But we're happy to consider a draft as well.

Will you edit my post? We'll edit for content and clarity, doing our best to preserve your voice. We may also add an affiliate link or two. You'll be able to see any edits in the Google Doc.

Should I write a headline? That'd be great! We might tweak it for SEO or style, but your suggestion makes our job easier.

Do I need to include a photo? No need — we'll add one.

Anything else I should keep in mind? Please include links via anchor text (like this: *relevant keyword)* instead of HTML. Only use one space in between sentences.

Why do I need to submit through Google Docs? We use Google Docs because it allows us to easily collaborate with several people without passing around new versions of a Word Doc. Plus, you'll be able to see any changes we make to your post.

If you've never shared a Google Doc before, here are easy instructions. (Remember to give us editing power.)

Pro-Blogger (http://jobs.problogger.net/)

The ProBlogger Job Board is where bloggers looking for jobs and companies looking to hire bloggers meet.

ProficientWriters.com
(http://www.proficientwriters.com/writing-at-home)

Creative people seldom march to the same drummer as those with jobs that don't require those same abilities. One of the reasons that employers appreciate good freelance writers is that they don't require much supervision. ProficientWriters.com only wants people who are capable of writing at home and delivering good content in the timeframe agreed upon.

Quarasan
(https://www.flexjobs.com/jobs/telecommuting-jobs-at-quarasan)
(*Flexjobs requires a membership fee to see the job description and to apply for the job*)

Educational publisher offers editing and writing jobs that can be done from home.

Resmatic (http://www.resmatic.net/resmaticinc/detail.php?id=34)

We have an ongoing need for HTML coders working offsite on a CON-TRACT basis.

- Hand-write basic, clean html code on a contract basis.

  Work with designers and customer reps to make modifications and updates to existing and new client's websites.
- Use your internet skills to search and compile information from the web.

Qualifications:

- This is a telecommuting opportunity. You'll need your own computer, workspace and internet connection.
- You have experience succeeding at projects as a freelance contributor.
- Mastery of html, Photoshop, and working knowledge of installing and configuring pre-written per scripts.
- Knowledge of pier and JavaScript a plus.
- This is a contract "as-needed" position that requires that you be reachable during normal business hours.

Resume Edge.com (https://www.resumeedge.com/work-for-us/)

About Us ResumeEdge provides professional resume writing and editing services for job seekers worldwide. We are the leading provider of resume writing services and have written and edited thousands of resumes over the years. ResumeEdge is owned and operated by Nelnet, a publicly traded education services company. Nelnet helps students and families plan, prepare, and pay for their education—and find jobs after they graduate from college.

About the Job
You will write and edit resumes, cover letters, and LinkedIn® Profiles using customers' existing resumes and additional information submitted via a questionnaire. You will interact with customers using a ResumeEdge-provided email address. Some assignments will require telephone interviews with

clients; calling cards are provided. Self-paced, ongoing training resources are available on our online resume writer portal.

Requirements
Writers must have a strong background in one or more of our 40 job industries or have past experience writing and editing resumes and cover letters. Certified Professional Resume Writers (CPRW) and National Certified Resume Writers (NCRW) certification is preferred, but not required. Our writing standards are high; ResumeEdge holds all writers to a proprietary certification process that includes adhering to quarterly quality checks. You must have access to a computer and the Internet, and be an expert in Microsoft Word. Excellent verbal and written communication, patience, data organization, and critical thinking skills required. Benefits As a freelance resume writer, you have the flexibility to work from anywhere. You set your own hours and schedule and take as few or as many assignments as you like. ResumeEdge writers may also accept/continue freelance assignments with other businesses. Pay is per assignment; bonuses are available for resume writers with excellent customer feedback.

How to Apply
If you meet the above requirements, we'd love to hear from you. Submit your resume and a "before" and "after" of a resume you've edited or written. If selected for further evaluation, you will be contacted via email. The evaluation process includes a resume edit, critique, and phone interview.

Scripted (https://scripted.com/writers/sign_up)

Scripted offers significantly higher pay, but they have fewer jobs and topics to choose from. You have to apply for each category you wish to be allowed to accept jobs from, but once you are in you can make anywhere from $10 up to however much a client is willing to pay for one blog post. Also, they often send out private emails to writers who do well on certain topics, offering to let them accept jobs before they are posted on the job board.

When you write for Scripted, you are a ghostwriter for their clients who are in need of content, so you don't get your name published on what you create and all rights to the content are transferred over to the client upon article acceptance.

Payment at Scripted

The amount you earn will vary depending on a lot of different things including the type of content, the length, and the topic, but from what I understand there are many assignments that pay upwards of $20 per piece.

Scripted states that you can expect payment for the content you create bimonthly, on the 15th and last day of each month. Payments will be made via Bill.com beginning in April 2013. The company has decided to move away from PayPal.

If you are asked to do edits, Scripted promises to pay within two days after the edits are completed and approved. If their clients reject your edits, you will still be paid 50 percent so your work won't have been for nothing.

The Application Process

To begin writing for Scripted, you have to fill out the writer registration form and also submit a writing sample (one that has never been previously published). If you are in the U.S. you will also need to fill out a W-9 (you are considered an independent contractor for Scripted.) You are free to apply if you live outside the U.S., and of course the W-9 is not required if you are not a U.S. resident.

When you apply, you must select different industries you feel you are qualified to write in and a sample reflecting your ability to write within each industry you select is required. So if you select three different industries, you'll need to submit three different samples for each one. The current industries you can choose from are art and design, business and finance, internet and software, environmental, government and politics, law and legal, lifestyle and travel, media and entertainment, and sports and fitness. You may only apply to each specialty once. If you get rejected for an industry, you can't ever attempt to apply to it again.

After you've been approved, you'll see that you have a writer score that is assigned to you based on the quality of the sample(s) you submitted when you signed up. The higher the score, the better because sometimes writers with high scores get a chance to claim jobs before writers with lower scores do. Also, you might get more email invites if your score is high.

Grabbing Assignments

Once your application has been approved and you are officially in the system, you should be able to see by logging in some jobs that are available within each industry you got approved for. Scripted also occasionally sends out email invites letting you know when something is open that they think you would be a good fit to write.

Clients can additionally "favorite" you if they really like your writing, then this will give you first dibs on assignments from those clients.

Smart Brief (http://www.smartbrief.com/)

Discover a work experience where diverse ideas are met with enthusiasm, and where you can learn and grow to your full potential. We're looking for individuals who enjoy the entrepreneurial thrill of invention and who enjoy working as a team to create a satisfying outcome for our customers.

SmartBrief hires editors, often as part-time telecommuters, to comb through the day's business news stories from a wide range of sources and distill the news related to a specific industry into a daily newsletter.

Studio D Talent Network (http://talent.studiod.com/)

Studio D (formerly Demand Studios) accepts applicants with writing, editing and filmmaking skills. They are assigned to produce made-for-the-Internet content that appear on sites like eHow.com, LIVESTRONG.COM and dozens more sites. Writers are paid both on a flat fee and revenue sharing basis.

Suite 101
(http://www.examiner.com/article/suite-101-offers-freelance-writing-jobs)

Suite101 is an online magazine written by freelancers who are experts in many fields. Writers must submit 10 articles in every three month and are paid based on ad revenues for their work.

Textbroker (https://www.textbroker.com/authors)

Textbroker.com is exactly what the name implies: It's a site which acts as a broker between individuals or companies that need a bit of writing done and freelancers who will gladly spit out 200-400 words or so for pay. Texbroker. com rates your writing sample on a general scale of 2-5, with a "5" rating reserved for professional writers.

Triond.com (http://www.triond.com/)

Triond publishes user generated content on a network of websites, enabling users to reach a wider audience, gain more recognition and earn more revenue.

UxBooth (http://www.uxbooth.com/contribute/)

If you've ever had the goal to make the world a more user-friendly place, you have the expertise we're looking for to become a UX Booth author.

Send us a paragraph on the topic you're passionate about, and include a thesis and research that backs it up. We're excited to work with you!

Article Template

All UX Booth articles follow the following template:

- [Lead+thesis]: Here's where you grab the reader's attention, and let them know how this topic relates to his or her life.
- [Intro]: In the introduction you summarize the main points of the article, to prepare the reader for what's to come.
- [Main points]: In the body of the article, you'll go through 2-3 main points, each supporting the main thesis.
- [Next steps]: Instead of conclusions, at UX Booth we offer "next steps," or suggestions that will help the readers to implement the information you've provided.

Questions to Consider
Before you start writing your article, consider:

- What do you want to share with readers?
- Who is your audience?
- How did you learn about this?
- What else has been written on this topic?

- What examples can you think of that support your main point?

Guidelines

- **Length:** UX Booth articles are between 1200-1800 words long.
- **PoV:** UX Booth articles are written from a 3rd person point of view as much as possible. Obviously any narrative you tell about your own experience should be in the 1st person, but that said, we avoid second person like the plague, and as such write sentences such as "Including usability testing in the process helps designers observe more" as opposed to "if you include usability testing in your process, it will help you observe more."
- **Research:** We rely on research to support our theories, so please link to relevant articles if you are making a statement that someone else has also made, or provide your own data if your team has learned something through practice.
- **Show, don't tell:** Rather than telling the readers, (for example) "content audits are important," we ask that authors show us through examples. Tell a story about a time that creating a content audit made a difference in the course of a project.
- **We aren't the place for sales**: Articles aren't the place to showcase your cool new product. Articles are the place, however, to share the user-centered thinking behind your cool new product.

The Fine Print

Drafts submitted to UX Booth must be original – they may not have been previously published elsewhere. Once published, you grant an exclusive, royalty-free license to UX Booth to be the sole publisher of your article online. You may republish extracts; however, the article in its entirety must not appear elsewhere. You consent to the full article, extracts, samples or examples from it appearing in other sites, products, and services.

Vitac (http://www.vitac.com/careers/index.asp)

Realtime Captioners - Remote

Realtime Captioner employees are highly skilled court reporters who specialize in translating video into text "on the fly". Looking for skilled real-time reporters with advanced English grammar skills and typing speed greater than 50 wpm.

Wildjunket.com

(http://www.wildjunket.com/magazine/editorial-guidelines/)

Destination Features: Inspirational first-person, narrative accounts of your travel experience through a country/region – examples include trekking through the Amazon Jungle and traveling overland in Central Asia. The piece should encompass all-rounded aspects of travel: adventure, culture and history. The anecdote should be entertaining and informative.

- Photos: 10-15

- Writing: 1,800-2,200 words including boxes and sidebar

- Payment: US$150

- Sidebar: Getting There, Getting Around, When to Go, Cost of Travel, Packing and Accommodation

Photo Essay: Using striking, high-quality photos to showcase a destination or culture. Whether they are portrait shots of people in Nigeria, landscapes images of Antarctica or wildlife snapshots from the Galapagos Islands, they should piece together to tell a story.

- Photos: 15-20

- Writing: Introduction (400words) and short captions for each selected photo

- Payment: US$80

Travel Guide: A practical guide on a destination with a general introduction, list of must-see attractions and suggestions of up to 5 itineraries around the country. Itineraries can be themed (wildlife, culture, cities etc.) or based on geographical locations (north, central, south etc.) The style should be lively but informative. Include how long each itinerary takes, and what type of traveler it caters to.

- Photos: 10-15

- Writing: 1,800-2,200 words including boxes, sidebar and list of must-sees

- Payment: US$150

- Sidebar: Getting There, Getting Around, When to Go, Cost of Travel, Packing and Accommodation

Dispatches/ Just Back: Short first-person narratives of an unusual experience such as coasteering in Wales or staying in a temple in South Korea (narrower scope than destination feature).

- Photos: 8-10
- Writing: 1,300-1,500 words
- Payment: US$80
- Sidebar: Getting There, When to Go and Accommodation

Under the Radar: A short feature on a country/region that has yet to be discovered by mass tourism and have reasons to be in the tourist limelight. This is a general overview of what to see and most of all, why go now. Style should be factual but lively and includes some narratives.

- Photos: 8-10
- Writing: 1,300-1,500 words
- Payment: US$80
- Sidebar: Getting There, When to Go, Must-See Attractions

Feast: Stories that bring you on a journey through a country's gastronomy. Story scopes range from street food in Seoul to bizarre eats of Marrakech to award-winning tapas joints in Barcelona. It should be narrative and quirky yet informative.

- Photos: 8-10
- Writing: 1,000-1,200 words
- Payment: US$50

Smart Travel: This section discusses travel-related topics: from tipping to couch surfing. Article should be thought-provoking and evocative.

- No photos needed
- Writing: 700 words
- No payment

Snapshots: On the first few pages of our magazine, we feature contributions from readers who are interested in showcasing their photos. We look for very striking and outstanding images of landscape, people or culture. Photos must be landscape oriented and bigger than 4MB.

- Writing: A 200-word explanation of how, when and where you took the photo
- No payment

GENERAL GUIDELINES

All articles are written in American English. Prices should also be stated in local currency and USD.

- Please include sub-headings and boxes (at least 1 per feature).
- An author's bio and headshot will be included on the magazine's first page. Please keep
- your bio short (2-3 sentences).
- Articles should be submitted in a Word document and high-res photos (either in RAW or
- jpg of at least 4MB) via *YouSendIt.com.*

PUBLISHING RIGHTS

- Contributors will retain the rights to your articles or photographs.
- Please state if the article or photographs you're pitching are original or have been
- published previously. While we do not have a first run only policy, please assure that all
- parties involved are aware of the republication.

QUERY PROCESS

Once you've read through our past issues to get a good understanding of the style we're looking for, please send us a brief query summarizing the scope of your story with a proper title, subheading and bullet point summary of the content.

Please include links to photos that would accompany your story or send us low-res versions of the photos. It's advisable to include your credentials and samples of your previous writings or blog links to give us an idea of your writing style.

CONTACT DETAILS

For all magazine pitches, please contact *Nellie Huang at* editor@wildjunket.com.

Wordy.com (https://wordy.com/wordy-for-editors/)

Wordy is a real-time, human, copy-editing and proofreading service for everything you write. Wordy optimizes the accuracy, consistency and readability of content from Fortune 500 business reports to website copy.

As an editor on Wordy we expect you to have an excellent, professional working knowledge of the language, grammar, usage, punctuation and standard editorial conventions (e.g. New Hart's Rules, Chicago Manual of Style, etc.).

Writer's Domain (https://www.writersdomain.net/)

Writer's Domain is another site that offers a job board with fairly broad topics to write on. Most of their jobs are fairly uniform in that they are required to be around 250 to 300 words and include the keyword two times. Pay is $3 for each article from 250 to 300 words. Ratings are done by editors, and each article receives from 1 to 5 stars on both content and grammar. Those who get 4 or 5 stars on grammar get a $.30 bonus on that article. This means you could easily make $3.30 for one 250 to 300 word article. They pay via PayPal once per month, on the 5th. However, once you hit $100 in earnings you have the option to click a "pay me now" button and get paid right then. Another big difference here is that, in addition to a writing sample being required for the application, there is also a basic grammar test. Writer's Domain is tightening up on their content requirements beginning in September 2012, so be aware of that also.

Zerys.com (http://www.zerys.com/writers/)

Interact Media's Zerys platform gives you the opportunity to earn steady side income, doing what you love... all from the comfort of your own home.

- No monthly fees
- No need to purchase bid credits - get unlimited access to writing jobs
- No need to submit bid proposals
- Get notified when new jobs are posted that match your profile
- Develop long-term relationships with clients and build a steady source of work

Chapter 6

JOBS FOR TEENS/COLLEGE STUDENTS

(http://www.onlinejobsteenagers.com/)
(http://mysurvey123.com/kids-teens-paid-surveys-list/)

If you are of the opinion that looking for an online job for teenagers will involve a long, boring process of interviews, then let me tell you – that's just not the case. As a matter \ of fact, it is quite simple for teenagers to find online jobs and get started with earning money.

Unlike the offline jobs, there is no need for any paper work making it rather convenient for teenager to work online.

Most online jobs can be very educating too while being interesting. These jobs offer flexible work schedules without too much stress on deadlines and targets. This makes it convenient for teenagers like you to balance your work, study and entertainment as per your convenience.

(http://www.today-job.com/online-jobs-for-teenagers)

Here is a list of the best 10 online jobs which teenagers can use to make money online:

#1. Taking Surveys is one of the fastest and easiest way for high school and college students to earn extra money. Here is a list of survey sites especially for high school and college students:

American Consumer Opinion (Minimum age is 14 yrs.)
(http://www.acop.com/)

Get paid cash by check to take online surveys and participate in a focus group.

Cada Cabeza (Minimum age is 13 yrs.)
(https://www.cadacabeza.com/?id=32&srcid=21269&subid=10278a25e907
50d8b0146e4cd35bd2&ExternalRespID=3318)

This is a Latino survey site and networking site. Earn a chance to win cash.

Cash Crate (Minimum age is 13 yrs.) (http://www.cashcrate.com/)

Get paid to view videos, take surveys, and other tasks.

E-Poll (Minimum age is 13 yrs.)
(http://www.epollsurveys.com/epoll/clients/signup.htm?affiliateid=
HS1008/source=5436&)

Surveys vary and they pay in points that can be redeemed for cash (via Pay-Pal), gift cards and prizes.

Global Test Market (Minimum age is 14 yrs.)
(https://www.globaltestmarket.com/join.php?utm_source=panthera&utm_
medium=affiliate&utm_campaign=pantherauswg4&p=pantherauswg4&lan
g=E&CONTACT_COUNTRY=US&redirect=false&CID=3318)

Share opinions and earn points that can be redeemed for cash by check or via PayPal, or get Amazon, I-Tunes and other gift cards.

Harris Poll (Minimum age is 13 yrs.)
(https://join.harrispollonline.com/?sid=4bce4d2f-1573-4fd2-ba13-
3cdf9c640008)

Earn points for completing surveys which are redeemable for Amazon and other gift cards and prizes.

I-Poll (Minimum age is 13 yrs.)
(https://www.ipoll.com/registration_step1.php?P=902)

Earn cash by check or via PayPal, or get Amazon, I-Tunes and other gift cards.

Ipsos (Minimum age is 14 yrs.) (http://i-say.com/)

Get paid to take online surveys. Points are redeemable for cash (check or PayPal) or Amazon and other gift cards or prizes.

MindField Online (Minimum age is 14 yrs.)
(http://www.surveygizmo.com/s3/1866118/2403HO?sid=102c8e0d9ca0b4 6819b42c2355e9db&psid=3318)

Take surveys and earn cash via check or PayPal or Amazon gift certificates.

MySoapBox (Minimum age is 13 yrs.)
(https://www.mysoapbox.com/survey/html.pro)

Earn points for every survey completed and the points are redeemable for Amazon and other store gift cards.

My Survey (Minimum age is 16 yrs.)
(https://www.mysurvey.com/)

Share your opinion and get paid in gift cards, e-certificates, vouchers, money and PayPal and Amazon e-certificates as well as electronic, home and personal care items.

Opinion Plus (Minimum age is 13 yrs.) (https://opinionpl.us/)

Earn points that can be cashed out for cash paid via PayPal.

OpinionSite (Minimum age is 13 yrs.)
(https://opinionsite.com/survey/index.pro)

Members earn points for taking online surveys; points are redeemable for **cash (via check)** for taking surveys. Minimum cash out is $10. Earn $1 for registration and $2 for completing basic profile.

Opinion World (Minimum age is 13 yrs.)
(https://www.opinionworld.com/)

Panel members earn points for taking surveys; points convert to cash via PayPal, gift cards and prizes.

Paid Viewpoint (Minimum age is 13 yrs.)
(http://paidviewpoint.com)

Paid for every answer given…. after $15.00 or more is earned, it is paid to PayPal Student Account. Parents set up this account for their teenager to receive and withdraw funds.

PanelPolls.com (for teens 13 to 17 yrs.)
(http://community.panelpolls.com/registration.php?rc=MjE5)

Earn points that are redeemable for cash paid by check.

SpringBoard America (Minimum age is 14 yrs.)
(https://www.springboardamerica.com/S.aspx?s=5727&r=wO9Fx2P3pD6F 2XA6uE34Ms&so=true&a=7080&fromdetect=1)

Take online surveys and get paid cash via check or PayPal.

SurveyDownline (Minimum age is 13 yrs.)
(http://www.surveydownline.com/rg/lp2.aspx?fn=)

Get paid cash via PayPal for completing surveys.

SurveySavvy (Minimum age is 14 yrs.)
(https://www.surveysavvy.com/?m=1635869&c=120)

Get paid to take surveys and earn cash (check) and earn extra cash by installing Savvy Connect app on your desktop/laptop or smart phone and tablets for 90 days.

TeensEyes (Minimum 13 yrs. old)
(http://www.teenseyes.com/registration.aspx)

Operated by the same company for Kidzeyes, TeensEyes.com is an online survey panel for teens between 13 and 17 who lives in the United States. Members earn points for taking interesting surveys, and points can be exchanged for cash via check. A Great teen survey panel!

Toluna (Minimum age is 13 yrs.) (https://us.toluna.com/)

Test products and share opinions on surveys. Earn cash and rewards.

Valued Opinions (Minimum age is 13 yrs.)
(https://www.valuedopinions.com/)

Earn cash and rewards by sharing your opinion.

VIP Voices (Minimum age is 13 - 16 yrs., depending on the survey)
(http://www.vipvoice.com/Toluna.MR.TrafficUI/MSCUI/Page.aspx?pgtid=1&utcoffset=7)

There is a teen survey panel for specific surveys. They pay in points for cash and prizes sweepstakes.

YouGov (Minimum age is 14 yrs.) (https://today.yougov.com/?stay)

Share your opinion... Get paid in cash, points and rewards.

#2. Take notes and sell them

You are good at writing notes and attended all lectures; you can sell your class notes via these websites:

Flashnotes.com (http://www.luvolearn.com/) (minimum age is 13 yrs)

Take notes and sell them, or tutor. On this site, students can post a variety of "products" including notes and flashcards after they've signed up through Facebook, Google+, or any email address. The site also employs students to provide live tutoring and video tutorials. The seller has the power to set his or her own prices.

They pay out every Friday at 5 pm and sellers keep 70% of their earnings.

NoteUtopia.com (http://www.noteutopia.com/)

NoteUtopia is the perfect student community. We offer an organic document marketplace where students can upload and download all of their class documents, including class notes, study guides, handouts, reports, quizzes and more. We are unlike any other study site in that our documents are specific to your class. Students can find documents by looking up their class or professor, and then download the document. NoteUtopia is the key for you to Study Better

One Class (https://oneclass.com/)

OneClass is one of the most popular websites to buy and sell notes. It gloats that it has helped over 90% of students improve their grades using over 200,000 lecture notes. You can sign up through Facebook or using any email address.

You will earn $5 every time someone views your notes!

You will earn this $5 in the form of OneClass credit (to buy other notes) or in gift cards to a variety of stores including Starbucks, Best Buy, and Amazon.

Student Notes (http://www.studentnotes.com/)

To work for Student Notes, a student must have a minimum cumulative GPA of 3.4 and have outstanding class attendance.

Student Notes is a little different in that it pays per test and gives a flat-fee based on the number of pages in the bundle of notes. Additionally, students earn 5% of net sales.

Student Notes is a relatively new site and has not expanded to many colleges quite yet. Keep checking in to track its progress and your job opportunities!

Study soup (https://studysoup.com/marketing/sell_on_studysoup)

Take diligent notes to help students and make some money.

Other ways to make money taking notes:

Check with the Office of Disability Services

Get to Know the Office of Disability Services: In order to accommodate disabled students, universities will pay other students to take notes or prepare study materials and share it with the class. Each university will have its own requirements for note-takers. Generally, note-takers must maintain a certain GPA, have received an A in the course, send in sample notes, and/or fill out an application.

The offer varies depending on the level of the course; graduate students will often receive more for their notes. On average, a student will receive anywhere from $40 to $150 for an entire semester of notes.

This is class-specific, though you may be able to contact the office directly if you're looking for some extra cash. Usually the Office of Disability Services will send out an email early in the semester requesting a note-taker for a single class.

Make Your Own Flyer!

If you've built up your street rep (umm…in the hallways…) as a successful student, your peers could definitely be interested in your notes. You can hang flyers in residence halls or ask your professors to hand them out.

You definitely set your own prices and get your payments in cash!

#3. Work for **UHaul** (http://jobs.uhaul.com/job_detail.aspx?aval_job_id=137607&) There are customer service type online jobs for teens at least 16 yrs. old. Need a computer with high speed internet and a USB headset. Base pay is $7.50 to $8.50 per hour. Can earn bonuses.

#4. Listen to Music and give your opinion with **Slice the Pie**. (https://www.slicethepie.com/splash.html)

Be at least 17 yrs. old. Slice the Pie pays $.05 to $.20 for each music track you review. Earn more depending on the length of review, quality and your member rank. Payments are made every Tuesday and Friday via PayPal after earning $10.00.

#5. Creative Writing. One of the best online jobs for teenagers is creative writing. If you are good at putting English words together, and have basic internet research skills, then a freelance article writing job may be for you.

Some creative writing sites that will accept teenagers are listed below:

Helium (Minimum age is 13 yrs.) (https://www.heliumnetwork.com/)

We match you to freelance assignments that are right for you. Qualified writers, editors and fact-checkers work on a wide range of projects through RRD Content Source. Freelance professionals like you provide content for newsletters, articles, blogs, retail product descriptions, customer websites and more. Our clients range from major newspapers and national department store chains to small businesses and local or niche publications.

HubPages (Minimum age is 18 yrs.) (http://hubpages.com/)

Revenue sharing for articles written---must have parental consent.

#6. Comment on forum or a blog on **Postloop.** (http://www.postloop.com/)

Get paid each time you post a comment and get paid via PayPal after earning $5.00, equivalent to 100 points.

#7. Tutor students online on **Enroll.** (https://enroll.com/Tutoring)

Minimum age is 15 yrs. Do not need prior teaching experience, be knowledgeable in a subject where you can tutor other students online.

#8. Do several different tasks on **CrowdSource**. (http://www.crowdsource.com/) Writing, translating, data entry, etc. They pay starts $.05-$.10 per task. Writing tasks pay $.02 to $.35 per word. Earn pocket change and pay is via PayPal---the more you do, the more you earn.

#9. Do different tasks and get paid $5.00 per task on:

Fiverr. (https://www.fiverr.com/) Fiverr is a reputable marketplace where people post services they are willing to complete for $5. Teens are allowed to sign up and post a variety of services such as: graphic designs, writing, music solos, and much more.

Fiverr is open to everybody and you can offer a 'gig' for $5 to anyone. The fun thing about Fiverr.com for teenagers is the 'gig' they offer can be anything and sometimes the most unusual ones turn out to be the most popular.

You can offer to do video impersonations, create artwork, take zany pictures; pretend to be someone's girlfriend or boyfriend on Facebook (believe it or not that's a very popular gig!) In fact almost anything goes, as long as it is not illegal or pornographic.

There are many people that make a living from Fiverr. Fiverr pays you thorough PayPal and after all the fees, you will earn around $3.80 for every $5 order you receive and complete. Some of the articles you might come across about online jobs for teenagers suggest joining a freelance site like Odesk or Elance and looking for writing jobs or other freelance work. The problem with that though (and something that is often not mentioned in those articles) is that those sites require that everyone who works on the site is over the age of 18. There is no faking it either as you are required to provide the proper proof!

#10. Watch advertisements online and get paid by Jingit. (https://www.jingit.com/home/) – Jingit is an income-earning program that pays teens to watch advertisements online. Teens that are at least 13 can sign up for Jingit. You can also earn money taking short surveys, downloading the mobile app, and scanning items at Walmart.

#11. Edit and Proofread.

This is a great idea for teens if you have great grammar and are good at proofreading. There are several companies that will recruit teens for editing research papers and essays. It could All you need to do is edit and proofread the material and mail it back.

Here are some companies where you can find online proofreading jobs:

Elance
(https://www.upwork.com/signup/create-account/freelancer_elance_direct)

Textmaster (https://www.textmaster.com/)

Guru.com (http://www.guru.com/)

(Amazon) **MTurk.com** (https://www.mturk.com/mturk/welcome)

#12. Create a Viral **YouTube** Video. (https://www.youtube.com/) – Making money from the advertising revenue that YouTube videos can earn is another way that teenagers can use their own personal creativity to make money online. As anyone who goes on You Tube knows almost anything and everything has the potential to go viral and a lot of teens have already made plenty of cash, and a name for themselves, with their videos. These days anyone can opt to 'monetize' their videos and then it's just up to you to promote, promote, promote!

#13. Paid to Click Sites –Joining a pay to click site. Basically you sign up for an account and then are presented with a series of websites that you literally have to click through. It is not always that interesting and the money you earn is not a great deal but if you get into the habit of visiting a site regularly you can earn some extra pocket money. READ ABOUT THE PTC SITES BEFORE JOINING. Some of them may be scams. Here are two websites that list PTC sites:

http://www.best-ptc-sites.org/

http://www.top-site-list.com/bestptc

Here are the 6 best paying sites in 2015 according to (http://moneyconnexion.com/top-10-ptc-sites-in-2012-earn-money-with-trusted-ptc-web-sites.htm):

ClixSense (http://www.clixsense.com/)

Inbox Dollar (http://www.inboxdollars.com/)

Traffic Monsoon (https://trafficmonsoon.com/ad_plans)

Paidverts (https://www.paidverts.com/how_it_works.html)

NeoBux (https://www.neobux.com/)

BuxP (http://buxp.org/)

#14.   Etsy (https://www.etsy.com/)- Lots of teenagers, even in the age of the Internet, like to make things. Jewelry, buttons, artwork, all kinds of things. Etsy is an online marketplace for all of these things and more. If you are under 18 you will have to have an adult set up a 'store' for you but once they do it's all yours to run. Etsy provides you with a lot of cool tools to help you build a great online storefront and all you will need is a PayPal.

#15. Start a Blog --- Of all the ways that a teen can make money online blogging is the one that will take the longest to become profitable and it will also probably require the most work. However if you really, really know what you are writing about and can then write about in the long run all the effort can be worth it.

#16. **Video Game Play** surveys. (https://www.gameplaysurveys.com/)

Register for free (get paid $5.00). As a member, you will be emailed surveys for video games, movies, and other products to share your opinion. A cash reward will be placed in your GamePlaySurveys account for each survey you complete. When you earn $25.00 you can redeem it for cash, gift cards or virtual currency credits.

You will need a computer, internet access, a subscription to one of the many free websites that offer this opportunity, and most of the time a PayPal account were you can get paid. The amount of money you can make here depends on your writing skills, motivation, knowledge on a particular field, and TIME you devote to writing.

Chapter 7

JOBS FOR DISABLED WORKERS

Even though you may have limitations such as not able to stand or sit for extended periods of time, or can't lift, or can't hear or speak, you do have abilities. With the right kind of work at home job position, you will be able to earn an income despite your work limitations.

As a job seeker looking for work at home online job opportunities that fit with what your abilities are, then you will be set. There are some websites that are available to help you:

Ability Jobs (http://abilityjobs.com/finding-a-job-for-a-person-with-a-disability.htm)

ABILITY Jobs is the first and largest employment website for job seekers with disabilities. Since 1995, we have provided a place where people with disabilities can seek employment, confident they will be evaluated solely on their skills and experience. Posting your resume and searching jobs are *Free.*

Disabled Person (https://www.disabledperson.com/)
This is a disABLEDperson.com a premier Job Board for People with dis-ABILITIES since 2002. We boast over 40,000 active jobs with hundreds of new jobs posted every day from all across the U.S. posted by companies who are looking to hire people with disabilities. Disability Employment is our passion as we work closely with employers to place their job openings for you, the disability community.

We work closely with disABILITY Organizations and State Vocational Rehabilitation Departments again from all across the U.S. We hope you enjoy your experience on our site. Register, post your resume and begin your job search.

Employment Options (http://myemploymentoptions.com/)

Employment Options is a Certified Social Security Administration (SSA) Employment Network in the free Ticket-To-Work program. We help citizens on SSDI or SSI who are 18-64 return to work in either Work-at-Home or On-site Community employment in 47 states. From pre-screening qualifications to resume prep and job placement; we offer a complete package and valuable tools for success.

GettingHired.com (http://www.gettinghired.com/)

This site offers a searchable, well-populated database of jobs specifically for people with disabilities. Though you do have to register in order to view the actual job listings - and in some cases you must have "an active jobseeker profile" (a resume) in their system to use resources such as the career assessment - this may be worth it in order to gain access to the sheer volume of listings they have available.

Hire Disability Solutions
(http://hireds.monster.com/homepage?where=remote)

This is a website that lists work at home job opportunities for people with work limitations. Must type "remote" in the location box.

Indeed.com
(http://www.indeed.com/q-Disability-l-Remote-jobs.html)

This is a website with a listing of work at home online jobs for people with work limitations.

NTI: National Telecommuting Institute
(http://www.nticentral.org/work-at-home-jobs-disabled.shtm)

NTI provides job opportunities for Americans with disabilities that require home-based work.

Who should apply?
If you're an American who is disabled and would like to work from home, you may qualify for an online job in customer service, technical support, medical transcription, quality control, or many other types of work.

Legitimate at-home jobs
NTI, a nonprofit organization, has worked for over 15 years with employers, Social Security Disability Insurance, and with vocational rehabilitation services that work with disabled individuals. We match people like you with legitimate work-at-home opportunities suited to your situation and requirements.

Apply now
New job openings are arriving all the time. Apply now to be a part of NTI's database of pre-screened, pre-qualified applicants. We'll follow up to identify what jobs you're interested in and try to match you with a suitable work-at-home opportunity.

Source America

(http://www.sourceamerica.org/?gclid=CNi304mt7skCFYwvgQodMcE JKg)

SourceAmerica is the national leader in creating job opportunities for a dedicated, high quality workforce for people with significant disabilities.

Chapter 8

JOBS FOR VETERANS

There are many companies hiring veterans for work at
home online jobs. Here is a list of some of them:

CenturyLink

(http://www.centurylink.com/Pages/AboutUs/CompanyInformation/
Careers/callCenter.jsp)

This provider of broadband, entertainment and voice services to consumers
and businesses in 33 states offers work-at-home positions for virtual call center agents who perform sales and customer service. The company actively
recruits veterans and provides them special training. Activated reservists
receive full difference between civilian and military pay for one year.

Deloitte

(http://www2.deloitte.com/ca/en/pages/careers/articles/flexibility.html)
On Fortune's "100 Best Companies to Work For" list in 2011, Deloitte is the
best of 100 when it comes to telecommuting--with 86 percent of its workers telecommuting for at least 20 percent of the work week. The company
actively recruits veterans and has special mentoring programs and training
for vets.

The Hartford (http://www.thehartford.com/careers/)

This large insurance company offers work at home positions for nurses,
adjusters, sales people, attorneys and claims consultants. (Use the keyword
"remote" to search the company's job listings.) According to the Military
Times website, it has a hiring program for spouses and it pays reservists
a combination of full civilian pay and the difference between civilian and
military pay.

Health Net (https://jobs.healthnet.com/)

Heath insurance company operating in 27 states hires nurse case managers, data entry and care coordinators with the option to telecommute. (Use "telecommuting" or "work from home" as a search keyword of company's job database.) Company actively recruits military spouses.

Humana (https://www.humana.com/about/careers/military-initiatives)

Humana, which includes Humana Military Healthcare Services Inc., offers many telecommuting positions, particularly for nurses. The company also has opportunities, which may allow telecommuting, for medical coders, chart auditors, licensed insurance reps, accountants, physicians, writers, human resource recruiters and benefits consultants, website specialists and sales people. The company pays activated reservists the difference between their military and civilian pay without a limitations.

Intuit (http://careers.intuit.com/) ----use the keyword "remote"

Intuit has a variety of remote positions in software engineering, sales, marketing and finance in the U.S. and Canada. Qualifications, salaries and requirements will vary widely. However, its work-at-home, online tax advisor jobs support its Turbotax product.

Online Tax Advisor Qualifications and Requirements:

These 500 to 1,000 tax advisor positions are for certified public accountants (CPA), enrolled agents (EA) and tax attorneys, who will support TurboTax products via phone, chat and email (with no required upselling) and provide written summaries of tax solutions to customers.

Unlike a typical tax preparer job, these experts will give advice but won't actually do tax preparation.

Full- and part-time, seasonal positions are available. Some seasonal agents are promoted to permanent managerial positions. During tax season expect 30 to 40 hours per week of work. The season begins with paid training, which consists of training sessions taking place from November to January, and the season ends in late April. A variety of established schedules that cover the hours of 5 a.m. to 9 p.m. Pacific Time, seven days a week are available. However flexibility to take extra work during peak hours may be required

Successful applicants for the online tax advisor must have active credentials as an enrolled agent or CPA and a preparer tax identification number (PTIN).

Additionally tax advisors need a minimum of 5 years of experience preparing federal and state returns, extensive knowledge of tax laws, experience using tax preparation software, excellent verbal and written communication skills and the ability to work with minimal supervision and to research IRS and state publications, regulations, and GAAP publications.

Lockheed Martin (http://www.lockheedmartinjobs.com/)

Lockheed Martin employs more than 25,000 veterans, and more than 20 percent of its executives are vets. The company pays activated reservists the difference between their military and civilian pay without a limit. It supports telecommuting in its workforce but doesn't necessarily let new hires telecommute. To find telecommuting jobs, search "telecommuting" in its jobs database.

Met Life
(https://www.metlife.com/careers/index.html?WT.ac=GN_careers)

This large insurance company hires underwriters and controls analysts for work from home positions. However, the company also has flexible workplace options (including telework) for other employees as well. (Use "work from home virtual location" as a keyword in the employment database.) Metlife actively recruits veterans and has a military spouse hiring program. It pays full differential pay for activated reservists for one year.

Simply Hired
(http://www.simplyhired.com/k-veteran-work-at-home-jobs.html)

This website lists open work at home online jobs for veterans.

U-Haul
(http://jobs.uhaul.com/moonlighter.aspx) (http://jobs.uhaul.com/job_detail. aspx?aval_job_id=137607&)

Are you looking for another job to supplement your income? If so, U-Haul is the right place for you! Moonlighters are important and valued members of the U-Haul Team because they help us meet our customers' needs - which are significantly greater on evenings, weekends and holidays - with skilled, talented people who will provide excellent customer service.

Whether your "regular" job is a full-time or part-time position at another company, being in the military, going to school or being a stay-at-home parent, the flexible schedules available at U-Haul will make it possible for you to join our team. We have a variety of positions available for moonlighters and the flexible schedules we offer provide many options.

Vet Jobs (http://vetjobs.com/)

VetJobs services makes it easy to reach transitioning military, National Guard, Reserve Component Members and veterans that have separated over the last several decades and, due to the services provided by VetJobs, are now productive members of the civilian work force in all disciplines as well as their family members.   Look for "Work at Home" jobs in the jobs category.

Chapter 9

WAYS TO MAKE EXTRA MONEY
WORKING AT HOME

These methods are paid per task and are generally
not paid per hour or as a salary.

D. #1. E-Juror

Jury Talk (www.jurytalk.com)

JuryTalk.com, which is run by the Wilmington Institute Network, a trial
and settlement psychology firm, is looking for Research Jurors to provide
opinions on current legal cases and participate in focus groups or mock trials. Many of the research studies can be completed online; others require
participation at their research facilities in Houston or Dallas, Texas. The
sign up form for this paid mock jury site is very quick and easy.

JuryTest.Net (http://www.jurytest.net/index.cfm?action=howjur)

Jurors for JuryTest.net may be asked to provide their opinions on legal
cases in several ways, including online questionnaires, recorded voice
feedback via a toll-free phone number, online chat room discussions, or
teleconferences (also by way of a dial-in 800 number) in which he or she
will discuss the case with other jurors for the researchers to witness live.
Payments vary according to length of the case, but typically range from
$5 to $50 and can be paid by check or PayPal. Please note: In order to
participate in the paid mock jury research studies through JuryTest.net,
you must have RealPlayer installed and operational on your computer.

Online Verdict.com (http://www.onlineverdict.com/jurors.php)

Act as a prospective juror and review cases for payment of $20 to $60 per case. Sign up and when your profile matches a lawyers need you will be invited to sit on the "virtual jury."

Trial Juries (www.trialjuries.com)

The online jury review opportunities for mock jurors offered by TrialJuries.com vary in length as they do with most other mock jury sites, but will usually take about an hour commitment of your time. Rate of pay is typically $30, with the chance to make more for longer or more complex cases. Participants are paid via PayPal.

Trial Practice.com (http://signupdirect.com/)

Sign up to be a mock juror and get paid $100-$150 if you are selected. However, this is not an online review of a case but a live one so you would have to travel outside the home for the 8-10 hour session.

Virtual JuryTM (virtualjury.com)

VirtualJury.com is currently accepting application for mock jurors to participate in online focus groups. The website does not offer much information for jurors upfront; it only states that once you've signed up, you will be notified of any studies you are invited to, and that compensation details will be provided at that time. Payments will be in the form of written checks which will be mailed to jurors within two weeks of their participation.

#2. Miscellaneous ways to earn money online

A. E-Mail

Avail Mail (http://www.avamail.com/cgi-bin/add.cgi?refid=17112)

Make 7 cents for each email you read. 3 Referral Levels - 2 cents from all the emails your referrals read.

Cash 4 Offers (http://www.cash4offers.com/)

Cash4Offers gives you several ways to be rewarded for your online activity. You can get paid to read emails, take surveys, complete cash offers, play online games, refer your friends and more...

All you have to do is sit back and enjoy the extra income working with your computer on the Internet from the comfort of your home.

Cash For Action

(http://www.cashforaction.com/membersignup.php?RefID=19615)

Minimum payment of one cent and five levels of referral commission... pays out regularly.

Donkey mails

(http://www.donkeymails.com/pages/index.php?refid=)

Get paid to read emails, play games, clicking on ads, and referrals.

Email Pays U

(http://e-mailpaysu.com/members/index.cgi?sidneyon)

Make 2 cents for each email you read. Free $10 Sign-Up Bonus. Two Referral Levels - 1 cent from all the emails your referrals read.

Inbox Dollars (http://www.inboxdollars.com/)

Sign Up ($5.00 instantly), read e-mail (1 to 10 cents each). Refer your friends and earn $5.00 each.

I Won (http://www.iwon.com/home/home.jhtml)

You could win up to $25 million just for checking your email, reading horoscope or catching up on the latest news.

NOCS (http://www.nocs.us/)

Receive up to 25 e-mails per month containing 1 task each. They are usually simple tasks (i.e. asking you to visit a website). Tasks are different each time and they are chosen according to member's personal interests.

Below are companies that pay you just to read your email. You choose what topics you want to be informed about and advertisers will pay you from $0.50 to $0.02 per email. Make even more money by telling your friends and family about these great programs. Sign-up for one or all of these programs. Start making money today! Anyone is eligible to sign-up whether you live in Sidney, Unadilla, Bainbridge, Delaware County, Otsego County, Chenango County, or anywhere else in the U.S.

Paid to read (http://www.paid-to-read-email.com/)

Register – get emails ---read emails----get paid.

Sidney online.com (http://www.sidneyonline.com/email.htm)

Get paid to read emails and refer others.

Send Earnings (http://www.sendearnings.com/)

Users "Get paid to read emails." $5.00 sign-up bonus.

Spice 2 mail (http://www.spice2mail.co.in/)

Register and read emails and SMS daily, get paid weekly.

B. Decoy

Become a Decoy: Companies want to keep track of what is being sent and to whom. As a mail and email decoy you help them with their research. They pay in cash, gift cards and stamps. Must be organized and have someone you trust to substitute for you when on vacation. See the 4 companies that give you this opportunity:

The Hauser Group (http://www.hausernet.com/opportunities.html)

We provide various promotion tracking and marketing intelligence services for major national firms. They are interested in a number of things, such as the delivery date and condition of their advertising mail. From time to time, some sample merchandise to check on delivery of customer orders. We also protect their mailing lists against mis-use. In other cases, we track what other companies are doing in the way of advertising in the mail. These are essential services, many of which are also in the public interest.?

All you have to do is mark the date received on each special piece as it comes in, enter it on our Web site, and save the mailings for a period of time. We may occasionally ask that you send us specific items. you get?

Participants are credited for each valid item accurately reported. Any mailing costs are reimbursed or, we may make use of UPS call tags, etc.

There may be extra potential opportunities. From time to time some participants get to keep test shipments of merchandise, or get free copies of magazines.

Honestly, you won't get rich as a decoy agent, but many people are delighted to get some extra spending money doing something that's fun with hardly any effort. (We cannot promise any particular amount as this depends on clients' needs for your location and a number of other variables.)

If you are interested in being considered, please fill out and submit the Agent Application Request Form found on the website.

Be sure to include your name, phone number, country and city. We will contact you if there is an immediate need for coverage in your area.

Quad Readers Club (no known website)

Collect and report mail to them and earn free postage stamps, plus free magazines. Reports of mail are made by phone and the whole process is quick and easy. If you are interested in becoming a volunteer, email them at quadreaders@qg.com with the subject line: Quad/Readers Mail Decoy Program. Let them know you are interested in joining this program as a volunteer and include your name, address, city, state, zip, phone number and email address.

Quotas

(http://www.world-mail-panel.com/portal?lg=en&action=show.about_
survey)

Postal quality surveys

For our international postal surveys we are looking for participants acting as receivers of test mail (and for some projects as senders).

Your task

In most studies you will receive a certain amount of letters over a specific time period, in some studies the participants also send test letters. Your task is to confirm the receipt of each test letter (and possibly the posting dates of test letters) here at this website.

We kindly ask you to enter the data as soon as possible, at least once a week.

What kind of information do we need from you?

In order to guarantee a smooth course of the survey we need your complete postal address and your email-address. If you are interested in participating please register at this website! In case of further questions just send us an e-mail: panel@quotas.de.

What do I get?

For your participation we will credit you points to your User account depending on the scope of the study. These points can be redeemed for gift vouchers or online payments. We are cooperating with the online payment systems PayPal and Moneybookers and in the field of gift vouchers with Amazon and Globoforce (provider of a variety of vouchers). Furthermore, we can also donate your bonus to the medical aid agency "Doctors Without Borders".

Data Protection

Your data will be used exclusively for our surveys and treated according to the ESOMAR (European Society for Opinion and Marketing Research) rules of data protection.

US Monitor (http://www.usmonitor.com/agentform/)

Make some extra money being a decoy for our clients. When a mail agent is needed within your geographical area, you will be contacted.

Small Business Knowledge Center (SBK Center) (http://www.sbkcenter.com/consumer.html)

They pay for certain "junk mail" and junk email sent in to them: Insurance, Investments, Loans & Banking, Credit Cards, Telecommunications (utilities) and travel. They also pay for referrals.

Reach 2000 points and exchange them for $20 gift cards to major stores, restaurants, etc.
Join SBKC with an application. Not everyone gets accepted, it depends on demographics. Once accepted, you start sending them to SBKC and accumulate points.

C. Expert

Ask Me Help Desk (https://www.askmehelpdesk.com/register.php)

Payment is done by promoting your business. Consumers are not charged for asking questions.

BrainMass (https://brainmass.com/)

This is an online academic academy where experts can make money by assisting university, college, and high school students though an online library, one-on-one help, or via their e-book library. Experts must be working on, or have obtained a graduate-level degree from an accredited university. To get started, register online, watch a training video, take a quiz, then send in your credentials and proof of education. Once you're approved, you'll be able to generate content for BrainMass. The academic expert pay rate works on a sliding scale. Payments are paid on the 15th day of the following month via PayPal or check.

Clarity (https://clarity.fm/browse)

This is an online marketplace where people can sell small business advice to entrepreneurs. Simply create a profile through LinkedIn, set your rates, link up your PayPal account, and wait for calls to come in. Topics you can speak on are Business, Tech, Sales and Marketing, Funding, Product Design, Skills and Management, and Industries. Clarity hosts over 30,000+ verified experts, including Mark Cuban, Eric Ries, and Cameron Herold. Clarity takes 15% of the fee collected from the call and you get the rest. Payments are made via PayPal every 15 days.

Createpool (https://www.createpool.com/)

This is an online marketplace for information selling in the following areas (pools): Programming, Academics, Auto Repair, and Legal Advice. To become an expert, create an account, search online for questions, give advice, and then make money. Createpool deducts a 20% service fee from each transaction and payments are made via check or PayPal.

E-Lance
(https://www.elance.com/php/landing/main/login.php?redirect=http%3A%2F%2Fwww.elance.com%2Fmyelance 0)

A marketplace for various services from software development to being a personal assistant.

Epinions (http://www.epinions.com/)

Write and rate brutally honest and unbiased opinions. Earn cash for your expert advice.

Ether (http://www.ether.com/)

This is a company that lets you sell advice and content by phone, email, or through your website. Sign up for a free account, then set up your Ether Phone Number where calls will be forwarded to you. Set your rate and hours, and answer questions, Ether takes a 15% fee of what you make. Payments are made via check and direct deposit. Some examples are a therapist, doctor, nurse, tax expert, teacher offering their expertise to customers.

Guru.com (http://www.guru.com/)

Connecting freelancers and consultants with contract projects. Advice on how to run your business effectively.

Maven (http://www.maven.co/consultant#how-it-works)

This is a micro-consulting platform that allows you to profit from your knowledge and connections. To get started, sign up for an account, select an hourly consulting rate, and answer some questions, which are sent to you through the Maven match-up feature. Payments are made via Pay-Pal, check, and direct deposit. Maven charges a $4 – $25 fee per month based on usage. Maven is a member of the Better Business Bureau and has been featured on Forbes, the Wall Street Journal, and The New York Times.

Pop Expert (https://www.popexpert.com/features)

This is an online video portal where you can sell you knowledge on Meditation, Marketing, Music, Relationship, Career Mentoring, Language, Nutrition, Productivity, and Style. Set up your profile, set your rates for a 50 minute video session, let others know your availability, then instruct your lessons via video. Popexpert's fee is 3% when you have a session with a client and when they refer a new client to you, their fee is 20%. Popexpert pays will transfer money into your bank account 21 business days after your video session has ended. Popexpert has been featured on USA Today, Mashable, and the Daily Muse.

Presto Experts (http://www.prestoexperts.com/)

This is a unique service that connects individuals who have questions to people who are qualified to answer them in Health, Technology, Business, Education, Counseling and Design. People needing answers posts questions and experts post proposals with the amount of fee to read the answer. Presto Experts takes a percentage of the fee you charged then pays you the rest via check on a monthly basis.

Thinkific (https://www.thinkific.com/features/)

This is an online campus that allows users to create, market and sell beautiful online courses on your own site. You have your own private online space for training people. It's free to create an account and payments made to you by your students are yours. There are 4 different packages with 3 of them charging monthly fees billed annually.

Udemy (https://teach.udemy.com/)

Udemy is an online teaching platform that allows individuals to teach on a variety of subjects (business, design, art, education, music, etc.) Instructors create their content, publish it on the site, and then promote it. As an instructor you'll set your rates and promote your classes for which you'll receive 100% of the revenue. If a class is promoted through Udemy and a sale is made, they keep 50% of the revenue. Using Udemy is free, except for a small processing fee for accepting payments. According to their site, most instructors make an average of $7,000 annually. Udemy has been featured on Mashable, the Wall Street Journal, and The New York Times.

Yondu (http://www.yondo.com/)

Yondu is an online platform where experts can sell their knowledge through teaching videos. This site gives professionals a platform to market, schedule, accept payments, and instruct individuals all in one place. Totally free to join, you decide when and where to teach, and how much to charge. There are fees charged to use this platform.

D. Field Agent (https://fieldagent.net/for-agents/)

Sign up for an account with **Field Agent** and get paid to do small tasks around town for different clients. Those usually involve scanning barcodes with your Phone, checking prices at your local drug store and conducting field surveys. Your earnings vary from assignment to assignment and depend on the area you are based in. For example, one listing offers $9 for 4 pictures of any products in the toothbrush section of the local Target in Mission Viejo, CA; while taking one picture of $19.99 & under video game display taken in any Toys "R" in NYC will earn you $5.50.

E. Focus Groups

20/20 Research Incorporated (http://www.2020research.com/)

Online bulletin board and focus group (online chat) capabilities. There are also in person focus groups in Nashville, TN, Miami, FL, and Charlotte, NC.

Accurate Data Marketing, Inc. (http://www.accurdata.com/)

Focus Groups in Glenview, IL and online surveys.

Digital Research, Inc. (http://www2.digitalresearch.com/)

Online research is a specialty. Web surveys and moderated chats. (All North America)

Focus Groups.Com (http://www.focusgroup.com/)

Marketing Research Services listed market by market. Database of many companies. Not all want to hear from you as they do not keep a database. This list is for clients to hire companies.

Focusline (http://www.focusline.com/)

Conducts web based surveys, one-on-one interviews, and group sessions. Surveys usually take about 10 minutes to complete. Group sessions and one-on-one interviews are conducted in a chat based environment and usually last for 30 minutes to an hour. You'll be financially rewarded for your participation, typically between $25.00-$45.00 for your participation.

Pragmatic Research
(http://www.pragmatic-research.com/?page=home0)

Internet surveys and in person focus groups in St. Louis, MO.

Qualitative Insights (http://www.q-insights.com/)

Focus groups online and Sherman Oaks, CA.

What is your story? (https://whatisyourstory.us/)

Focus opinions via online surveys.

F. Give out Answers

Cha Cha (http://becomeaguide.chacha.com/)

When you join the Cha Cha Community, you can learn interesting things and share your knowledge. Connect with people.

Advice runs the gamut from solving puzzles to answering questions on set subjects. Payouts can be small but steady.

Building a following on ChaCha is the hardest part. You're listed along with 62,000 other experts. Also, ChaCha rates are pretty slim, ranging from 1 cent to 20 cents per task. Though savvy experts can make money online, don't give up your day job.

Log in whenever you want for as long as you want.
Put some extra money in the bank.

Just Answer
(http://www.justanswer.com/expert/credential/become_an_expert.aspx)

We invite you to join a community of professionals who answer questions on JustAnswer and Pearl.com. You will answer questions on your own time, and get paid by our rapidly growing customer base of more than 20 million people and counting. Answers come via email or text message.
To join the community of professionals, you will need to:
Complete an online application and online profile
Take a short subject matter test
Verify your credentials

KGB Answers
(http://www.kgbanswers.com/collections/jobs/37018)

You become an expert after taking a brief test. At these websites, a customer asks a question and receives an answer from an "expert." Answers come via your smartphone.

G. Listening to Music

Hit Predictor (http://www.hitpredictor.com/)

You can listen the music through this website and rate the music / artist after listening the song. In short by taking polls you can earn in this website. The earned points can be redeemed in the form of CD's, DVD's and debit cards. You will get 3 points normally while listening one song and if you are in the poll point you will earn 5 points for each song.

Music X Ray (https://www.musicxray.com/)

This is a very useful platform for undiscovered artists to help them get famous and on the other hand by listening to their music people will earn money through reviewing their music. This website gives a head start to new artists where they can start their career. People can sign up in this website and make their accounts /profiles and listen to music whatever they like. You will receive a song from an artist that will be according to your taste and you will also receive a mail for the acknowledgement. The rate of this website is 10 cent per song. You can withdraw your payment when it reaches threshold of $20.00.

Radio Loyalty (http://www.radioloyalty.com/)

Through this website people are not only welcome to listen to the music but they can also watch videos of their choice. You will get the points for listening to the music and watching videos. This website will give you an opportunity to transfer your points into gifts cards or transfer it into your debit card, This way is not that simple to listen the music. You have to call and place the order for transferring your points into your payment.

Slice the Pie (https://slicethepie.com/splash.html)

This website is for the people living in the US and Europe. They can easily create an account in this website and can start earning instant money while listening to music online. The online music service is available 24/7. After listening to the music for about 90 seconds you can write a short review about the music and earn money. The rates for each song are 15 cents. You can only withdraw your payment when it reaches 10 dollars. You must have PayPal account to withdraw your money.

G. Using Phone Apps

Bookscouter (http://bookscouter.com/)

If you have old books you want to get rid of, use this app to sell them. Scan the barcodes with your smartphone, and Bookscouter will let you see comparisons of payouts from more than 20 book buyback companies. Once you find the best offer, fill out some information about where payments should be sent, and ship the books to the buyback companies.

Cash for Computer (http://www.cashyourlaptop.com/)

You can make extra money by selling your old laptop, and this app will let you do it. Simply select the type of device you wish to sell, add a description of the device, pack it up and ship it (free of charge), and get paid with a check or PayPal.

Expensify (https://www.expensify.com/)

If you are having problems with your expense reports, you can save time and money by using Expensify. This app lets you capture receipts, track time and mileage, track business travel, create expense reports, and more. Using this app will allow you to get these things done quickly, so you can spend more time actually making money.

Field Agent (http://www.fieldagent.net/for-agents/)

This is a great app that can help you earn money. From the main navigation window you can locate jobs through the "Jobs List" or through the "Map View." Select a job to see additional details and accept it. Once a job has been selected, you will have two hours to complete the task. Be sure you're near the objective before you start the task.

Foap (https://www.foap.com/photographer)

This is an app that allows you to make money by taking photos. You can charge as much as you like per photo, which means that your money-making opportunities through Foap are virtually limitless.

People are always looking for a huge variety of photos, and you may be surprised at how much money you can make with a photo of your cat.

Ibotta (https://ibotta.com/unsupported)

Take photos of your receipts and receive rebates using this app. Sign up for a free account, download the mobile app, and click on "Rebates". Here you will find loads of great offers. Rebates will vary depending on the product and the promotion.

i-Say Mobile (http://www.i-say.com/)

When you need a survey app, this is definitely the one to choose. It is from the Ipsos company, which does much of the polling during presidential races. If you have some free time, you can make money completing surveys. Or, you can collect points, and redeem them for gift cards from Amazon, iTunes, etc., or cash them in through PayPal.

NeponLine (https://www.ncponline.com/panel/US/EN/Login.htm)

Earn rewards points as a panelist for Ncponline. Scan your purchases, and send the data in to get points. You may also be contacted occasionally for opinions. You can make money through this app, and it only takes an hour each week. You get points for every interaction, and when you have enough points, you can cash them in for rewards.

Receipt Hog (http://receipthog.com/)

This is a lot like Ibotta, because you can take photos of receipts and get rewards points for PayPal or Amazon gift cards. Unlike Ibotta, you don't have to shop at specific stores. You can shop anywhere, and still earn points. But, it is slower to cash out than it is with Ibotta.

H. Merchandising & Product Demonstration

Volition (http://www.volition.com/merchandise.html)

This is a website listing companies that hire people to demonstrate products and conduct merchandising tasks. Browse the list and apply for working with the companies.

World Alliance for Retail Excellence & Standards
(https://www.retailworldalliance.com/)

This is another website where you can sign up for FREE and sees the available merchandising jobs. These types of jobs are usually part time.

I. Mystery shopping

Volition (http://www.volition.com/mysteryUSA1.html)

This is the one and only website you need to start mystery shopping. It is FREE to see the companies A – Z and apply for work.

J. Other ways to earn money online

Café Press (http://www.cafepress.com/cp/info/sell/)

Are you funny? Can you draw? Design some t-shirts, mugs, and mouse pads and CafePress will set up a store for you. It's free and easy to set up. When you build a store, let us know and we will list it on the "Friends with CafePress Stores" page.

Commission River
(http://www.commissionriver.com/publisher_signup.html?crid=13195)

Show your friends how to save money on their phone bills, internet service and many other things. And make great money in doing so.

Models.com (http://models.com/)

You can make money as a model. Get YOUR 15 Minutes of Fame.

Movie Rewards (http://www.disneymovierewards.go.com/)

Get stuff from Disney by joining and accumulating points. You get points by buying Disney videos and seeing Disney movies in theaters. (Enter code GOOFY for 50 bonus points.)

Pay Spree (https://payspree.com/)

Get paid to sell products and earn instant commissions. Earn up to 100% instant commissions promoting the products in our ever expanding product directory.

Perfume Emporium

(http://www.perfumeemporium.com/beautybucks/index.cfm?referrernum= 19165&AID=4082810&PID=136899)

Get $5 just for registering for their Beauty Bucks Program. For every $1.00 spent, you will receive 500 Beauty Bucks. You can use these Beauty Bucks to get free products on their site. Refer your friends, because you'll get 10% of their Beauty Bucks.

Tupperware (http://www.tupperware.com/)

Host your own Tupperware Online Party and qualify to receive FREE products! Your Online Party is active for two weeks. Your guests receive e-mail invitations from you with special offers that help qualify you to earn FREE Tupperware® products.

O. Selling your Photos

Dreamstime

(http://www.dreamstime.com/sell-stock-photos-images#res8374337)

Anyone can join our community and sell their photos, images and/or videos. Just create an account and upload your media file.

For each transaction, the contributor receives 25-50% Revenue Share, which is calculated based on the net sales amount for the transaction. Exclusive files receive an additional 10 % bonus, while exclusive contributors enjoy a 60 % Revenue Share for all sales and an additional bonus of $0.20 for each approved submission.

Foap   (https://www.foap.com/photographer)

Get the app for free and upload your photo. You can sell them on Foap. com. Download the Foap app, upload your photos and make them available for purchase on Foap.com. For each photo you sell you make $5 and you can sell the same photo an unlimited number of times.

Fotolia   (https://us.fotolia.com/Info/Contributors)

Submit your content and sell across all Abode platforms to reach millions of users.

Submit content and sell it on both Adobe Stock and Fotolia.com.Adobe Stock offers integration into Creative Cloud: sell directly from Photoshop CC, Illustrator CC and other great apps.
Learn from our community:
We'll help you to reach your full potential by giving you access to fantastic tips and the most valuable seller information. The higher the quality of images you upload, the more cash you'll earn.

Make money:
Contributors are the heart of our marketplace. We are committed to distributing fair royalties so our contributors can dedicate themselves to their creativity.

Shutterstock
(https://submit.shutterstock.com/?utm_medium=Affiliate&utm_campaign=
KirbysMarketing&utm_source=102882&irgwc=1)

Shutterstock is a global marketplace for artists and creators to sell royalty-free images, footage, vectors and illustrations. Our customers are increasingly requesting both HD and 4k video content, including location-based, driving shots, green screen and more. Our customers are always searching for local, authentic images that include cityscapes, families, landmarks and more. Vectors are always in high demand, whether they are icons, textured backgrounds or illustrations.

The following photo earning apps are available via Google Play: (*from the website: https://play.google.com/store/apps/ similar?id=com.depositphotos.clashot&hl=en*)

Blurb Checkout/Blurb Inc.

Blurb Checkout is the background purchase and checkout app for Samsung's book-making app that comes preloaded on the new Galaxy S4 phone.
The Checkout app lets you:

- Order your book and process your transaction by credit card
- Set billing and shipping information
- Order in seven different currencies
- Get your book delivered in just 7 to 14 days (in most locations)

PLEASE NOTE: Blurb Checkout is a separate app from Samsung's book-making tool. We welcome feedback on your Checkout app experience here; comments related to Samsung's app should be provided to Samsung directly.

Champcash

Best Affiliate Program To Earn Money By Just referring to Your Friends. Install App => Refer To Friends => Earn Unlimited

Funda is SImple , We are Giving Money of Advertisement. Users Installs the Apps and Advertisers Pay us and We Pay Users. You can Earn Unlimited without investing any money...

To Become Champcash Associate You don't Have to Pay anything . Its 100% Free Business and If someone Ask you for Any type of Payment to Join in Champcash then it is illegal and let us know about that.

Features :

1. Earn by Referring Champcash to friends.
2. Earn when your friends refer someone.
3. Withdraw Payment by Bank, recharge and Gift cards.

Before Installing ChampCash (earn unlimited money free) / Giving Any Bad Review Please Read Full Detail And Watch Promo Video:

Champ Cash (earn unlimited money free) is 100% Free Networking Application Through which Anyone Can Earn Unlimited Money By Just Referring Champ Cash (earn unlimited money free) To their Friends .Just Refer Champ Cash (earn unlimited money free) to Your Friends and Ask them to Complete the Challenge (By installing & Opening 8-10 Apps in their Android phone), You will Get its payment Within Few Minutes.

As Networking is the Best Way to do any Business we have Implemented Networking Concept in This application.

We are Aware of Many Networking Companies Who are Doing Fraud with Their Clients By asking them To Give money for joining. Here in Champ Cash (earn unlimited money free) If we are Not taking any Money and Only Distributing Money To Whole Network By installing some Apps . So, As we are 100% Free in the same way We are 100% Genuine and Legit Company to Earn Unlimited Money.

How We are Distributing Money , Even We are Not taking Any Charges From User :

This is the Main Point and will comes in Everyone's Mind. Here is Your Answer : Other Companies are Giving money directly to their Users if they install Apps in their Phone . We Have Changed this Scenario, we are not giving any Money to the User who is Installing Apps in his phone But we are Distributing that money in Whole Network.

In Champ Cash (earn unlimited money free), There is no limit on Direct Referrals. Means You can Join Unlimited Friends at Your Level 1 and In the same way Your Direct Referrals can Join Unlimited At their Direct and You will get benefit of All.

Earn cash real Money referring apps through networking free recharge ChampCash (earn unlimited money free).

Steps To Earn Unlimited With Us

  1 : Install Champ Cash (earn unlimited money free)
  2 : Open Champ Cash in Your Phone

3 : Signup

4 : Enter Refer ID of Your Sponsor

5 : Accept The Challenge

6 : Install Apps Given in the Challenge

7 : Open Installed App For At-least 1 Min.

8 : Install And Open All Apps Step By Step.

9 : As You Installs All Apps You Will be Eligible to Use our N/W System

10 : Go To Invite And Earn Menu (To invite your Friends)

11 : Choose Any Message And Select Social Media Profile where you want to Share the Message.

12 : If Any of Your Friend Click on Your Shared Link And Completes The Challenge then You Will Instantly Get its Payment.

13 : Ask Your All Friends to Open All installed Apps one by one for 1 min. Otherwise you won't get its payout.

Earn cash real Money referring apps through networking free recharge Champ Cash (earn unlimited money free)

Clashot

Shoot and upload, sell and earn money using the app. The free Clashot app helps you to take, publish and sell your photos.

Depositphotos

Now Depositphotos goes mobile to offer you the best photos, vectors and videos on the go!

No longer tethered to desktop computers, designers can now get instant mobile access to more than 27 million leading-edge, royalty-free stock photos, vector graphics and video clips. Now anyone – media professionals and desktop designers alike – can search and download stock files from anywhere, at any time.

Dreamstime

Earn cash for doing what you love: taking pictures! Sell your photos on Dreamstime – the leading stock photography community.

- Make money from your photography

- Reach millions of potential customers
- Real time sales notifications
- Quick account set up & sign in
- Easily upload from your smartphone or tablet
- Optimize images for prime visibility in the marketplace
- Track sales and earnings
- Track image statistics

The Dreamstime Companion empowers pro and aspiring photographers to make money by selling their own original photography and images. With Dreamstime Companion you can easily upload images (min. 2.5MP) directly from your smartphone into the Dreamstime Stock Photography marketplace, making them available to millions of customers looking to buy great photography just like yours.

Dreamstime Companion also allows you to track your current earnings and image statistics while on the go. Download now and sign up for a FREE account or sign into your existing Dreamstime account. It only takes seconds to start making real money selling your photographs!

Earn Talktime

Introducing 'Earn Talktime™' the app that gets you 'FREE MOBILE TALKTIME' for apps downloaded from its own personal dashboard.

Earn Talktime™ helps you take advantage of the app that you've download for fun or work. Just download an app from Earn Talktime™ and earn real cash that you could use to redeem free mobile talk time instantly. You will never have to pay for your mobile recharge again. Supports mobile recharge for the following mobile networks: Aircel, Airtel, Idea, Reliance CDMA, Reliance GSM, Tata Docomo, Vodafone, BSNL, Uninor, Videocon, MTS.
How to recharge mobile using Earn Talktime app in free?

Install Earn Talktime™ app into your mobile.
Go inside offers, Install and open your favorite Android app.
Amount will credited into your wallet.

Use wallet amount for fill talk time into any mobile.
Want to full your mobile with recharge?
Refer app to your friends and get up to Rs 1000 or more free recharge.

Key Features:

- Instant free mobile recharge across all operators in India.
- Refer friends through Whatsapp, Facebook, twitter or Email and earn extra.
- Take a look time and again for "special offers" - we also usually send out notifications for these!

Earn Talktime/RationalHead

Over 1.3 crores Earn Talktime users have earned more than Rs.55 Crores of talk time. Earn Talktime makes it easy to earn money by downloading the best free android apps, reading horoscope, tarot, bollywood gossips, filling surveys etc. from your mobile earn talk time is the first app to give you unlimited mobile prepaid recharges, DTH top-ups, postpaid bill payments and much more.

How does it work:

- Earn unlimited money: install apps, complete short surveys etc., invite friends
- Spend your money: mobile prepaid recharges, DTH recharges, mobile postpaid bill payments

Invite friends and earn more…

- Earn money for every friend you get to download the earn talk time app
- Invite friends through whatsapp, Facebook, WeChat or SMS
- Earn more money when your friend uses earn talk time

Redeem your unlimited earn talk time balance from your mobile number: Prepaid mobile operators: Airtel, Vodafone, Reliance, Idea, Aircel, BSNL,MTNL, Tata Docomo, Uninor, MTS, Videocon, Loop

DTH operators: Airtel Digital TV, TATA Sky, Dish TV, Sun TV , Videocon D2H

Postpaid mobile bill payments: Airtel, Vodafone, Reliance, Idea, Aircel, BSNL,MTNL, Tata Docomo, Uninor, MTS, Videocon, Loop

iCash-Earn Cash/NelsonBolson

iCash is an easy way to earn cash free rewards and make money online by getting paid for completing various tasks and micro jobs.

Have you always dreamed about making money online and get paid for the time you spend in your mobile device? With today's technology and the billions of dollars spent in the advertising industry it's very easy to get a piece of it for yourself.

With iCash you get access to unlimited and unique offers that will get your rewarded for completing them. Earn enough points and redeem your reward instantly. Repeat the process and you'll have a stable and very good source of income, and you don't risk anything and it's even not requiring too much time, only a few minutes per day can bring your some nice $$$ every day.

iCash offers you a revolutionary method to make money by using your Android mobile device. It's Free, Fast and Easy!

- How exactly do I get paid from iCash?

By using iCash app you earn money every time you install an app or game, when you share on social networks(Google and Facebook), when you redeem your daily free bonus gift, when you refer friends and they enter your invitation code, when you watch rewarded videos. There are endless possibilities.

- How much can I earn daily?

You can make from $1 to $50+ daily, everything depends on how many offers will you complete and of your location. It's a well know factor that users from Tier 1 countries have more offers available and thus getting paid more.

- I have completed an offer but didn't received my coins

Some of the offers pay instantly upon completion, but please allow up to 24 hours for the iPoints to be credited into your account. If after 24 hours you still didn't received your reward then please contact us.

- PayPal isn't accepted in my country, can I choose another reward?

Absolutely yes! We have a various selection of rewards you can earn. If PayPal does not work for you then you can choose from this rewards: Payza money, Webmoney wallet, QiWi , Amazon gift card, Google Play gift card, and Playstation and Xbox promo codes.

So to sum up what iCash does and what you need to do to start earning free money and gift cards rewards:

- Install iCash on your Android device
- Complete various tasks like installing and trying out free cool apps and games
- Answer quick and fun surveys
- Watch awesome videos and get rewarded
- Share your experience on Facebook and Google
- Invite friends and get paid
- Exchange your iPoints for real money in your PayPal account or any other reward

So what are you waiting for? Get on board with iCash and start earning **free cash** rewards and get paid for your time!

Insta Square/Insta Photo

Frustrated that you have to crop your portrait and landscape photos before posting them to Instagram?

Insta Square Maker is an easy and fast way to upload your entire photo to Instagram or similar social networks without having to crop away any piece of it. It puts frames around your photos to make them square shaped.

Key features:

- post entire photos without cropping.
- choose any color for background.
- change image position inside the square frame.

- crop tool
- shadow effect
- make blurred background from photo
- more than 20 filters to make your photos more beautiful
- share created square photo directly to Instagram with just one click of a button.

Never crop photos again to make them compatible with Instagram.

Follow us on Instagram and add #InstaSquareMaker hashtag to your photos before posting to get more likes and followers!

* Caller ID
Insta Square Maker has free caller ID. It identifies callers for you - even the ones not in your contact list. Caller ID results are shown after calls and also allow you to save the contact details directly to your address-book. You can also go to create beautiful photos in Insta Square Maker with one click from the Caller ID screen.

You can adjust or disable caller ID to your preferences in the settings menu any time.

Ladoo/Airloyal

Ladooo is sweet & simple! Earn free recharge for just checking out some of the best Android apps, watching videos and completing simple polls and surveys. Or participate in contests and win! With ladooo, you will get INSTANT free mobile recharge in minutes!

Never pay for recharge again!

No complex registration required. More than 3 million users have earned crores of rupees already.

New offers are updated multiple times a week, so you can keep earning free mobile recharge and talk time.

Recharge your mobile free or become popular among friends and family by gifting recharge to any other mobile in India instantly.

We take our promise to give instant free recharge seriously. If you have trouble using the app, contactsupport@airloyal.com or use the support feature within the app for quick resolution.

Key Features:

* Instant free mobile recharge across all operators in India
* Supports Airtel, Aircel, BSNL, MTNL, Idea, Loop Mobile, MTS, Reliance, Tata Docomo, Tata Indicom, Uninor, Videocon, Virgin Mobile, Vodafone
* Refer friends through Whatsapp or Facebook to install Ladooo or other apps and earn
* Post-paid customers can use wallet money for recharging any pre-paid mobile for self, family or friends
* Topup any of your DTH accounts with free DTH across Tata Sky, Videocon d2h, Dish TV, Sun TV, Reliance Big TV, Airtel DTH
* Built-in support features to quickly resolve any issues on your own or chat with us for any issues from within the app

Free Tips to Earn Maximum Free Mobile Recharge:

* Check the app every day to see new offers and install them.
* Refer friends in addition to offers to earn extra

Magazine Cover/Thalia Photo

Your dream is to become a superstar or a model? You fantasize about the chance to put your picture on a "magazine cover"? Your dream will finally come true: Magazine Cover Photo Montage is here! Our real simple magazine app allows you to edit a cover photo for a famous magazine. You can easily design cover pictures and put your own photo on a magazine cover. Feel like a glamorous model with this "photo magazine app". Download Magazine Cover Photo Montage for free and create a zine cover photo with your face on it today!

- You own cover image maker!
- Take a picture or choose one from your phone gallery!
- Select from variety of magazine templates and adjust your pic!
- Easy photograph editing controls!
- Plenty of front page designs for various zine types!
- Share your new fake mags on Facebook, Twitter, Instagram & any other social network app you have on your phone!
- No Internet connection required!

Amazing magazine "photo effects" will leave you and your friends breathless once you're done with the free photo montage. Choose your favorite magazine headline, the best image filter for your pic and watch the magic happening on your phone! You can share your masterpiece on Facebook, Twitter or Instagram so your friends can see the fabulous "magazine wallpaper". Make male photo magazine covers to beautify your boyfriend's pic with this magazine picture cover or you can choose magazine for girls and do a "professional picture editing" on your image.

Your photograph can end up on the front page of your favorite fashion zine. Live the life of a celebrity for a moment and customize the whole picture not just a part of it. If you ever wondered how to do a photo montage then you can download Magazine Cover Photo Montage for free and have your own picture montage maker on your mobile. This "cover photo maker" will make you look like a famous singer or a rock star. You do not have to be bored with the same old photo effects on your smartphone because our new magazine effects will beautify any picture within a second.

You do not need online picture editor to create a cover photo nor you need a professional photo editor when you can have all that on your own phone. If you love to make a photo collage and you want to be creative with your images then get this text cover image maker free of charge. Glamorous photo effects in this "magazine editor app" will make every image super sophisticated and fancy. Making your own zine has never been easier and you can do it like a pro with Magazine Cover Photo Montage. Place your picture on a magazine front page and watch all of your friends like it once you share it on social networks.

Be creative and try to make a parody magazine! Take a goofy photo of yourself or your friends, choose a funny photo effect and start laughing! You can also restore an old photograph to look brand new on a fashion zine front page or you can choose a "vintage photo effect" for your new image- the possibilities are limitless! Plenty of free magazine picture frames and picture covers are available in just one photo editing app. You can do face photo montage and look fabulous on every picture you make. Place your photo on a beauty zine and get a high quality photo montage.

Edit your pics like a pro using this magazine cover photo frame maker! Apply cool photo effects on your selfie and let the world admire your fame and beauty! With this pic studio you can change the frames any time you want because the internet connection is not required. One of the best "photo montage" software is within a few taps on your phone. Download "Magazine Cover Photo Montage" for free and let the magic begin!

Money Photo/Photo Frames

Become really rich with money photo editor that will decorate your images with interesting money picture frames! Money Photo Frame Editor will make all of your dreams come true! You can be a millionaire if you download this photo montage maker & start editing pictures! This frame collection is rich in wonderful money frames and other photo effects that can make your pictures look stylish & expensive! Get this free photo editor right away and enjoy moneybags, dollar bills & coin photo frames embellishing your dearest images! Hurry up!

Photo frame editor's features:

A frame collection full of amazing money picture frames for cool photo manipulation!

 High quality & the coolest design of photo frames!
Money photo montage maker you will learn how to use in a couple of seconds!
Upload a selfie or a photo from your phone's photo gallery and start adding money frames!
Capture new images with your camera straight from this photo editing software!
15 money photo frames you can choose from when you start editing!
20 wonderful picture filters you can apply over your money images!
Don't forget to save all the images you edit to your personal money photo album!
Use some of these framed images as your wallpaper pictures!
Feel free to share your money photo montage to different social networks! (Facebook, Instagram, Twitter)!

Be the richest man on the world with Money Photo Frame Editor!
This free photo montage software is the only app that offers you really expensive looking photographs completely free of charge! Put your

photo on money & you can rule the world! Becoming rich has never been easier! With the best money picture editor the sky will be your limit! Get this photo collection of free images of money you can use to decorate your photos & selfies! Make money photos easily- it will only take you a couple of seconds to edit your favorite pics!

Enjoy your customized money pictures you can create right here for free!
Frame all your photos with excellent money borders for images available in our brand new photo gallery! Use your free photo montage maker to create images all your friends will admire & get virtual wealth that will bring you many likes & shares on social networks! Download Money Photo Frame Editor & let the photo fun start this instant! Finally, you can make the coolest images with fun & unique money picture frames! Don't wait any longer to get this money photo lab you needed all your life!

Pic Collage/Cardinal Blue

Make your holidays even happier with PicCollage! With exclusive holiday content, PicCollage has everything you need to commemorate the season! New Christmas and Hanukkah stickers, holiday backgrounds, and easy-to-use templates make PicCollage the perfect app for the holidays (and any time of year)! Join over 100 million people who use Pic-Collage to combine photos, YouTube videos, funky fonts, sassy stickers and cute cutouts to create the prettiest collages you'll ever see on a mobile device.

You can also PRINT your collages into greeting cards to send to your loved ones anywhere in the world, or turn your collages into phone cases, magnets, posters, and MORE!

Awesome features:
* Import photos from your photo library, Instagram, Facebook and web image search
* Simple touch gestures to rotate, resize, flick to delete
* Double-tap a photo to edit photo with Aviary photo effects, clip photo, adjust borders, copy/paste images, and "flip" stickers
* Just tap on the lower-left Frame icon, and swipe to select a frame to make an instant collage!

* Clip photos by outlining the area you want with your finger
* Lots of backgrounds and stickers to choose from!
* Choose Templates to create themed collages easily
* Share your creations to Instagram, Facebook, and Twitter.

* Make your creations into personalized products- phone cases, prints, magnet, greeting cards or posters!

PicsaStock

PicsaStock is your marketplace to sell and buy the world's best authentic photos and discover creative royalty free images.
"Want to earn some money from your photographs? PicsaStock is an excellent starting point"
(148apps.com/2014)

"An easy way for hobby photographers to sell their images …"
(venture village/2014)

We offer you a simple and safe way to upload your unique photos and sell it thousands of times to millions of people. Our photo community can change the world of royalty free images through simple and innovative products that help you to sell and discover the world's best photos.

Upload your images right NOW and be astonished on how easy earning money could be!

Finding inspiration has never been easier - swipe down on any picture to see similar images!

Features:

Upload & Sell your photos:
- simply upload photos from your camera roll, Instagram, flickr, 500px or dropbox
- earn 50% commission per sale
- stay informed about your statistics

Discover awesome images:
- find beautiful royalty free photos and photographers

- discover tons of high quality images in the stunning landscape modus
- Browse through images in different views
- always find the photo you need - tag and color Search make it possible
- like your favorites

Inspiration from other photographers:
- found a photo you like? Swipe down to unveil more inspiration.
- add inspirational photos to your collections with a single tap

Picture Gallery:
- create and manage your own gallery
- easily present your photos with tags & titles
- Redesigned User Galleries - more eye pleasing than ever before
- Keep yourself informed with the new statistics slide
- Collections! Create stunning collections of your favorite images

Share your photos
- advertise your gallery by using our sharing functions (via Facebook, Instagram etc.)
- easily share images, galleries and even your collections with all your friends

Pictive

Where mobile photographers thrives.

Publish your best photos for sale: Sell your photos through your own gallery

Shoot for paid projects: Respond to calls for submissions from brands and agencies offering premium payouts.

Showcase your portfolio to the world: Find an audience, get exposure, and be discovered.

Quick Cash/My Earn

You spend hundreds of hours using your mobile, but what if there was an easy way to get paid for it? App companies are spending BILLIONS of dollars every year to get people use their apps but you see NONE of this money. QuickCash empowers YOU to change that reality and claim that money back to your pocket. It offers a wide variety of simple and fast ways to leverage your social contacts (i.e. on Facebook or Whatsapp) to earn money and exchange it for PayPal cash or use it to recharge your mobile.

QuickCash is a revolutionary way to make money with your mobile, fast and easy!

What Is QuickCash?

QuickCash is the most simple and fastest way to make money on your social networks. We pay cash every time you or your friend installs an app. The more friends get to download the apps you recommend the more cash you earn. We'll also give you lots of fun and quick ways to post on your social networks and make money with just a few taps.

How Much Can I Earn?

You will make your first $5 in less than 5 minutes. A couple of minutes each day will make you over a hundred dollars cash each month.

What To Do When I Didn't Receive My Coins?

Due to proliferation of different partners we cooperate with, it happens that you can miss some Coins once in a while. In case it happens, please check what third-party offer wall the offer came from and contact them accordingly:

Supersonic Offer

Open up the supersonic offer wall again and click "Missing Coins" at bottom of the screen.

Aarki

Please fill out the following information and contact customer-service@ aarki.net with the following info:

1. Name:

2. Offer Name:

3. Date when the offer was completed:

Superrewards

Go to the offers page and click on the "Get Help" link. You will be redirected to player.superrewards.com. Click on the "?" help icon for the offer in question and proceed to the offer inquiry page. Follow the steps.

TrialPay

Go to the app and search Earn Cash tab, click "Help". You will be redirected to a new window, find "Check Your Offer Status" and click on it. Find the offer you didn't get Coins for and click "Report a Problem" next to it. If you don't see your offer, click on "Contact Support" at the bottom of the window.

How Do I Earn Coins?

Remember to login every day and collect your daily rewards and Coins. There are a lot of fast free ways you can make money on your mobile and get easy rewards with QuickCash for you and your friends:

- Install new Android apps.

- Recommend new apps to your friends.

- Login in every day.

- Invite your friends to install SocialCash.

- Fill in invitation codes.

How Does It Work?

1. Install QuickCash on your Android.

2. Fulfill in-app tasks and collect your free Coin rewards.

3. Exchange Coins you earn for the real-life money via PayPal.

Recommend Apps to Your Friends and Earn Money Fast and Easy! The More Coins You Collect, The More Money You Earn!

****Please, remember that you can receive Coins only if it's the first time the app is installed on your or your friend's device.****

What Users Say:

'I made my first $10 in just a few minutes! It's an amazingly simple and fun app to use and make money on mobile.'

'I didn't have to put much effort really; just a few clicks and my friends basically made real cash for me. There's no catch, they really pay for your social contacts trying new apps.'

SnapCape/Digital Belly

Snapcape is a make money online photo app in your pocket that helps you to earn money. Just Take Pictures and sell them in various photo contest & earn money! Make money fast by selling photography to Editorials/Brands through your Smartphone.

Participate in photo contests & tasks organized by various brands. You make money online once your images are sold & then your wallet will be upgraded by the selling price.

Snapwire

Snapwire is a platform that connects a new generation of photographers with brands and businesses around the world. Photographers get access to real-time, paid photo Requests and Challenges. Photographers can also sell photos directly from their own portfolios and in our growing stock photo Marketplace. Snapwire is your home for selling all your creative photography.

Authentic photography has been proven to boost engagement and increase conversions, so your best authentic photos are in high demand.

Start as an Explorer and submit your best photos to Snapwire Challenges. Level up to participate in paid buyer Requests. If your photo is nominated, you earn points and if its purchased you get paid quickly and fairly. Build your reputation by getting more points and level up. Levels give you access to other app features such as: the ability to be invited to Requests, direct commissions, and better exposure.

With Snapwire you can:

– Participate in Snapwire Challenges and earn award money
– Level up and get exclusive access to paid photo Requests from popular businesses and brands
– Submit photos from your gallery, camera, or cloud
– Build a beautiful portfolio and sell images directly from it
– Share your personal portfolio with friends, fans and clients
– Sell your best photos from our growing stock photography Marketplace
– Get real-time notifications about Requests
– Connect, communicate, and engage with photographers and creatives around the world
– Become part of this quickly growing community of talented photographers

– Get paid fairly with one of the highest market payouts when your photos are purchased
– Unlock features by earning points and level up

Stock Photos/Dreamstime

Creativity happens when you least expect, we're only a tap away. Create on the go with the Dreamstime app.

- Advanced search & zoom-in on 37M+ photos&illustrations
- Save and share favs
- Quick account set up & intuitive navigation
- Fast and easy download on smartphone or tablet
- Download archive and invoice history always at hand
- Content from 200K+ contributors worldwide
- Standard and extended licenses for multiple usages and users

With the Dreamstime app, inspiration is always in your pocket. You can easily browse, search, download and license amazing images from contributors worldwide directly on your smartphone or tablet.

Download now and sign up for a FREE account or sign into your existing account.

Say Eurekaaapp! Creative ideas are now possible anywhere.

Ugento/Apogaeis Tech

Uento is the best way to get rewarded by collecting android apps and playing games!

How to make money with Uento?

1. Get unlimited money by playing our Money Maker Game. Up to $1000 in daily prizes!
2. Downloads our app's offers on Google Play and get paid for it!
3. Unlimited Bonus FREE Points every day!
4. Invite your friends and get unlimited earnings!

TIP: If you invite your friends and they register using your referral code you can earn even more points every time they install an app! There are up to 2 levels of referrals, no earning limitations!

* Choose your own username and profile pic on PicCollage
* Follow others to discover more collages
* Remix collages with collages!
* We've also added a Contests section where you can Remix others with your own creations to get shoutouts and more followers, and stand a chance to win awesome prizes from our sponsors.

Watch and Earn/Gohil Software

What you do in your free time ???

Let's start making some money and enjoying new free advertising videos which is full of new apps, games, movie trailers, brand ads, trying new apps and many more and completing these offers may lead you some coins which interns bring you money.

These are the few steps towards your pocket money.

- Watch videos, try new apps, complete offers and earn some coins.
- Convert your coins into the rewards mentioned.
- These steps may lead you to get free shopping vouchers, recharge vouchers, online cash, movie vouchers and many more.
- There are special feature like playing jackpots through which you may earn tons of coins in a single touch.

We provide you your rewards in your own local currency through our various country supports.

You may get these many rewards from mentioned below :

+ Amazon vouchers
+ Paypal Cash
+ Steam vouchers
+ Google Play vouchers
+ Paytm cash
+ Mobikwik cash
+ Freecharge vouchers

+ Flipkart vouchers
+ Snapdeal vouchers
+ Bookmyshow vouchers
+ Many more

P. Pitch products online/Affiliate Marketing

Pitching other people's products is one of the Internet's best-paying gigs.

One method is being an affiliate at a mega-site such as **Amazon Associates marketing website:** (https://affiliate-program.amazon.com/gp/associates/join/landing/main.html/),where commissions are up to 25 percent.

Anytime anyone buys a product you're pitching, you get a cut. And you can choose from more than a million products, including gift cards or computers.

At **ClickBank** (http://www.clickbank.com/), commissions are even higher -- up to 75 percent -- and there are more than 50,000 products to choose from. Signing up is free.

Here are more Affiliate Marketing websites that allow you to pitch products:

AdMedia (http://www.admedia.com/)

Affiliate by Conversant (http://www.cj.com/)--formerly Commission Junction

Affiliate Future (http://www.affiliatefuture.com/)

Affiliate Window (http://www.affiliatewindow.com/us/)

Avangate (http://www.avangate.com/)

AvantLink (http://www.avantlink.com/)

Ebay Affiliate marketing website (http://pages.ebay.com/affiliate/referral.html)

Flex Offers.com (http://www.flexoffers.com/)

Impact Radius (http://www.impactradius.com/)

Link Connector (http://www.linkconnector.com/index.htm)

LinkShare (http://marketing.rakuten.com/affiliate-marketing)

One Network Direct (http://www.onenetworkdirect.com/)

Revenue Wire (http://www.revenuewire.com/)

ShareASale (https://account.shareasale.com/newsignup.cfm?)

TradeDoubler (http://www.tradedoubler.com/)

ValuLeadS (https://valuleads.com/)

WebGains (http://us.webgains.com/public/)

Q. Product testing

You will need to contact a company that offers these opportunities and sign up. Then you will fill out what they call a screener survey which basically lets them know if you qualify to be in the list of the next testing event for their products. Depending on the product and also the company, you can make between $3 and $125. In addition, the products are yours to keep!

Here are some companies you can test products for:

Bzz Agent (https://www.bzzagent.com/)

This is another great company. You sign up and then take several surveys. These surveys will let them know where they can place you since they have several "Bzz Campaigns" happening from time to time. Once they have accepted you, products will be sent to you and with them several different offers that you can give to your friends and family. Of course the more offers you share, the more they will send you free products.

iPoll (https://www.ipoll.com/)

This company previously went by the name SurveyHead. Opportunities here include product testing, online tasks and paid surveys. They also use a mobile app that makes it easier for you to see what tasks are available for completion, products that you can buy, which one you can test as well as review. When you sign up you get a $5 bonus!

Ipsos-I_Say (http://www.i-say.com/)

This is just an online money making gold mine. It provides opportunities to take paid surveys, product testing and several other ways that you can make some money on the internet.

Mindspay
(http://www.mindspay.com/uc?a=lpn&j=14&aff=590&saff=5436&affmid= #tA42)

You can actually have a steady stream of income with this company. They have great opportunities for both online surveys and product testing. They pay out two times each month in $50 multiples via PayPal. You do have to keep a $9.03 minimum balance.

My View (https://www.myview.com/login)

This company has both product testing and online surveys with the latter being more than the former. However, since the product testing opportunities are emailed to you, you will need to keep a close eye on your email account. They give Amazon gift cards, as well as Prepaid Visa gift cards among others.

Nielson Home Scan (http://join.ncponline.com/who)

This Company is based in Canada. It sends you a free scanner that you use at home to scan all of the household purchases you make. They then offer you free electronics and other rewards for doing so.

Pinecone Research (https://www.pineconeresearch.com/index.asp)

This is a great company that actually pays very well. You can do both product testing as well as take online surveys for them.   US males also have an opportunity for the same. More details can be found on their website.

Survey Spot

(https://www.surveyspot.com/Signup/Intake-SOI?jtype=s&cpid=6567
&offer_id=2651&affiliate_id=2316&transaction_id=102ef0ca9055051b11
5ec553b43fd1&aff_sub=5436&ip=184.60.17.131)

This site also offers both product testing and paid survey opportunities. Again, the online survey opportunities are more. The test products they send to you can include household items, foods and beauty products too. Reward is in the form of money via PayPal, store gift certificates and Amazon gift cards.

Toluna (https://us.toluna.com/products)

This company invites product testers from the USA, Australia and Canada. Once on their website you will need to click on the tab that reads "Rewards." From there click on the tab that reads "Test Products" in order to sign up. Invitations to receive their test products will come in your email. They offer gift cards as well as money as rewards.

Valued Opinions

(https://www.valuedopinions.com/eng/join/?ref=Panthera_Ban32_Share_
US&utm_source=Panthera&utm_medium=Affiliate%20Network&utm_
campaign=Panthera%20US&utm_content=Ban_32_Share_US_EN&utm_
term=Image%20or%20Banner&partner=5436)

If you love beauty products this is just the ticket! You get to test a variety of them and if you are part of their focus groups, you get even higher pay.

R. Research the Internet

There are different ways to get hired to research on the web. Using Job Boards, apply with question and answer research web sites and have your own business are three ways to make money doing research online working at home. The following list is from (http://www.theworkathomewoman. com/internet-research/):

Online Job Boards

Flex Jobs (https://www.flexjobs.com/?sub=1033) –a membership fee is charged

This is an online job board that caters to flexible working arrangements. Simply use their job search function and enter "Internet Research" or "Internet Researcher". This will take you to a page that lists all the jobs in this category. While it does cost a small fee to join, it's well worth it. All jobs are hand screened, so you know that you're dealing with legit opportunities.

Indeed

(http://www.indeed.com/jobs?utm_source=publisher&utm_medium= organic_listings&utm_campaign=affiliate)

This is one of my favorite sites to use when searching for telecommuting jobs, here's why. It's an aggregated job board, which means their platform pulls job listings from all the other major job board sites. This means you save tons of time, because you don't have to search each job site individually. While the jobs are not screened for legitimacy, Indeed does requires that all listings contain a company name, location, job title, and complete job description.

To find Internet Research jobs just use the keywords, "work at home" and "internet research".

Upwork (https://www.upwork.com/)

There are freelance jobs board sites that cater to freelancers. Simply register for an account (it's free), search for Internet Research positions, and submit your bid. If your bid is accepted, you'll complete the work and get paid through the platform, minus a small fee (usually 10%). While many freelancers complain of the low rates on these sites — it can be a great way for you to establish yourself in the field, and to work with repeat clients.

Answer and Research Questions websites

There are a bunch of sites that hire independent contractors to answer questions on various topics. So if you have experience in a certain area that will be extremely helpful when you're applying. With these opportunities you're not only researching answers for people, you're also writing the answers online — so you'll need to write well.

Experts 123 (http://www.experts123.com/SignUp)

This is a revenue sharing platform, so the more popular your answer they more you'll get paid. Payments are made via PayPal.

Just Answer (http://ats.justanswer.com/landing#)

Pays 20% – 50% of what the person is willing to pay for the answer (if it's accepted). Payments are made via PayPal. Has an A+ rating with the Better Business Bureau.

Small Biz Advice (http://www.smallbizadvice.com/)

Browse questions and make a bid. Payments are made bi-monthly via PayPal, minus a 5% commission fee.

S. Surfing the Web

CashSurfers (http://www.cashsurfers.com/)

Earn points while you surf the internet. Points are converted to cash at the end of each month.

Groupon
(https://www.groupon.com/?z=dealpage&utm_source=rvs&utm_medium=afl&utm_campaign=136899)

Provides a deal per day of great things to do, eat, see, & buy in your area. Refer Friends and Get $10 Groupon Bucks.

Memolink (http://www.memolink.com/)

Complete surveys, answer trivia, signup for free trials and in return, you earn points toward gift certificates at places such as The Home Depot, Olive Garden, Red Lobster, Best Buy and more.

Search Cactus.com (https://www.searchcactus.com/)

Also pays you to do searches, and for telling your friends about it too.

S. Taking Surveys (Note: Never pay to take a survey)

American Consumer Opinion
(http://www.acop.com/?SSAID=114793&SSCID=c1jz_idbnc)

They invite you to fill out surveys online. Once finished with the survey, you will receive cash, a check, a gift, and/or an entry in a drawing (values typically range from $4.00 to $25.00 per completed survey). Even if you are not selected for a survey, your name will be entered in a monthly drawing.

The Business Research Lab
(http://www.busreslab.com/index.php/research-services/online-surveys/survey-panels)

Various surveys and online mystery shops. We have no experience with this company yet. Feedback wanted.

BuzzBack (http://panel.buzzback.com/)

Just a 5 minute survey about a product you use, a web site you've visited, or a reaction to a new idea. Your completed responses earn you $5.

Cash Crate (http://www.cashcrate.com/lp13)

Take surveys, paid to search, fun contests, games for cash and prizes—easiest and highest paid program.

Clear Voice Surveys (http://www.clearvoicesurveys.com/)

Pays you for each survey you participate in.

Clickin (http://www.clickin.com/)

Focused dialogue, market research and opinion polls. Incentives include phone cards, gift certificates, cash, and drawings.

ConsumerViews (http://www.consumerviews.com/)

Provided by Solomon Wolff Associates, Inc. Typically, participants will receive a check for $5.00 or perhaps coupons worth $5 or more on the client's products. In some situations, participants may receive larger payments. Solomon Wolff Associates is a full service marketing research and marketing support firm providing data gathering and analysis in addition to related marketing support services.

Employee Surveys (http://www.employeesurveys.com/)

Brief e-mail surveys, usually about work related topics. Each time you participate in a survey, your name will be entered into a drawing. We have no experience with this company yet. Feedback wanted.

Epinons (http://www.epinions.com/)

Write and rate brutally honest and unbiased opinions. Read buying guides, professional reviews and web resources. Read pros and cons about the products you buy. Earn cash for your opinions.

E-Poll (http://www.epollsurveys.com/epoll/clients/index.htm)

Provide feedback on new products, services, celebrities and entertainment. It's free to join and we never share your personal information. Receive surveys via email, take surveys and earn points, then cash in your points to get free gift cards.

E-Search (http://www.esearch.com/)

The Internet Consumer Research Company. Register for cash prize drawings.

EyeCloud Consulting (http://www.eyecloud.com/)

Payment for participating in online surveys can be either in the form of a sweepstakes or a set amount which ranges between $1 - $10.

FGI Research (http://www.fgiresearch.com/)

Online surveys range between $5-$10 or will be a Prize Drawing.

Global Test Market (https://www.globaltestmarket.com/?lang=E)
Earn rewards for taking paid surveys

Earn Marketpoints to be redeemed for rewards for products available in the US reward catalog: Amazon, PayPal, Macy's, Kohl's and UNICEF charity donation.

GoZing (http://www.gozing.com/)

Survey you about movies, sports and products.

Grace Market Research (GMR) (http://www.gmrnet.com/)

They do TV viewing studies. Register for TV Pilot Tests and surveys and cable tests about television shows. They do not say that they pay.

Harris Poll (http://www.harrispollonline.com/)

Take cute online polls and get points. Then redeem your points for stuff. Not cash, but some useful stuff and the surveys are fun.

Ipsos i-Say Panel (http://www.i-say.com/)

One of the ten largest research firms in the world. Give feedback about their client's products and services and tell them how they can make them better. They also want to know your ideas on current events and social issues. Cash prizes. (USA only)

I-Think, Inc. (http://www.ithinkinc.com/)

Each time you qualify and complete a survey, you'll be paid. In addition, they have regular drawings for cash prizes (usually around $100).

Lightspeed Research/My Survey (http://www.mysurvey.net/)

Take online surveys and earn points that can be redeemed for cash and prizes. Join today to earn an entry into the $5,000 Sweepstakes.

Mar's Research (http://www.marsresearch.com/)

Your time will always be rewarded with products or cash.

Memolink (http://www.memolink.com/)

Complete surveys, answer trivia, signup for free trials and in return, you earn points toward gift certificates at places such as The Home Depot, Olive Garden, Red Lobster, Best Buy and more.

Mindfield Online (http://mindfieldonline.com/)

Earn cash and prizes for each completed survey.

Mintvine (https://mintvine.com/)

Get paid cash for participating in online market research surveys, and with more earning opportunities.

The Net Panel (http://www.mdxresearch.com/the-net-panel/)

Just for signing up, you enter to win prizes. Then get rewarded for your opinions.

NFO World Group
(https://www.mysurvey.com/index.cfm?action=main.join&R=DEFAULT_CLOSED)

Over 50 year old company, who invented consumer panels back in the 1940's. You will be automatically entered in the "Your Opinions Count Sweepstakes" upon joining.

Nielsen Digital Voice
(https://digitalvoice.nielsen.com/us/en/home.html)

Nielsen family members have been influential in determining the popularity of television programs for over 50 years. Here's your opportunity to participate in Nielsen's panel for the Internet. (USA only)

Nielsen Home Scan
(https://www.homescan.com/panel/US/EN/Login.htm)

Earn valuable gift points, which are redeemable for electronics, household items, jewelry, toys and more.

NPD Online Research Team

(https://www.npd.com/wps/portal/npd/us/about-npd/consumer-panel/)

Your opinions will be heard by decision makers worldwide. And, you'll have a chance to WIN CASH - starting with the chance to win $1,000 for registering to join.

Opinion Outpost (https://www.opinionoutpost.com/)

Opinion Outpost bridges the gap between your opinions and the companies who need them. You can earn cash and rewards for the time you spend taking online surveys with points you can redeem for cash or gift vouchers to popular brands.

Opinion Square

(https://www.opinionsquare.com/Home.aspx?action=cookieTest&trackid=520016217&sitegroup=2&siteid=2000&languageid=1)

Earn cash and prizes for each completed survey.

Panda Research (http://www.pandaresearch.com/)

- Earn Money by successfully completing our paid surveys and offers
- Learn how you can receive coupons, discounts, and giveaways with your participation in our offers and surveys
- Refer your friends and earn additional income
- Earn Additional Income by reading emails (Maximum $25 per payout)
- Get paid by the 1st and 15th every month though Paypal.

Planet Panel (http://www.planetpanel.net/index.php?lang=en)

A global community survey website where you can interact with people around the world.

Playtex In-Home Testing Program

(http://www.playtexproducts.com/)

You'll receive Playtex products such as Banana Boat, Woolite Rug Cleaner, and Baby Magic, to test in your home, in exchange for your opinion about the product. Unfortunately, at this point, they're only interested in the opinions of females who reside in select states.

Product Testing Services (http://www.product-testing.com/)

With product beta testing, there is always an incentive for you. Usually, you get to keep the product. In the case of testing products with little actual value, additional incentives are usually offered.

Resolution Research Panel
(http://panel.resolutionresearch.com/)

The compensation for participating in research studies vary with the length of involvement and difficulty of the tasks.

Supermarket Guru (http://www.supermarketguru.com/surveys/)

Has a Consumer Taste Panel. Asks your opinions on different supermarket items each month. Ten people get a t-shirt each month and one gets a big prize once per quarter.

SurveySavvy (https://www.surveysavvy.com/?ref_email_id=373623)

The online division of Luth Research, a leader in market research for nearly 25 years.

Survey Club (http://www.surveyclub.com/)

Free membership. They will help you find out about simple and fun online surveys.

Survey Head (http://www.surveyhead.com/)

Join today and get $5 instantly in your account. Survey Head provides you with real market research studies and you will get paid for your participation. Survey Head believes that your time and opinions are worth getting paid for.

Survey Panel Group (http://www.savingsandcoupons.com/)

Surveys earn cash, coupons or prizes.

Survey Spot (https://www.surveyspot.com/)

Express your opinions and beliefs while earning cash prizes and rewards.

Toluna (https://us.toluna.com/)

Paying people to fill out their surveys online.

Vindale Research (https://www.vindale.com/v/index.jsp)

Looking for qualified survey panelists to evaluate products and services, take simple online surveys, and enjoy compensation for their efforts.

Zoomerang.com (http://www.zoomerang.com/)

This site lets you create and take surveys. Get points for each survey you take.

Zoom panel (https://www.zoompanel.com/how)

Register – Take surveys – Earn Points --Redeem points

T. Teach English (as a) Second Language (ESL)

Berlitz (http://www.berlitz.com/Careers/33/)

Berlitz, a large company with more than 550 locations in 70 countries, offers a variety of individual language classes and children programs. The pay is around $13 an hour for the ESL tutoring position. You must be a native English or French speaker. Most positions require a four year college degree and experience in the language you will teach. Teaching experience is not required but is preferred.

Englishunt (http://www.englishuntusa.com/apply.html)

This company was founded in 2000 in Korea and currently offers both live phone and video classes. A Teaching certification and a four year degree is required for most video programs, however a teacher certificate is not needed for their phone English programs. Typically for the live video class, the students are young learners from kindergarten through high school. The typical students for live phone classes are adults. No teaching certificate is required to be an instructor for the phone classes.

GoFluent (http://www.gofluent.com/web/us/jobs-in-the-north-america)

GoFluent is a company that also hires people for home based ESL tutoring. This company is limited to hiring in certain areas. You must work a minimum of 5 hours per day, Monday through Saturday. They are now seeking tutors who speak fluently in Chinese, Italian, Japanese, Korean, or Portuguese, and also have excellent English.

iSpeak u Speak (http://jobs.ispeakuspeak.com/)

iSpeakuSpeak is a company that offers English as a Secondary language to everyone worldwide. Typical students are adults who need to learn English for their careers. Trainers work from home teaching classes by phone and are provided with all materials that are needed. As far as scheduling, you may work up to 30 hours a week and choose the hours you prefer to work. Applicants must be native English speakers, understand the concept of IT technology, have educational experience, and possibly some business experience.

Italki (https://www.italki.com/teacher/apply)

Italki is the world's largest marketplace for online language teachers. With over 100 different languages offered, anyone speaking any language can teach! Set your own rates and schedules.

Language Development System (http://wetutorenglish.com/)

Language Development Systems, started in 2005, is a way to teach English to international students online. All applicants must have a four year teaching degree or English degree preferred. Typical students are college students or professionals.

If you are a person who loves language and helping others, the option of working from home as an ESL tutor can be the perfect home based job for you.

Teach English Online (www.teachonlineenglish.com)

Teach English online and earn a second income. There are prepared lesson plans for teaching conversational to people who are learning English as their second language.

Teach English Online with Kuku Speak
(http://www.kukuspeak.com/online-esl-jobs/)

Teach English to non-English speakers using a dynamic online classroom. Apply using this link: http://www.kukuspeak.com/online-esl-jobs/form.html

TutorGroup (http://recruit.tutorabc.com)

Teach conversational English online from home. There are non-English business people who need to learn English and be conversational in English. Multi-national business corporations need for their employees to do business in the USA speaking English, and you can be their teacher.

V. Tweeting — Earn money by tweeting

If you have a relatively large following on Twitter you can get paid somewhere from $.50 to $20 for tweeting sponsored tweets and content to your audience. The rate depends of the amount of followers you have and some other factors e.g. the age of your account. You can earn with SponsoredTweets; PaidPerTweet and some other services alike.

Here are a few programs that can help you make money on Twitter: (from the website: http://www.jeffbullas.com/2012/05/24/5-ways-to-make-money-with-your-twitter-account/0)

Ad.ly (http://adly.com/)

This is another ad service that lets you send out advertisements in your tweets. However, you don't get paid-per-click. Instead, you create a profile of your interests, then advertisers can choose your account to publicize a campaign. You agree to send out a specific number of tweets on a specific schedule, and you get paid a lump sum.

Ad Dynamo (http://www.addynamo.com/en/)

Ad Dynamo offers advertisers a single marketing platform: reach a targeted audience throughout Africa across thousands of relevant online & mobile publishers, & take advantage of our social offering with direct access to Facebook & Twitter.

MyLikes (http://mylikes.com/)

This is an extensive ad platform can be used on Twitter, Tumblr, YouTube, and your blog. You get to choose ads from thousands of advertisers, and you get to schedule the time the advertisement will be tweeted from your account. You can earn as much as $0.42 per click, and you can get a payout weekly.

Paid Per Tweet (http://paidpertweet.com/)

Get paid to create buzz for companies! You can set your price to Tweet website links, press releases, products promos, services, and companies and help companies gain exposure. PaidPerTweet allows you to monetize your social network accounts.

Rev Twt (http://revtwt.com/)

This is a Twitter-based advertising service and is a pay-per-click platform. The more followers you have and the higher reputation you have, the greater access you will have to higher-paying campaigns. Payout is made via Paypal when you have reached $20 in earnings.

Sponsored Tweets (https://sponsoredtweets.com/)

This is a well-known ad service for Twitter allows you to set your own price-per-click for ads that you tweet. You can choose the ads you tweet from a list of available ads that are updated regularly. You must have at least 50 followers, 100 tweets, and an account that is at least 60 days old to sign up for this service.

Twittad (http://www.twittad.com/)

You are able to set your own cost-per-click, but you have to wait for advertisers to accept your bid. You will also have to identify your niche so that advertisers can match their products with you appropriately. Payment is made via Paypal when you have reached $30 in earnings.

There are many other ways you can make money with your Twitter account, including selling banner ads on your profile page, setting your own rates and selling direct sponsored tweets, charging to send a personal message to your followers, or charging for access to your private list of followers. These advertising services can also help you make money through pay-per-click advertising, which can be especially lucrative if you have a large following.

W. Foreign Exchange Student Coordinator

Here are 8 different non-profit exchange organizations to check out:

American Institute for Foreign Study
(http://www.academicyear.org/local_coordinator/about.asp)

- Established in 1981.
- Must be 25 years or older to apply.
- Earn financial compensation for each full year International student you place and supervise.
- Incentives and International and domestic travel bonuses available.
- A+ rating with the Better Business Bureau.

Aspect Foundation
(http://aspectfoundation.org/become-a-coordinator/)

- Established in 1985.
- Must be 25 years or older to apply.
- Coordinators are compensated with a stipend for each student that is placed and supervised.
- Additional opportunities for bonuses and incentive training trips.

CCI Greenheart

(https://www.cci-exchange.com/host-families/work-with-exchange-students/)

- Established in 1985.
- Must be 26 years or older to apply.
- Earn up to $1,000 for each exchange student that you place and monitor throughout the year. Or become a Group LC and earn $2,000 – $5,000 per group.
- Receive discounts on travel.

CIEE (http://www.ciee.org/highschool/404/)

- Established in 1995.
- Earn financial compensation for each student placement and additional compensation for supervising during the semester.
- Earn travel rewards and free trips for the successful placement of students.

EF Education First

(http://www.efexchangeyear.org/be-a-coordinator)

- Established in 1965.
- Compensation is based on student placement and supervision during the school year.
- Earn travel rewards and other benefits.

Educational Resource Development Trust

(http://www.erdtshare.org/become-a-coordinator/)

- Established in 1974.
- Earn $200 for each student that is placed. Additional compensation for monthly monitoring and mentoring.
- Earn cash awards, points, gifts, gift certificates, and more for personal goal achievements.

International Cultural Exchange Services
(http://www.icesusa.org/employment/)

- Established in 1991.
- Receive monetary compensation for each student placement.
- Earn other benefits such as goal-based National and International annual group trips.

STS Foundation (http://www.stsfoundation.org/)

- Established in 1986.
- Receive up to $1,000 per student placement and supervision for the full program year.
- Earn International travel incentives.

Chapter 10

KEEPING AND ADVANCING IN
YOUR WORK AT HOME JOB

It is a time of elation and celebration when you get a job, especially a work at home online job! Now, you have the job, you want to keep that job and maybe even advance in the company, right?

Allow me to share 7 habits of highly successful work at home online job workers:

1. Always be working in accordance with your scheduled hours.
Your employer counts on your performance on the job. If there is a time you cannot be at work, you need to contact your supervisor in advance and let him or her know what is happening and when you expect to be back at work.

2. Never be late for your work session.
Just like with an onsite job, your online job employer expects you to be at work, on time and prepared to perform your job tasks to the best of your ability. Should there be an occasion when you cannot be at work on time, you need to contact your supervisor as soon as you know you will be late. Be specific when it is you will be working, and honor the time commitment.

3. Be in tune with your team and events taking place in their families.
Working at home often times makes you feel isolated and working in a vacuum. So, you need to stay in contact with not only your supervisor, but with your team of co-workers too. This builds and maintains a cohesive and highly productive virtual office environment.

4. Perform your job duties with excellence.
You were hired because the company or organization believes you to have the right fit for them. This means that the level of your skill and the quality of your personality means a lot to them and their work to accomplishing their missions, goals and objectives.

5. Volunteer for projects to benefit the company/organization.
The more you are involved with the company or organization, the more valued you are. It is very important to build and maintain your perceived value. The best way to do that is to "volunteer" and be more engaged to help meeting the company's or organization's productivity goals.

6. Be looking for additional training opportunities.
The company or organization has invested in you with time and effort to train you for the position you were hired. After establishing your value to them, and when there is an opportunity to do so, it is wise for you to inquire and apply for additional training to "cross-train" into more job responsibilities. Then, when an opening for a position that would be a promotion for you becomes available, you will be a perfect candidate.

7. Be aware of job openings in other positions requiring additional training and experience.
Most companies and organizations have job openings posted on their websites. After you have established yourself (usually after 6 months) with your employer, and have built and maintained your work value, then look at the job postings. Just as you did for getting hired initially, look for the job position that matches with your job skills and work experience. Make sure to update your resume listing your present position before applying for a new position with your employer. It is also recommended you write a cover letter mentioning what job tasks you are working and how much you enjoy being a part of the team and the company or organization.

I have learned these 7 habits while being employed to work at home. In every job capacity I have been promoted and received raises and bonuses, so I know from personal experience these habits are highly effective.

Another tip for being successful with a work at home online job is to take breaks. It is best that you not over work and make sure you not sit in one spot for longer than 2 hours at a time. Even as an employee working with a headset, you can take a few minutes to stand and stretch. Taking breaks will help you to always perform your job tasks with maximum performance, which will no doubt lead to greater success.

Chapter 11

DIRECTIONS FOR GETTING
A PAYPAL ACCOUNT

Start with going to this website:
(https://www/paypal.com/webapps/setup-paypal-account/onboarding/
execution=els1)

Register for personal account

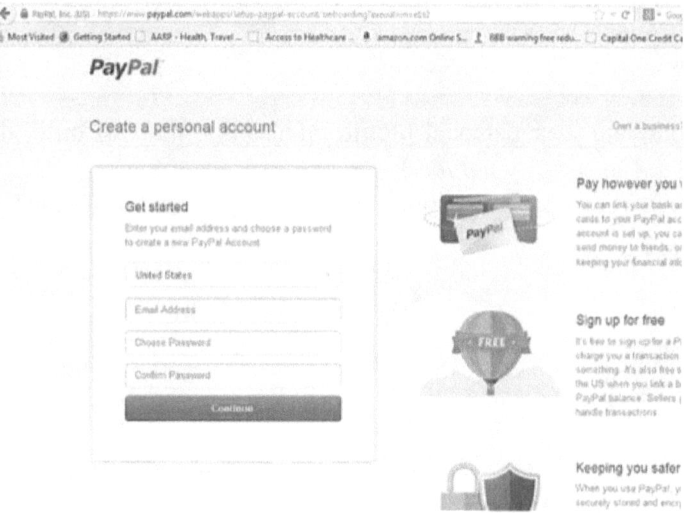

Type in your email address
(This email address will be your login to PayPal)

Create your password then Continue

Next, complete your personal profile information (date of birth, the last 4 digits of social security number)
Review the Terms and Conditions and then "Agree and Continue"

Type in your email address (this email address will be your login to PayPal)
Create your password
Continue

Next, complete your personal profile information (date of birth, the last 4 digits of social security number)
Review the Terms and Conditions and then "Agree and Continue"

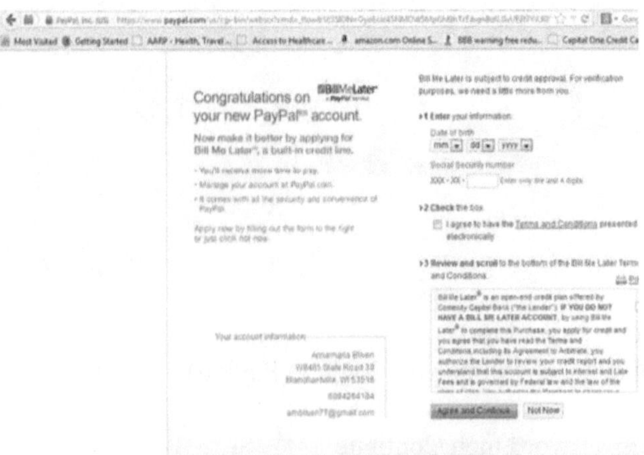

Then you will need to complete the PayPal Account set up:
Confirm PayPal Mobile
Confirm email address
Add your bank account

Set up your security questions

It is highly recommended that you write down your login credentials, questions and answers to security questions in a safe location……this is so you will always have them handy.

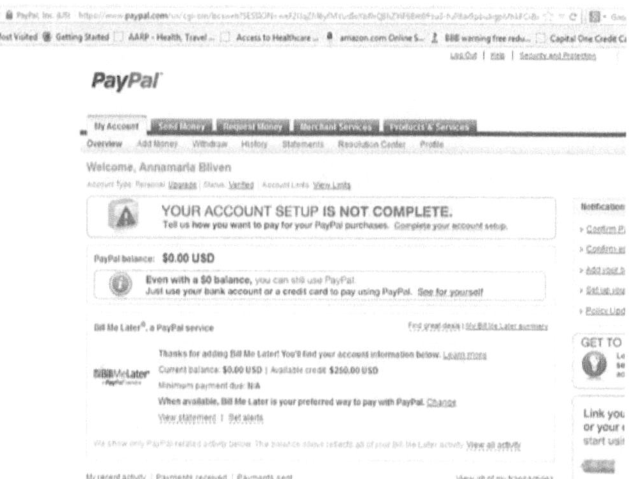

Confirming PayPal mobile is done with a text message or phone call from PayPal

Confirm your email address (with an email that is sent to you from PayPal)

When you add your bank account, you will need the routing number and account number and will be asked to confirm your bank account with two deposits under $1 within a few business days.

Setting up security questions is self-explanatory.

At this point, you are ready to receive payment from doing online work.

Chapter 12

MICRO TASKS

(THESE TASKS TAKE A SMALL AMOUNT OF TIME TO DO AND PAYS INSTANTLY)

IF YOU NEED IMMEDIATE CASH, OR YOU HAVE A CRIMINAL BACKGROUND OR CANNOT PASS A CREDIT CHECK ---IT IS HIGHLY RECOM-MENDED YOU DO MICRO TASKSTHEY PAY INSTANTLY***

Amazon Mechanical Turk

(https://www.mturk.com/mturk/welcome)

Type of micro job: Online tasks, crowd sourcing
Pays in: US dollars, Indian rupees or Amazon gift certificates, depending on your location.

One of the earliest and best known *crowd sourcing* marketplaces, Amazon's Mechanical Turk, also called MTurk, and utilizes what it calls the "human intelligence" of an army of independent contractors who complete small online tasks. These online tasks are things that its "requesters," or clients, need real people, not computers, to do. This work-at-home division of Amazon is part of Amazon's Web Services division and is separate from the online retailer's home call center employees.

Types of Work-at-Home Opportunities at Mechanical Turk: Online workers at Mechanical

Turk accepts HITs, or "human intelligence tasks," and is paid small sums for each. Though Amazon is a U.S.-based company, workers (and requesters) come from all over the globe. Because of this global diversity, what HITs pay and what they require can vary greatly. Some jobs might pay 1 or 2 cents but take only minutes to complete and require very little expertise of the worker. Other HITs require workers to gain qualifications before being allowed to work on them. Qualification may be a test but it could also simply be approval or rejection based on your previous work, location, profile, etc. Jobs with qualification presumably pay more. Unlike some other micro job sites, which may offer real-world and online tasks, Mechanical Turk is completely online.

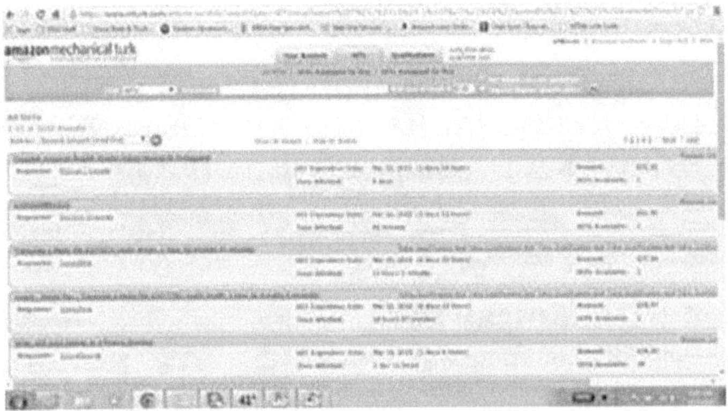

The types of task might include:
Surveys
Blog comments
Transcription
Short editing and writing jobs
Keyword searches
Photo captioning and tagging

How Mechanical Turk Works:
To begin working for Mechanical Turk, go to the Mechanical Turk website and simply choose to accept a HIT. It will then prompt you to sign into your Amazon.com account or to create one. In taking this step, you agree to the Mechanical Turk privacy notice.

Browse HITs looking for ones that interest you. [Note: Change the display to read "Reward amount (most first)] then click "Go."

Examine the "Reward" field to see what it pays.

"Time Allotted" tells you how long you have to finish the task before it is considered abandoned and is assigned to someone else. This is not necessarily how long it will take. Many HITs will give an estimated time for completion in the full description but some do not.

Click on the name of the HIT for a very brief description and click on "View a HIT in this group" to see a full description. On this screen you can choose to accept a HIT or you can skip it and look at other HITs from the same requester.

You can search HITs by keyword or sort them by reward amount or qualifications required.

Payment:
Payments from Mechanical Turk are based on a digital piece work model in which workers receive a fixed fee for each job completed. Because this work is for independent contractors there are no minimum wage protections. Another caution is that requesters may reject work
and refuse to pay.
Immediately after a HIT is accepted by the requester, the worker is paid into an Amazon Payments account. However, the time between submitting a HIT to approval can vary from a few hours to a few days.
For U.S.-based workers, money can then be transferred to a U.S. bank account. Workers in India can elect to receive a check in Indian rupees. For all others not based in the U.S. or India, earnings can be transfer to an Amazon gift card.

App Rewards (http://www.apprewardsclub.com/)

Type of micro job: Rewards program for using cell phone apps
Pays in: Points on RewardsDen and Kiip

Clickworker (http://www.clickworker.com/en/)

Type of micro job: Crowd sourcing in writing, translating, data entry and research.
Pays in: US dollars or euros, monthly

Industry:
Data entry, translation and writing, using in a crowd sourcing platform
Company Description:
Global company uses *crowd sourcing* to distribute micro tasks (aka micro labor) in fields such as writing, translating, data entry and research to more than 300,000 "clickworkers" worldwide. The company's clients--which include Honda, Groupon, PayPal and T Mobile--contract with it to have a larger project completed and then Clickworker breaks the project down in to smaller tasks, which can be completed by many different freelance workers.

Types of Work-at-Home Opportunities at Clickworker:
As is typical in crowd sourcing marketplace micro jobs, the freelancers at Clickworker choose small tasks from the pool of available projects. What tasks are available for a freelancer to choose from is based on the qualifications of that freelancer. Qualifications are determined by his or performance on assessments and on previous work completed.

The types of services performed by Clickworker's freelancers for its clients include:
Writing:
SEO text creation and optimization for online marketing
Product descriptions and the categorization of products in e-commerce
Data Entry and research:
Structuring large amounts of data by categorizing and indexing
Categorization and tagging of videos, audio content, image
Address enrichment, data validation and online research for databases
Data verification and research
Translation

Pay and Benefits:
The company states "On average, we expect that a Clickworker earns $9.00 per hour." However, workers are not paid by the hour; payment is on a per

piece basis, which means this could vary significantly depending on how fast a freelancer can work. Workers receive a fixed fee for each job completed. According to the company, fees "can range anywhere from a few cents to double-digit Euro sum." The company pays in either Euros or US dollars. Because Clickworker hires independent contractors, there are no benefits and no guarantee of minimum wage for workers. Payment is made on the 7th or 8th day of the month (or the first non-weekend day after that) for money earned as of the last day of the previous month. You will need to have earned €10 or $10 USD in order for a payment to be processed.

Qualifications and Requirements:
There are very few requirements for Clickworkers. You must be legally able to work in the jurisdiction where you live and have a computer with Internet access. If you live in the United States you must be age 18, but this requirement may vary based on legal age in your country. However, workers must also pass assessments in order to have access to work.
The company hires worldwide, but you must have a bank account in a SEPA (Single Euro Payments Area) country or have a valid PayPal account and that can accept payment.

Applying to Clickworkers:
Depending on your language preference, choose the website: Clickworker in English or Clickworker in German. Choose the "For Clickworkers" tab and hit register. Fill out the basic information of name, address and email and agree to the terms of service. You will receive an email with a link to log in to Clickworker. You will then have to take assessments to see which projects you can work on.

ClixSense (http://www.clixsense.com/en/Tasks)

Type of micro job: Online task site
Pays in: US dollars, twice weekly via PayPal, Payza, Liberty Reserve; month for checks; minimum cash-out requirements with fees.

CrowdFlower (https://tasks.crowdflower.com/auth_central/login/new)

Type of micro job: Various

Pays in: USD via PayPay; withdraws require an $84 minimum and can be processed 15 days after payment is made.

Crowd sourcing: (http://www.cloudcrowd.com/)

Crowd sourcing company offers micro jobs in general writing, marketing writing, and editing (Chicago Manual of Style). Writers and editors sign up using Facebook. They must pass a series of assessment and build a credibility score to access each type of work, which each pay a small fee and possibly a bonus.

CoinWorker (http://coinworker.com/)

Type of micro job: Online task site
Pays in Bitcoins (BTC); earn points at 1 point=$0.1USD; at 180, points are converted to bitcoins at the prevailing BTC/USD exchange rate.

Gigs Bull (http://gigsbull.com)

Type of micro job: Online task/services marketplace
Pays in: Amounts calculated in USD into a PayPal or Payza account

EasyShift (http://easyshiftapp.com/)

Type of micro job: Real-world task site via mobile phone
Pays in: US dollars in PayPal account

Embee Mobile (http://embeemobile.com/)

Type of micro job: Mobile micro task websites
Pays in: Points redeemable for mobile airtime or other services

Fittytown (http://www.fittytown.com/)

Type of micro job: Online task/services marketplace

Fiverr (http://fiverr.com/)

Type of micro job: Online task marketplace
Pay is: Calculated in USD and paid via PayPay with a 2% or $1 fee
(whichever is less) in the currencies that PayPal works with.

Fivesquids (http://www.fivesquids.co.uk/)
Type of micro job: Online task/services marketplace
Pays in: Pounds via PayPal with a 2% or £1 fee (whichever is less)

Field Agent (http://www.fieldagent.net/)

Type of micro job: Real-world and online tasks via mobile phone
Pays in: PayPal account; jobs pay $3-12 each

Gigwalk (http://gigwalk.com/)

Type of micro job: Real-world and online micro tasks via mobile phone
Pays in: PayPal account; tasks typically pay $3-5 per gig

Inbox Dollars (http://www.inboxdollars.com/members)

Type of micro job: Surveys, rewards program
Pays by: Check on a monthly basis
Participants earn a few cents for each search performed or more by watching
ads, taking surveys, shopping online redeeming coupons, receiving emails
and playing games. Caution: Inactive accounts' payments may be forfeited
and company charges a $3 payout fee.

InstantBucks (http://www.instantbucks.com/)

Type of micro job: Surveys, rewards program
Pays in: "Virtual bucks" redeemable for gift cards

Ipinions (http://ipinionrewards.com/)

Type of micro job: Surveys on mobile phone
Pays in: Reward points, which can be redeemed for cash in a PayPal account
at 100 reward points to one dollar; minimum to redeem is of 500 rewards
points. Download the free app; fill out the profile with information such as

such as your name, address, gender, and birthday and employment status. You will then be contacted by email, push notifications or phone to participate in surveys that match your profile.

IZEA (https://izea.com/)

IZEA works in addition to a blog or on its own. You get paid to blog, tweet, take photos and take videos. The pay is mostly based on your following, so if you want to make money with your tweets, you'll need to grow your Twitter following. Likewise, if you want to make money with blogs, you'll need substantial blog traffic (more on blogging below).

Microworkers (http://microworkers.com/)

Type of micro job: Online tasks
Pays with: Money bookers or Alertpay; must have earned $9 to make a withdraw Micro workers put the "micro" in micro jobs. These jobs typically pay a few cents each.

Mylikes (http://mylikes.com/)

Type of micro job: Social media advertising
Pays in: Cash in PayPal or Amazon gift cards

Playgroups USA
(http://www.flexjobs.com/jobs/telecommuting-jobs-at-playgroups_usa)

Please note: Flex Jobs requires that you pay for a membership.

Playgroups USA was started by parents that saw the irreplaceable benefits of playgroup years ago and wanted to bring these opportunities to everyone wishing the best for their children. By providing resources and intuitive site tools, visitors can search every US zip code for a playgroup nearby or create their own. Playgroups USA also has an event division called WeeBoogie. WeeBoogie events inspire parents by encouraging music and dance early in a child's life while also supporting local nonprofits that serve young families. Playgroups USA have home based event and account manager opportunities in many major cities around the US as well as remote volunteer opportunities.

Project Payday (http://www.projectpayday.com/home.cgi)

Go ahead and create your account above so you can get started right now - with **NO out-of-pocket cost** - before it's too late. *You truly have nothing to lose.* Sign up and get started right now at no cost to you. Our "QuickStart" Training Guide is approximately 65 printed pages, but you'll only need to read the first 17 pages in order to start making money today.

QuickTate (http://typists.quicktate.com/transcribers/signup)

Type of micro job: Crowd sourcing, transcription
Pays: $.0025 per word or 4 words for 1 cent

Redlr (http://pin.redlr.com/signup)

Type of micro job: Online services marketplace, online tasks
Pays in: USD via PayPal or Payza; withdraws may incur PayPal fees

Reward TV
(http://www.rewardtv.com/welcome/sampleGames.sdo)
Play trivia for cash and prizes
Watch your favorite
TV shows then visit RewardTV the next day!
Win cash & prizes like gift cards and electronics in our Auctions, Shopping Sprees, and Sweepstakes! You'll earn an entry into our $10,000 Sweepstakes each day you play TV Trivia!

Scribie (http://scribie.com/jobs)

Type of micro job: Crowd sourcing, transcription, transcription review and proofreading
Pays: $1 per 6-minute audio segment via PayPal

Shopkick (http://www.shopkick.com/)

Type of micro job: Rewards program, online and real-world tasks via mobile phone.
Pays in: Points redeemable for discounts and coupons

Short task (http://www.shorttask.com/)

Short Task connects online job seekers with providers. Workers can work at home and make money from thousands of tasks and jobs.

Skyword (http://www.skyword.com/writers/)

Type of micro job: Writing
Pays in: PayPal account twice a month
Articles earn around $10 plus very small amount for traffic. These micro jobs for writers are probably best for beginners because of the pay scale.

SwagBucks (http://www.swagbucks.com/)

Type of a micro job: Rewards program
Pays in: "Virtual currency" redeemable for gift cards, coupons, etc.
Users earn SwagBucks by playing games, doing surveys and shopping.

Zaarly (https://www.zaarly.com/howzaarlyworks)

Workers fulfill tasks starting at $5 per job similar to Fiverr.

WRAP UP AND DISCLAIMER

According to the GlobalWorkplaceAnalytical.com website (as of September 29, 2015): http://globalworkplaceanalytics.com/telecommuting-statistics:

- 50% of the US workforce holds a job that is compatible with at least partial telework and approximately 20-25% of the workforce teleworks at some frequency

- 80% to 90% of the US workforce says they would like to telework at least part time. Two to three days a week seems to be the sweet spot that allows for a balance of concentrative work (at home) and collaborative work (at the office).

- Fortune 1000 companies around the globe are entirely revamping their space around the fact that employees are already mobile. Studies repeatedly show they are not at their desk 50-60% of the time.

- Regular work-at-home, *among the non-self-employed population*, has grown by 103% since 2005 and 6.5% in 2014. This represents the largest year over year increase since before the recession.

- 3.7 million employees (2.5% of the workforce) now work from home at least half the time.

- The employee population as a whole grew by 1.8% from 2013 to 2014, while employees who telecommuter population grew 6.5%.

- About 22% of the self-employed population work primarily from home.

I included pertinent information about each company and made sure to list the website for you to get more details and register for the jobs. Every link in this book was first tested ----and led accurately to the company's website. I cannot guarantee that all the websites and jobs listed in the book will be available --- things in the business world are always changing. Please read each job listing carefully ---there may be locality restrictions and you may need to be living in a specific area to qualify for the job. Not all telecommute/remote jobs are like that, only some of them.

DISCLAIMER: I do not guarantee you will be hired but if you follow these tips, you are likely to get hired and keep your job:

1. Be positive ("it takes work to get work") and that is not any different when looking for an online job.
2. Make sure to apply for only the jobs you have experience, skills and ability.
3. Make sure to submit all the paperwork required to be hired in a timely manner.
4. You may have to take an assessment test and go through some training before you are fully hired.
5. Be sure to perform your tasks with excellence.
6. Be sure to cultivate healthy working relationships with your supervisors and co-workers.

   Keep in mind that even though you are not sharing an office space, you are sharing a "virtual" working environment.
7. Work with diligence and integrity ---it will definitely pay you dividends!

   Some of the companies in the book are listed more than once. This is due to the fact that the companies employ online workers in different capacities.

PLEASE NOTE: Most of the information for this book came from several different websites. In most cases, the information on these websites was cut and pasted into this book. Some of the websites have more information than others. You are invited to go to these company websites and see all the details found on them.

Here are some other websites you may want to bookmark and **monitor for additional telecommute/remote jobs** as they become available:

www.workersonboard.com

http://www.nextjobathome.net

http://jobs.monster.com/v-part-time-q-work-online-from-home-jobs.aspx

http://www.wahm.com/

http://www.moneymakingmommy.com/

http://www.makemoneyfromonlinejobs.com/

http://www.allyou.com/budget-home/money-shopping/online-jobs-work-from-home-00411000073600/

http://www.onlinejobsteenagers.com/

http://jobsearch.about.com/od/workfromhome/tp/work-at-home.htm

http://voices.yahoo.com/huge-list-paid-online-jury-opportunities-8066268.html?cat=3

http://www.spi-global.com/jobs/career-opportunities-in-madison

http://workathomemoms.about.com/od/workathomecareers/ss/wahjob-directory.htm

http://realwaystoearnmoneyonline.com

https://www.elance.com/r/jobs/

I invite you to research on your own to find more job opportunities you can work from home and work at home. Remember the steps? If not, refer to Chapter 3: Three Basic Steps to Seeking, Finding, and Applying for WAH Online Job.

ABOUT THE AUTHOR:

AnnaMaria Bliven (AKA: Prosperity Princess) is someone who for the past 14 years has discovered the "secrets" to getting and keeping a real work at home online job. She is teaching people how they can seek, find, apply, get and keep legitimate online jobs to work at home. Her first book: The Guide to Mystery Shopping has helped hundreds of people start and sustained their own mystery shopping business. Her second book: Get a Real Job Online has helped hundreds of people locate legitimate work at home job opportunities and has a 5-start rating. This is her third book and includes chapters on getting hired to work at home, and keep and advance in their job position. It is meant as a job seeking resource and a guidance for people who are needing to work at home earning income from part time, full time and flex time job positions.

She served with distinction in the U.S. Army, Army Reserve and Army National Guard for 26 years and is a mother, grandmother and soon to be a great-grandmother who has always had a heart's desire and passion for teaching people knowledge and skills needed to advance in their chosen careers. She is also a "Champion for Changed Lives." For a more detailed view of her credentials and passion, visit her LinkedIn website: https://www.linkedin.com/in/annamariabliven.